THIS
TIMELESS
MOMENT

THIS
TIMELESS
MOMENT

A PERSONAL VIEW OF
ALDOUS HUXLEY

LAURA ARCHERA HUXLEY

CELESTIAL ARTS
MILLBRAE, CALIFORNIA

Acknowledgment is made to the copyright owners of the following illustrations:

Page 2,   Photograph© Philippe Halsman
Page 26,   Associated Press
Page 138, Philip Lieberman
Page 178, Drawing by Don Bachardy
Page 190, Douglas Glass, London
Page 200, Robert M. Quittner — Black Star
Page 216, W. Suschitsky
Page 228, T. McArdle Photo

This edition published by arrangement with Farrar, Straus & Giroux, Inc., by Celestial Arts, 231 Adrian Road, Millbrae, California 94030

First Printing: February 1975
Manufactured in the United States of America

Library of Congress Cataloging in Publication Data

Huxley, Laura Archera.
        This timeless moment.

        Reprint of the ed. published by Farrar, Straus & Giroux, New York.
        1. Huxley, Aldous Leonard, 1894—1963--Biography.
2. Huxley, Laura Archera. I. Title.
[PR6015.U9Z726 1975]   823'.9'12 [B]   74-32396
ISBN 0-89087-022-5

At a gallop we charge up the shingle,
At a gallop we leap the sea-wall,
With a mad exultation we tingle,
For we, we can overcome all.

Aldous wrote these lines at the age of thirteen, a flower child of his time. To the flower children of all times—with their open hearts and open minds, with their ageless, timeless love and hope — this book is offered.

CONTENTS

ACKNOWLEDGMENTS

"Gratitude is Heaven itself." With what pleased conviction would Aldous quote this from Blake! As the years pass, the enormous significance and feeling contained in those four words become clearer and deeper to me. It is this feeling that I want to express to:

Ginny Pfeiffer, who, with her understanding of my intent and her editorial skill, had an essential part in the writing of this book.

Christopher Isherwood for his penetrating, limpid criticism and marvelous support.

Juliette Huxley, in whose counsel, regardless of difference in opinion, I always felt an ego-less good will.

Sybille Bedford, Thornton Delehanty, John Ervin, Ellen Giffard, Richard Meigs, Betty Wendel, and master jester, Alan Watts, who, in various ways, gave expertly and generously.

L.A.H.

Making Passes

MY FIRST ENCOUNTER with Aldous took place some time in 1948. I had gone to see him and his first wife at their home in the mountains, to interest them in a film I hoped to make in Italy. My experience in films had been unusual and varied. Now I was eager to integrate what I knew in a rather ambitious project of my own: it was going to be the most beautiful, intriguing film on the *Palio,* the famous horse race run in Siena every year—and I brightly hoped Aldous Huxley would write it. I had heard how much he loved Italy and especially Tuscany, where he had spent several years. Now he was living in Wrightwood, only two hours from Los Angeles.

I prefer to meet people directly, so I declined a friend's offer of an introduction to Mr. Huxley and wrote him a note myself. From the moment I mailed it I waited impatiently for an answer. A long week passed; none came. It was disconcerting. Couldn't Aldous Huxley feel the beauty and urgency of my project? I decided to call him. There were only two telephones in the little town of Wrightwood, and the Huxleys did not have one, but my message was relayed to him and he called me back. It was on the long-distance phone that I heard for the first time that sensuous and beautifully modulated voice. I must have been able to communicate my urgency, for he asked me to come see him the next day and gave specific directions on how to get there.

I had an old car which my friends had baptized Laurissima. It just made the steep mountains and I arrived punctually at a brilliant high noon.

Maria, so small, so lively, greeted me in Italian; she was preparing lunch and she mentioned a new diet; I hadn't started yet the unending study of the effects diets can produce on our physical and psychological being and was fascinated by the subject. Then, I don't know how it happened, but I was following Maria, I thought, to the dining room, when she turned into a corridor and suddenly we were standing at the bathroom door. There, for the first time, I saw Aldous: unreasonably tall, washing his hands in the sink too little and too low, his strange light eyes looking at me, curious and amused, through a romantic lock of hair.

During lunch we spoke about Siena and its centuries-old horse race, run twice a year in honor of the Virgin. I had no idea Aldous had written a lovely essay about the *palio* some twenty years before I saw it. Tactfully and typically, as I was to find later, neither Aldous nor Maria told me how well they knew my subject, so I kept talking. *Il Palio* is a bold, fantastic competition between ten of the seventeen *contradas,* or districts, of the enchanting medieval town of Siena. Each *contrada* has its chapel and its flag. The flag bearers, attired in the most fanciful, tasteful livery of the early quattrocento, made of silk and velvet, look and act as though they had just stepped down from a fresco of the period. These young men, with renaissance (or Sunset Strip) hairdos, don't just walk; they slowly and nobly dance through the stone- and brick-paved streets and piazzas, elegantly tossing their psychedelic flags "like the painted wings of an enormous butterfly" high in the air, with graceful, nonchalant skill, "daring, brilliant and yet always right, always irreproachably refined."[1] The leaders of each *contrada* take their horse to church the day before the race, for the blessing. Unfortunately the horse of the *contrada* with which I had become involved was so unambitious and indifferent that he would not relieve himself in church, a traditionally reassuring omen for winning the race. Now came the climax of my story—and the Huxleys were all ears, I hoped. It was at this point of "no show" that, to save the situation, I had confidentially told the captain of the *contrada* of certain pills (Benzedrine was much used then) that the Americans take when they must run and don't feel like it. By comparing the horse's weight with mine, 111 pounds, we computed the dosage, and in the dark of the night a secret messenger came to my room for every pill I had. The next day, our horse arrived second, which was just right as far as I was concerned; for had he failed, I should have had to run out of town, and if he had arrived first, I would have become suspiciously and dangerously popular.

By the end of lunch, we had enough material for several films. After lunch, Aldous and I went into his workroom, and he began choosing music for the film—early Italian music, to blend with the Sienese

[1] Aldous Huxley: "Il Palio at Siena," *Collected Essays* (Bantam).

architecture. Maria joined us, and we listened to some madrigals. Occasionally the fleeting thought passed through my mind that I must not forget to impress the Huxleys with my business acumen as a producer, for that was the role I had assigned myself at the time; but I kept forgetting about it and losing opportunities, for there was so much to talk about and especially to hear. How wonderfully comfortable, and exciting at the same time, it was to be with these two people!

By the time I was taking leave, our plans for the film were completed—and marvelous. There was only one flaw. As we were standing near old Laurissima, Maria said: "I am a little worried about you. How are you going to do this—you are a musician, not really the type we imagine the Hollywood producer to be...."

"Oh, but I am," I protested. "Why don't you think so? What do you mean?"

"I mean," Maria answered, "that it takes a lot of money to make a film like this: where are you going to find it?"

Now, I thought, is the time to impress them with my business acumen. In a confidential tone I said: "I happen to know that M.G.M. has a lot of money frozen in Italy." (Later, I also happened to find out that this was no secret, and that others had been faster than I to warm up that frozen money.)

"Well, then," said Maria encouragingly, "find this money quickly, because nothing would please us more than to live a few months in Siena."

I drove back to Los Angeles in a golden dusk, feeling like a conquistador. Needless to say, M.G.M. never paid the slightest attention to my dream picture, which was never made. But something much better happened to me: a friendship with two marvelous human beings.

We did not see each other often, Maria and Aldous were very busy. They traveled a great deal, and besides, Maria had had a cancer operation and was often exhausted. Then in 1952, after the Huxleys had moved to Los Angeles, I found myself seated next to Aldous at a dinner party given by the motion-picture producer Gabriel Pascal, with whom I was working at that time. It was on this occasion that I first discussed psychotherapy with Aldous.

I myself had done considerable experimenting with various techniques of psychotherapy, my interest having been first stirred by the grave illness of a close friend. Aldous knew all about the orthodox therapies and was characteristically open-minded about the unorthodox ones. For example, there was a great deal of controversy at that time about dianetics. Aldous and Maria had experimented with it, and so had I. It is interesting to note here how Aldous was able to use in his writing almost everything that came his way. In the first chapter of

Island, his novel about a possible Utopia, the hero, shipwrecked and wounded, is found semiconscious by two children, who give him psychological first aid, a basic dianetic technique.

At dinner that evening we spoke about several techniques and Aldous asked me if I had ever experimented with magnetic passes. I had never heard of them. In his subtly powerful voice, soft and round as a ball of velvet, Aldous said, "You must try them sometimes—they are effective and disreputable—just like dianetics." And then he told me about Dr. James Esdaile, the English physician who practiced in India about a hundred and twenty years ago. Aldous had been deeply impressed, not only by the three hundred major operations Dr. Esdaile had performed without anesthetics and without pain to the patients, but also by the amazing number of recoveries and the low mortality rate from post-operative shock and infection. As Christopher Isherwood remarked later, Aldous had a subtle, unassuming way of telling you something as though you knew it already and he was only reminding you of it.

"As you know, before anesthesia was discovered, the mortality rate after surgery was twenty-nine percent; between chloroform in 1847 and Lister's discovery of aseptic surgery in the sixties, the death rate from post-operative shock fell to only twenty-three percent. During this period, Esdaile, who was working with undernourished patients, under even more septic conditions, without chemical anesthetics, and in a debilitating climate, had an unbelievably low rate of five percent." Years later Aldous expressed his admiration for Dr. Esdaile by portraying some facets of his life in one of the central figures in *Island*—old Dr. Andrews, who, with the Raja, was to make of Pala an ideal society. The description of the operation performed on the Raja is an almost verbatim report of an operation performed by Esdaile on June 3, 1846, in Calcutta.

Aldous continued, "And do you know, Laura, how the medical profession expressed appreciation for Dr. Esdaile?"

"Either they gave him a hospital or they hanged him," I answered.

"They boycotted and derided him. They never published his reports. And any English doctor who made use of hypnotism ran the risk of being hounded out of his profession," Aldous said slowly and incisively. It was not until 1892 that the British Medical Association accepted hypnosis as a therapeutic technique and sanctioned it officially. And not until sixty-four years later did the American Medical Association take the same action.

Our conversation about Dr. Esdaile, the "passes," and animal magnetism was going on between the veal paprika and the latest gossip about *Androcles and the Lion,* which Gabriel Pascal was then produc-

ing. At the other end of the table Pascal was telling of the trouble his
assistant film-cutter (myself) was giving him by getting dangerously
mixed up, not in the cutting room but in actual encounter, with his
three lions: the stuffed one, the trained one, and the really wild one.
Some of the guests in the middle of the table, caught between the basso
profundo of Pascal and the lyric baritone of Aldous, were thoroughly
confused.

I was fascinated by Aldous's description and enthusiasm and wanted
instructions on using these magnetic passes. Although I had been in
America long enough to have known, I was somehow not aware at that
moment that the passes we were talking about might be confused with
the other, common garden variety.

"Are these passes difficult to make?" I asked.

Across the table, a guest who had missed the beginning of our conversation was listening open-mouthed to the famous philosopher
teaching the serious young woman on his left how to make passes.

"Nothing is easier," answered Aldous animatedly. "Just have your
client lie down..." He was interrupted by a late arrival—I did not have
the chance to get the instructions that evening.

A few days later I saw Maria and Aldous again, this time at their
home. Their son Matthew, with his first wife and their enchanting little
boy, were visiting from the East. Maria had been, and still was, ill. The
child was delightful, but a handful. Matthew was having difficulty
finding a job suitable to his explosive type of intelligence. We spoke a
great deal that evening about psychotherapy, and Aldous recommended that I read Dr. Esdaile's book, *Hypnosis in Medicine and
Surgery* (originally entitled *Mesmerism in India*).

Unexpectedly, Maria said that she wanted to have a therapeutic
session with me. I knew she had had a cancer operation, and thought
probably she wanted to speak about that. A week later, when she came
up the hill to my studio, she said she was completely at peace with the
thought of dying: "To me, dying is no more than going from one room
to another." She seemed to have little interest in her illness, and I
hadn't the slightest idea why she wanted a session. We had an easy one,
without any signs of resistance on Maria's part. Naturally and smoothly
she relived pleasant memories of her recent and distant past, and only
touched on one dramatic incident of childhood. After an hour and a
half she opened her eyes and said in that peculiar manner of hers,
straight and subtle at the same time: "You do this very well."

I remarked that we had remained pretty much on the surface.

"I know," she said. "However, I can see that you are a good hypnotic operator."

I jumped. Like so many ill-informed people, I had a conditioned reaction to the word "hypnosis," although, of course, I wasn't aware of it. As though I had been unjustly accused of grave misbehavior, I said, "*I*, a hypnotic operator? Maria, I do not use hypnosis!"

Maria laughed. "What in the world do you think you were doing? Do you think I was in my normal state when I was walking in the desert here a few minutes ago and feeling—really feeling—the sand under my feet? Or when I saw—not remembered having seen—but *really saw* the nurse I had forty years ago?"

I didn't realize then that this reliving of past events is in actuality a state of light hypnosis. I didn't call it by that name then. In any case, I did not want to make an issue of it now and spoil my rapport with my "patient."

Maria said she felt refreshed, and indeed she looked it. She told me that she really did not want sessions for herself, although she might have a few more. She was looking, she said, for a therapist for someone about whom she was worried. And also, she added, Aldous might profit from a few sessions.

I was surprised. Aldous seemed so well and clear-minded, so peaceful and alert. "To improve his vision?" I asked.

"That also," Maria answered. "However, he practices the Bates system regularly and has his lesson with Mrs. Corbett every Tuesday. But what Aldous wants is to recover the memory of a two-year period around the age of eleven, of which he remembers very little. He needs to recapture this period for his writing. We have tried all methods with no success. He has such an extraordinary memory that it is all the more frustrating for him to know so little about those two years. Come over some day, Laura, and try *your* way. Sometimes a person like you, not so learned, can do better than the professionals with this sort of thing."

I was surprised and a bit nervous. As an acquaintance, Aldous was easy and gentle, generous and mysterious. But as a "case" he probably would be difficult—there was a legend that he knew everything. I did not know then of his ever present good will and openmindedness. It was precisely this willingness to give everyone and everything a chance that contributed so much to the depth of his knowledge and the variety of his experiences.

I did not realize then that one of Aldous's chief aims in life was the extension of consciousness. At this time he had not yet experienced the psychedelic materials (mescaline, LSD, and psylocybin) which later were to be so revelatory and directive.

Maria invited me to tea the following Wednesday—I would work with Aldous in the afternoon, she said, and then stay for dinner. I went to the Spanish house in Kings Road braced for a difficult session. I think Maria and Aldous sensed my nervousness and were amused by it. After giving us tea, Maria said, "Now you two go and do your work."

Aldous lay on the bed of the guest room, and I sat nearby. Aldous said that he wanted to be able to relive past events in the same way that Maria and many others did. He was, he said, only capable of remembering, of reconstructing circumstances, people, and surroundings, by mental organization. But he claimed that he had no visual memory and that to him it was puzzling and frustrating not to be able actually to visualize, or "see again," what he knew and remembered so well. How often we were to discuss this matter! Aldous had an infinite interest in and derived great pleasure from seeing, and he remembered in precise detail paintings, places, and people. In view of this, it was difficult to believe that he did it all by a mental reconstruction.

We tried various methods of entering into the period of his life of which he had so little recall. Aldous was attentive and willing to follow directions, but we were not succeeding. After about an hour I had what I thought was a brilliant idea. I suspected that he was not getting anywhere because he was a little embarrassed by my presence, by *my* conducting this "session." If, perhaps, he could do something for me, he would feel more relaxed afterwards.

"Aldous," I said, "it might be good to stop for a few minutes, let your subconscious do the work, and then start again. In the meantime, would you show me how you do those passes of Dr. Esdaile's?"

"Nothing easier," said Aldous, jumping off the bed. "Lie down."

I lay down, pleased with my strategy and with the fact that Aldous was pleased, too. I didn't really know what he was going to do—uppermost in my mind was the thought of being ready for the propitious moment to exchange place and role.

In making magnetic passes, the hands of the operator never touch the patient: they merely stroke the air about two inches above the patient's body and are effective through some agent other than the spoken word or the touch. Aldous started the magnetic passes, just as he described them ten years later in *Island:*

Dr. Andrew took off his coat, rolled up his shirt sleeves and started to make those famous magnetic passes, about which he had read with so much skeptical amusement in *The Lancet.* From the crown of the head, over the face and down the trunk to the epigastrium, again and again until the patient falls into a trance. ...Quackery, humbug and fraud, but all the same it worked, it obviously worked.

Yes, it obviously did!

But I could not *let* it work for, I kept reminding myself, I was there to give *him* a session. I was not going to let him skip it by this silly technique. This was only *my* strategy to handle *his* "stubborn subconscious resistance." In fact, I assured myself, I didn't really feel anything. It obviously wasn't working on me. Yet, how soothing it was to feel the warm vitality flow over my body from Aldous's hands.

Many thoughts were running through my mind, especially how odd and also how ridiculous all this was. I would surreptitiously open my eyes and see the long, bent figure of Aldous leaning toward me, with his interminable arms and outstretched hands stroking the air over my body. Too ridiculous for words! Still, I felt strange currents about my forehead. Unexpectedly a deep sigh came out of me. How comfortable it would be just to let go—to give in—to float away on this gentle river... I caught myself just in time.

I really didn't feel much of anything, I told him, but I was interested and would try these magnetic passes on a friend who suffered migraine headaches. With an effort I quickly got off the bed and Aldous lay down.

I sat nearby in a deliciously vague state of mind, but I was unable to enjoy the deliciousness. I am a conscientious worker, and I was aware that Aldous was now expecting some direction from me. But I couldn't focus my mind. Worse still, Aldous's forgotten years didn't seem so important now. He is in good health, I told myself. He writes well. He really doesn't need this. With the excuse that it was dinnertime, I concluded a very ineffectual session and went to help Maria in the kitchen.

Throughout dinner I was vague and felt strangely out of focus. It was a hazy, pleasant mood, certainly, but on my rare visits to the Huxleys I wanted to be on my toes. The next day I told a friend about the magnetic passes and the pleasantly relaxed state they had put me in. She looked at me, puzzled and said, "I don't know what these passes are, but you certainly look strange today."

Fortunately I didn't have to leave the house and floated through the day lazily and vaguely—which was unusual for me. In the late afternoon I saw my friend again, who said "You still have that faraway look, Laura. You're acting like a somnambulist."

"I feel like one, and I like it." I replied.

She insisted that I call the Huxleys and ask them what to do about somnambulism.

Maria came to the phone. I didn't know what to say beyond thanking her for dinner. On the extension phone, my friend helped by saying that I was behaving like a sleepwalker. Maria was quick to understand.

"Did Aldous give you the waking-up passes?" she asked.

"Waking-up passes—what are they?"

"He forgot to wake you up!" she exclaimed. And pressingly, with laughter in her voice, she called, "Aldous!"

I heard him running to the phone.

"Aldous," she repeated, brimming with fun and mockingly reproachful, "Aldous! You forgot to wake up Laura."

"She didn't give me a chance," I heard Aldous protesting mildly. "Suddenly she jumped off the bed and said nothing was happening!"

Then he came to the phone—we all were laughing: at me, at Aldous, and at our session. Aldous told my friend to give me a few reverse passes. "Simply pass your hands over her body, without touching it, beginning from the waist to the top of the head, in a rather quick motion."

However, I no longer needed to be awakened—laughing together at ourselves had been the awakening spark.

For me, the high point of this episode still is Maria's voice, bubbling with irrepressible laughter and quizzical disapproval: "Aldous! *You forgot to wake up Laura.*"

This Timeless Moment

IN THE SUMMER of 1954 I was in Rome. For several years I had been involved in motion-picture production in Hollywood. Now American producers had "invaded" Italy and there was frantic activity in Cine Cittá, the enormous Roman studio. It seemed logical that, speaking Italian and having Hollywood experience, I would get a job. I was so enthusiastic that I would have taken any job, no matter how small. One morning I received a postcard from Lebanon. It was almost illegible. After closer examination I deciphered the signature: "Maria H." Then I succeeded in reading the message, which gave me their address and the date of their arrival in Rome: they were already here!

I called the hotel and had lunch with Maria and Aldous. They were going to be in Rome for about a week. As usual, Aldous was full of ideas for sightseeing in town and exploring the country around Rome. I had a little Fiat, and we planned two one-day excursions. My friendship with Maria and Aldous became more intimate during that week in Rome than it had in our scattered meetings in Los Angeles over the years.

Maria was exhausted by the last few weeks of traveling. She was pale and thin, noticeably more so than a few months before when I had seen her in Los Angeles. When she had told me of her illness, she also said that she had had enough of life, that she was ready to go. However, it was not a feeling of sadness or bitterness—it was more a feeling of "mission accomplished" or "that's all for now." But I worried about the feeling and the illness, and wondered which had come first.

The Huxleys invited me to go with them to dinner at Sybille Bedford's. Maria said that they had been friends since Sybille was a young girl and that her mother was a principal character in one of Aldous's books. Now Sybille, a writer herself, was in the middle of an important novel, and was having some difficulty finishing it. Maria thought that perhaps a few sessions with me might be effective in releasing her creative energies. After the Huxleys left, Sybille and I became friends; she told me that they had asked her if they could bring a guest that evening, but had given no hint of sex or age. Maria had only said that it was someone who probably could help her over her difficulty. Sybille imagined that the guest would be a staid and bearded philosopher, and waited all evening for the wise man to appear. She thought I was just his daughter, who certainly had nothing to do with philosophy, and that he would arrive later.

It was that evening, on Sybille's terrace, fragrant with flowers and the ineffable sensuality of a persuading Roman night, that Maria told me, "Laura, I changed my mind since I saw you last; now I think I will live a little longer. I am paying attention to my health now—taking vitamins and eating more." As I was wondering whether she said this only to reassure me, she continued, "And I had a funny dream; I dreamed that Maria ascended into heaven." She looked at me, smiling and feeling my silent suspense. After a few seconds' pause she added quickly, "Then she changed her mind and came right back to earth!" For a moment I had a glimpse of Maria as a young girl, light and mischievous.

 I saw her efforts to "eat more" two days later when, on our way to Tarquinia to see the Etruscan tombs, we stopped in the country for lunch. I shall never forget that lunch. We were having spaghetti, and Maria was trying—trying so hard—to eat, but the food seemed so difficult to swallow. My heart sank. The memory of my mother, who for years had had the same difficulty and had died of a similar illness, gave poignancy to my feeling for Maria. How diligently they both tried to eat just one more mouthful....

We planned for another day together, driving to Monte Cassino.

"We like to go with you, Laura, because when we come back you don't ask us to attend some official dinner with all the diplomatic corps in Rome," Maria said. However, she explained, she was not going to go with us this time. "I think tomorrow I will stay in bed. You and your friend and Aldous go. I don't know *when* I will have another day to myself."

The next morning, as I was trying to park in front of the hotel, Maria came running out the front door. I was pleased to see her but she looked so exhausted I thought it might be better for her to stay home and rest.

"Good morning, Maria. I knew you would be coming." I spoke without thinking; it was just a spontaneous reaction.

"I decided to come," she said thoughtfully, "because if I didn't Aldous might feel that when so many times in the past I have gone, I really didn't want to." I did not answer. "Why do *you* think I am coming?"

I was not really thinking; I had just known she would be coming and said so without a second thought, but I was quick to answer, "For the reason you just said." She gave me a strange look, and then I did begin to think. Perhaps she is coming because there may not be many more outings with Aldous. She knows it. Does he?

He did not.

Toward the end of that day, before entering the city, Maria, perceptive as usual said, "Laura has been driving a lot; we must stop and reinforce her before attacking the Roman traffic." We stopped at a trattoria *all' aperto* for an afternoon pickup. It was lovely, sipping our drink, with the Campagna Romana, vast and quiet, at our feet.

But throughout the day I had seen Maria becoming more and more worn out—tired to death; and now her neck was tense and painful. It might help to massage it a little, we thought. It must have been a rather energetic massage I gave her, because when I finished she said, in that half-mocking, half-affectionate way of hers which left me wondering: "I see—you are the tempestuous type."

I never saw her again.

Maria and Aldous left the next day for Paris and we did not correspond. I stayed in Europe the rest of that year and flew into Los Angeles at one o'clock in the morning, on Saturday, February 12, 1955.

How limited is our consciousness! Involved with the immediate fact of my return to Los Angeles after a year's absence, busy with luggage, tickets, and similar details, I was unaware of what was happening at that moment to Maria and Aldous. These were her last hours. Bent over her dying body, Aldous was whispering to her words of love, joy and peace.

Two weeks later Aldous told me how she died. He also wrote an account of her death, which he gave to a few friends. It conveys the feeling that death is not the end of consciousness but rather an expansion of it. It is a touching document of human love which could totally change, in many persons, their tremulous attitude toward death. This is his account.

Maria was in the hospital for two periods of about two weeks each, with an interval of a week between them. During these two periods she underwent a long series of tests and was given twelve X-ray treatments to relieve the pain in the lower spine and to guard against the spread, in that area, of what was suspected to be malignancy. These treatments were tolerated at first fairly well; but the last of them produced distressing symptoms, due, as it turned out, to cancer of the liver. During the last few days in hospital Maria was unable to keep any food or liquid in the stomach and had to be fed intravenously.

She was brought home in an ambulance on Monday, February 7th, and installed in her own room. The nurse who had taken care of her after her operation, four years before, was waiting for her when she arrived. Maria had a real affection for this good, deeply compassionate woman, and the affection was warmly reciprocated. Three days later a second nurse was called in for night duty.

On the Monday afternoon her old friend L. the psychotherapist, came in for half an hour, put her into hypnosis and gave her suggestions to the effect that the nausea, which had made her life miserable during the preceding days, would disappear, and that she would be able to keep down whatever food was given to her. Later that evening I repeated these suggestions, and from that time forward there was no more nausea and it was possible for her to take liquid nourishment and a sufficiency of water for the body's needs. No further intravenous feeding was necessary.

The progress of the disease was extraordinarily rapid. She was still able to find a great and fully conscious happiness in seeing her son, who had flown in from New York on Tuesday morning. But by Wednesday, when her sister S. arrived, her response was only just conscious. She recognized S. and said a few words to her; but after that there was very little communication. Maria could hear still; but it was becoming harder and harder for her to speak, and the words, when they came, were wandering words, whose relevance was to the inner life of illness, not to the external world.

I spent a good many hours of each day sitting with her, sometimes saying nothing, sometimes speaking. When I spoke, it was always, first of all, to give suggestions about her physical well-being. I would go through the ordinary procedure of hypnotic induction, beginning by suggestions of muscular relaxation, then counting to five or ten, with the suggestion that each count would send her deeper into hypnosis. I would generally accompany the counting with passes of the hand, which I drew slowly down from the head towards the feet. After the induction period was over, I would suggest that she was feeling, and would continue to feel, comfortable, free from pain and nausea, desirous of taking water and liquid nourishment whenever they should be offered. These suggestions were, I think, effective; at any rate there was little pain and it was only during the last thirty-six hours that sedation (with Demerol) became necessary.

These suggestions for physical comfort were in every case followed by a much longer series of suggestions addressed to the deeper levels of the mind. Under hypnosis Maria had had, in the past, many remarkable visionary experiences of a kind which theologians would call "pre-mystical." She had also had, especially while we were living in the Mojave Desert, during the war, a number of genuinely mystical experiences, had lived with an abiding sense of divine immanence, of Reality totally present, moment by moment in every object, person and event. This was the reason for her passionate love of the desert. For her, it was not merely a geographical region; it was also a state of mind, a metaphysical reality, an unequivocal manifestation of God.

In the desert and, later, under hypnosis, all Maria's visionary and mystical experiences had been associated with light. (In this she was in no way exceptional. Almost all mystics and visionaries have experienced Reality in terms of light—either of light in its naked purity, or of light infusing and radiating out of things and persons seen with the inner eye or in the external world.) Light had been the element in which her spirit had lived, and it was therefore to light that all my words referred. I would begin by reminding her of the desert she loved so much, of the vast crystalline silence, of the overarching sky, of the snow-covered mountains at whose feet we had lived. I would ask her to open the eyes of memory to the desert sky and to think of it as the blue light of Peace, soft and yet intense, gentle and yet irresistible in its tranquillizing power. And now, I would say, it was evening in the desert, and the sun was setting. Overhead the sky was more deeply blue than ever. But in the West there was a great golden illumination deepening to red; and this was the golden light of Joy, the rosy light of Love. And to the South rose the mountains, covered with snow and glowing with the white light of pure Being—the white light which is the source of the coloured lights, the absolute Being of which love, joy and peace are manifestations, and which all dualism of our experience, all the pairs of opposites—positive and negative, good and evil, pleasure and pain, health and sickness, life and death—are reconciled and made one. And I would ask her to look at these lights of her beloved desert and to realize that they were not merely symbols, but actual expression of the divine nature; an expression of Pure Being, an expression of the peace that passeth all understanding; an expression of the divine joy; an expression of the love which is at the heart of things, at the core, along with peace and joy and being, of every human mind. And having reminded her of those truths—truths which we all know in the unconscious depths of our being, which some know consciously but only theoretically and which a few (Maria was one of them) have known directly, albeit briefly and by snatches—I would urge her to advance into those lights, to open herself to joy, peace, love and being, to permit herself to be irradiated by them and to become one of them. I urged her to become what in fact she had always been, what all of us have always been, a part of the divine substance, a manifestation of love, joy and peace, a being identical with the One Reality. And I kept on repeating this, urging her to go deeper and deeper into the light, ever deeper and deeper.

And the days passed, and her body weakened, her surface mind drifted further and further out of contact, so that she no longer recognized us or paid attention. And yet she must have still heard and understood what was said; for she would respond by appropriate action, when the nurse asked her to open her mouth or swallow. Under anesthesia, the sense of hearing remains awake long after the other senses have been eliminated. And even in deep sleep, suggestions will be accepted and complicated sentences can be memorized. Addressing the deep mind which never sleeps, I went on suggesting that there should be relaxation on the physical level, and an absence of pain and nausea; and I continued to remind her of who she really was—a manifestation in time of eternal, a part forever unseparated from the whole, of the divine reality; I went on urging her to go forward into the light.

A little before three on Saturday morning the night nurse came and told us that the pulse was failing. I went and sat by Maria's bed and from time to time leaned over and spoke into her ear. I told her that I was with her and would always be with her in that light which was the central reality of our beings. I told her that she was surrounded by human love and that this love was manifestation of a greater love, by which she was enveloped and sustained. I told her to let go, to forget the body, to leave it lying here like a bundle of old clothes and to allow herself to be carried, as a child is carried, into the heart of the rosy light of love. She knew what love was, had been capable of love as few human beings are capable. Now she must go forward into love, must permit herself to be carried into love, deeper and deeper into it, so that at last she would be capable of loving as God loves—of loving everything, infinitely, without judging, without condemning, without either craving or abhorring. And then there was peace. How passionately, from the depth of a fatigue which illness and a frail constitution had often intensified to the point of being hardly bearable, she had longed for peace! And now she would have peace. And where there was peace and love, there too there would be joy. And the river of the coloured lights was carrying her towards the white light of pure being, which is the source of all things and reconciliation of all opposites in unity. And she was to forget, not only her poor body, but the time in which that body had lived. Let her forget the past, leave her old memories behind.

Regrets, nostalgias, remorses, apprehensions—all these were barriers between her and the light. Let her forget them, forget them completely, and stand there, transparent, in the presence of the light—absorbing it, allowing herself to be made one with it in the timeless now of present instant. "Peace now," I kept repeating, "Peace, love, joy *now*. Being *now*."

For the last hour I sat or stood with my left hand on her head and the right on the solar plexus. Between two right-handed persons this contact seems to create a kind of vital circuit. For a restless child, for a sick or tired adult, there seems to be something soothing and refreshing about being in such a circuit. And so it proved even in this extremity. The breathing became quieter and I had the impression that there was some kind of release. I went on with my suggestions and reminders, reducing them to their simplest form and repeating them close to the ear. "Let go, let go. Forget the body, leave it lying here; it is of no importance now. Go forward into the light. Let yourself be carried into light. No memories, no regrets, no looking backwards, no apprehensive thoughts about your own or anyone else's future. Only light. Only this pure being, this love, this joy. Above all this peace. Peace in this timeless moment, peace now, peace *now!*" When the breathing ceased, at about six, it was without any struggle.

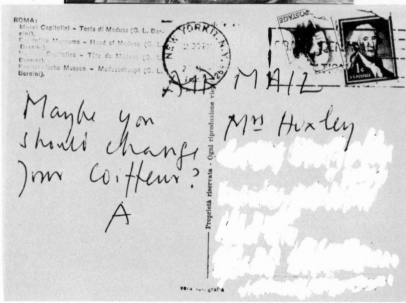

ROMA:
  Musei Capitolini – Testa di Medusa (G. L. Bernini).
  Capitoline Museums – Head of Medusa (G. L. Bernini).
  Musei Capitolini – Tête de Méduse (G. L. Bernini).
  Kapitolinische Museen – Medusenhaupt (G. L. Bernini).

Maybe you
should change
your coiffeur?
A

Mrs Huxley

The two sides of a postcard sent by Aldous to Laura in 1963. On the
front is a photograph of Bernini's Head of Medusa.

My One and Only

In the months that followed Maria Huxley's death in 1955, I dined quite often at Aldous's home. He was going through the most difficult period of his life. I saw then, for the first time, how Aldous applied his philosophy: Live here and now; do not be a slave of emotional memories of the past; be aware of what is going on now. "Let go," he had told his dying wife, "let go. No memories, no regrets, no looking backwards—go forward...."

The exhortation he had given to Maria, confronting death, was the same he now applied to himself, starting life again with the living. He succeeded much of the time. Once in a while he would lapse into a depressed silence. He did not speak much about his pain; he only said, "It is like an amputation." But, as he later wrote: "Amputation was no excuse for self-pity and, for all that Dugal was dead, the birds were as beautiful as ever and her children, all the other children, had as much need to be loved and helped and taught.... Henceforth she must love for two, take thought for two...."[1]

A few words, but it takes love, good will, and a youthful spirit to change those words into living. Aldous maintained throughout his life the best characteristics of youth: openness to ideas, an ability to let go of old habits, a desire to travel and learn firsthand from new cultures. It was perhaps this mental youthfulness that gave him physical resilience. When we were traveling, the schedule of meeting people, visiting museums, and generally trotting around was mentally and physically fatiguing. On one of these exhausting days, when we returned to the hotel to take a breath and get ready for dinner, Aldous took me to my

[1] Unless otherwise identified, all quotations are from *Island*.

room saying: "You rest a little, darling. I am going to take a turn around the block and will back in time to change my suit."

This natural abundance of physical and mental energy remained constant in Aldous through high and low periods of his life. Even a few months after the death of Maria he could write the following birthday letter to his brother:

June 22, 1955

Dearest Julian

Many happy and happier returns! Yes, it is hard to feel old—to be quite *serieux,* as the ageing bourgeois ought to be! We both, I think, belong to that fortunate minority of human beings who retain the mental openness and elasticity of youth, while being able to enjoy the fruits of an already long experience. Why there should be so few of these sub-species of homo sapiens, or why the majority of men and women, and even adolescents, should develop mental arterio-sclerosis forty or fifty years before they develop physical arterio-sclerosis is a great mystery. And yet the fact is obvious. Most people encapsulate themselves, shut up like oysters, sometimes before they have stopped being undergraduates, and go through life barricaded against every idea, every fresh and unconceptualized perception. It is obvious that education will never give satisfactory results until we learn how to teach children and adults to retain their openness. But the practical problem is as yet hardly considered by professional educators. I was pleased to learn, however, that the General Semantics people here—Hayakawa and the group which puts out that excellent little review "Etc"—have developed methods for training people to pass at will from conceptualized perception to direct virgin perception. The exercise keeps the mind fresh and sensitive and teaches a wholesome understanding of the function of language and its dangers, when taken too seriously, in the way that all pedants, doctrinaires and dogmatists invariably do, with such catastrophic results.

During that year of bereavement Aldous kept very busy. I think he made it a point to accept many social invitations; in the evenings he spent at home I was often there. As for the rest of our lives, we would speak of everything under the sun. I was then very active in psychotherapy. We discussed that; we listened to music, experimented with cooking. Marie LePut, the lovable and wise Bretonne who had helped Maria, came three times a week to Aldous. We always found delicious dinners ready in the refrigerator. (Monsieur is eating so much," she said to a friend. She did not know that often there were two eating her meals.)

One evening Aldous played a recording of his reading from *Time Must Have a Stop.* "It is my favorite book of Aldous's," Maria had told me the previous summer. It was a passage that has an extraordinary transporting quality. Now we would call it a psychedelic quality, but at that time the word had not yet been coined. The most amazing fact is that Aldous had written *Time Must Have a Stop* some ten years before he had taken mescaline, yet in the passage describing the transit between two states of consciousness the same preternatural quality of certain aspects of the psychedelic experience is conveyed. The door which later opened wide was already ajar. As mystics and poets had done for centuries before him, Aldous had written of psychedelics long before he had partaken of the sacred plant.

Another evening Aldous spoke about automatic writing—he was experimenting with it. In automatic writing, one sits with paper and pencil and waits for an involuntary impulse to make the hand move—to write or draw. Aldous said that nothing of value would come to him, but that it was refreshing and consoling to realize that part of his mind was totally detached from his present thoughts and feelings. The mention of automatic writing brought to my mind a strange event which had occurred to me in Rome the previous summer. One morning I had awakened with a complete poem in my mind. I only had to write it down. It was the first time I had written anything and the only time I have written a poem. When I read it, I was surprised and rather shocked by the clearness and polished brutality of its message from myself to myself. I searched for it among my papers and the next time I saw Aldous I told him about my experience in automatic writing and the unexpected way the poem had flowed out of me, concept, words, and rhythm, without effort. While I had been tensely and myopically staring at my superficial problems, the poem had suddenly appeared— a severe pointing finger commanding that attention be given to the *real* problem.

Aldous was almost as fluent in Italian as in English. So I read the poem as I had written it, in Italian, with the passionate feeling that those lines aroused in me. Aldous smiled the surprised, delighted, and somehow innocent smile that such phenomena of the human mind always called forth in him. I remember his comment verbatim. "Very good," he said, "and painfully true, for all of us."

Years later, when I was working on *You Are Not the Target* (at that time called "Recipes for Living"), I thought the poem would make a good springboard for a "recipe," and I asked Aldous if he would translate it into English. We discussed the differences in words—the

Italian incisive and sculptural, the English rounder and more mysterious. Here is the poem in both languages:

ODE ALL'IO

O Mio Unico Amatissimo IO

O tu che mi socchiudi gli occhi cosi ch'essi vedano come tu vedi,
O tu che fai si che le mie orecchie odano cio' che tu odi,
O tu che mi salvi dall'Eterno e dall'Infinito,
O tu che attraverso la realta pulsante della paura mi fai sentire
   la vita
IO Mio Unico Amatissimo IO, a te m'inchino, tuo volontario
   servilissimo schiavo.
Tu mi proteggi dalla immensa liberta
O mio unico amatissimo io,
Tu mi possiedi come un avido magnifico amante e
Invece della Gioia continua ed infinita
Mi dai ore di piacere lento e violento—
Mio unico generosissimo io
Tu vinci quando sei amato, tu trionfi quando sei flagellato.
Tua serva e la mio preziosissima pelle, che tiene ben avvolto
Il miracole del mia corpo per anche cent'anni—
O mio unico amatissimo io,
Sarei il profumo e la musica, il cielo e il mare.
Personale—
Definito—
Ineguagliabile—
O mio unico amatissimo io,
Tu mi dai la capacita
Di capire
Invece di essere
Di possedere
Invece di essere
Di esistere
INVECE DI ESSERE!

Laura Archera, Rome, 1954
English translation by Aldous Huxley, Los Angeles, 1959

ODE TO ME

My One and Only, My Most Beloved Me

My one and only, my best beloved ME,
You, who forever keep my eyes half closed
That they may see only as *you* see,
Who make my ears to hear only as *you* hear.
Oh, you, my saviour from the Eternal,
My preserver from the Infinite,
You, who reveal life through the throb of fear,
You, *my one and only, my best beloved* ME,
To you, your abject voluntary slave,
I humbly bow ...

From the huge threat of Freedom you protect me,
My one and only, my best beloved ME,
Like some fierce lover, avid and commanding,
You possess me ...
Instead of changeless infinite bliss you give me
The languor or violence of time-bound pleasure,
My one and only, my most generous ME.
You conquer when I love you
And when I hate you, you triumph still—
Your servant is my precious skin that wraps
The marvel of my body even for a hundred years—

Without you I would know eternity,
My *one and only, my best beloved* ME.
I would be all—fragrance and music, sea and sky ...
ME, personal
ME, the unmatchable
ME, the captive
ME, ME, ME!

You make me capable of knowing—
But not of being.
Of possessing—
But not of being.
Of existing—
BUT NOT OF BEING!

The Drive-in Wedding Chapel

"HAVE YOU EVER been tempted by marriage?"

I had never been asked that question in such a charming way. A woman, unmarried after thirty-five, is often asked why she is still single, but the innuendo in the question is usually, "Haven't you been able to catch a husband?" or "Do you think no one is good enough for you?" From the very tone in which the question is asked, one can often perceive much of the questioner's inner feeling, as well as the fact that very likely he has already answered his own question. But in wording and tone Aldous's question was charming and limpid—really interrogative and objective, making one want to answer as sincerely as possible.

It was an evening in the beginning of his widowhood. We had had one of those delicious dinners prepared in advance by Marie; we had finished with the dishes and were talking, this time about me. On the subject of marriage, our experience was so different. His marriage, a creative, thirty-five-year-long relationship, had just been ended by death. I had never been married. Aldous's question launched me into an autobiographical narration of some aspects of my life. It ended with the mention of two men—but these are other stories.

What had chiefly kept me from marriage was the fear of losing my freedom of action. As a child and an adolescent I had been almost completely deprived of freedom and had attained it not by the usual rebellion of youth but by unflinching arduous work. I valued liberty in an almost obsessive way.

Aldous rarely forgot anything. Months later, on a late Sunday afternoon in March 1956, we took off for Yuma, Arizona, to be married.

We planned to drive about a hundred miles that evening, then go on, the next morning, to Yuma. As we were driving in the dark, a diffuse anxiety overtook me, and I lapsed into a moody silence. Aldous sensed it immediately. After a while he said, "Are you worried about losing your precious liberty?" It is one of the few times, maybe the only one, that I heard in Aldous's tone toward me a slight overtone of irony.

"I won't," I answered darkly.

We drove until late that night and stopped at a motel about one hundred fifty miles from Yuma.

The summer before, Aldous had driven East with Rose, his sister-in-law. She told me later that one of the most amusing sights for him on the trip had been the Drive-in Wedding Chapel in Yuma. Later, when we decided to marry, Aldous had said, "Do you think it might be amusing to drive to Yuma and get married at the Drive-in?" Nothing could delight me more, I said. I have an anti-ritualistic streak in me, and a "drive-in marriage" was most unritualistically attractive. Considering Aldous's very British and Victorian upbringing, this suggestion was another revealing indication of his inner freedom.

After breakfast we stopped for a walk in the Arizona desert and arrived in Yuma at about one o'clock. I believe no two people could have been more naïve and uninformed about this kind of marriage. But we weren't in the least worried, or even aware of our ignorance. We were looking for a restaurant when, comfortably on our right, there it was—a little shack with big letters: DRIVE-IN WEDDING CHAPEL. INSTANT MARRIAGE. I slowed down and Aldous said, "I will go in and see—it might be necessary to make an appointment." I stayed in the car and waited.

Aldous was in the shack much longer than I had expected. When finally he came out, he was not alone. A lanky, underworldly fellow was with him. The mind is such a surprising organism—instantly, mine presented me with a ready-made, stereotyped television script into which fitted the present real events. Paradoxical and parallel, it co-existed with them. The Drive-in Wedding Chapel was a decoy; Aldous had been trapped; this man was obviously a gangster. What should our next move be? Aldous looked so serious!

"What happened?" I asked in a low voice. Aldous did not answer. Of course he heard me, but he had been ordered not to talk, I was sure. It must be a grave situation to make Aldous suddenly so serious. (The fact that he might be serious because he was getting married never entered my mind—it was not in *that* TV script.) The gangster sat in the front seat with Aldous and me, "to give directions." It was obvious we were being kidnapped. This fellow was typical of the underworld—pale, undernourished, and liverish; never exposed to the light of the day, smoking too much, passing the night in bars, He was devoured by ulcers, I quickly diagnosed, caused by the poisonous pangs of guilt inflicted on the sensitive lining of his stomach by the knowledge (conscious or unconscious?) of the ignobleness of his profession—luring innocent couples into marriage traps and then ... What a hellish life! What was he going to do with us? What could we do? Just do as we were told? Why would Aldous not talk?

"Who is he?" I tried in French.

Instead of answering in French, Aldous said, "He is taking us to city hall."

If the thought occurred to me, even for a split second, that city hall could be connected with marriage, it was immediately obliterated by that part of my mind furiously at work on the TV script. City hall, indeed!

"Turn right, dearie," creaked the gangster in a high voice, as though he were being strangled.

I was driving very slowly, trying to think of a way out. But how could I plan an escape from this nefarious character if Aldous refused to talk to me? I got bolder.

"But, Aldous, why does he want us to go to city hall?"

Aldous's answer was tense, quick, and—in a manner new to me—as though he were being put upon. "But, darling, this is the way it is done —we have to sign some papers."

Of course, the script went on—the ransom papers! There was no use in being cautious; better face facts; surely our situation could not be worse. On the other hand, the gangster was alone; we were two, although unarmed. Almost aggressively, and in a loud voice, I asked, "Sign papers for WHAT?"

"To get MARRIED," Aldous almost shouted.

"But you said you were going in just to get an appointment."

"Yes, I know." Aldous had never been so edgy. "But they want to marry us right now.

As I was about to answer, the strangled voice said, "Stop here, dearie."

I stopped and we got out of the car. I looked at the building. It *was* the city hall! With the same abruptness with which it had presented it, my mind dismissed the TV script. Obviously, the reality was much more thrilling. And it was going at a thrilling speed.

Swiftly we floated through several halls to a counter where a smiling woman, who seemed to enjoy her job thoroughly asked us whether we had been married in Arizona in the last twelve months—and how old we were? Then we signed a paper. When the woman saw Aldous's name, she became even more cordial and told Aldous she had read

Brave New World. Then we were guided back to the Drive-in Wedding Chapel.

"While we get ready," the ex-gangster said, "you may want to go to the rest room." Aldous was whisked to one side of the hall and I to the other. The ladies' room attendant asked me if I needed anything. I was dusty after the long drive and the walk in the desert. I thought of the lovely canary-yellow suit I had bought for the occasion. ("You must have at least *one* new dress to get married," Ginny had said. Ginny—Virginia Pfeiffer—our best mutual friend, was the only person I had told of our plans.)

I had delayed shopping until Saturday, the day before our "elopement." Five minutes before closing time, Ginny and I had found the very suit I wanted on a dummy in the window of Bullock's Wilshire. We had rushed in. "It's closing time," the tired saleslady had said. Ginny revived her by confiding to her that the suit was going to be used for an elopement the next day—Sunday. The saleslady was now willing to sell the suit, but union rules demanded that only a "specialized initiate" could undress the dummy. By now the "specialized initiate" had gone off for his weekend. Wondering what kind of initiating she could mean, I climbed into the window and undressed the dummy myself, while the dazed saleslady watched helplessly. As the doors were being locked, I signed the sales slip, and we left with the suit in my arms, unpackaged. And now it was in the trunk of the car. Would I have time to get it out and put it on? The quick tempo of the last ten minutes had infected me —I found myself feeling that everything must be done very fast. (Later, we wondered how many couples the Drive-in Wedding Chapel's director had seen change their minds at the last minute.)

The ladies' room assistant, overweight and motherly, was obviously accustomed to brides in need of reassuring; she told me I looked just right. I left the ladies' room and found Aldous sitting on a little sofa in the entrance hall. I sat down near him. "What now?" I asked.

"Now they are going to marry us at once."

Suddenly a new anxiety, different from that of the night before, came over me. Aldous was used to such a different person in Maria. I wasn't like her—Aldous knew this better than I—but the preposterous thought flashed through my mind that he might expect from me the same total dedication. I loved him and did not want to disappoint him, but now it was too late to discuss this. So I only said, "You know, darling, I love others, too."

Instantaneous, crystal-clear, and tranquil was Aldous's answer: "It would be awful if you didn't."

Silence. Wonderful silence, in which to love and be grateful. As throughout our life together, Aldous had dissolved my doubts and uncertainty in tenderness and gratefulness. A few seconds later, when the ex-gangster came in, I was different—and so was he. My suspicion had changed into compassion: no, he never was a gangster, he was a victim! He still had ulcers, but from a different cause—actually, because he was *too* nice. From childhood on, he had never exploded when all those powerful women kept telling him he was "such a nice boy." What fury and loneliness! The ex-gangster-victim handed Aldous a paper—the bill. Aldous took out his checkbook and wrote out a check.

"Now," the ex-gangster-victim said, "our minister is ready for you. You only need two witnesses."

Aldous and I looked at each other. We did not know a soul in Yuma. We had come here so as not to have witnesses. Aldous started to speak, but the ex-gangster-victim, who had undoubtedly handled the same situation many times before, cut it short. "I can be your witness," he said to Aldous, "and Miss —— will be yours." He called in the ladies' room attendant, who was not surprised.

"What a marvelous organization," I thought.

We were shown into the next room, the chapel, which was also, we gathered from the crumbs on the floor, a dining room, squalid and dark. After a moment a very long purplish flourescent light on the ceiling slowly lighted up. Instantaneously, we all looked cadaverous. In a dark gray suit, middleaged and nondescript, the minister came in. The Book in his hand, and a little ribbon over his shoulder, he was conservatively and mechanically playing his role.

Each of us was properly placed—the gangster-victim standing a little back of Aldous, and the ladies' room assistant a little back of me —all of us facing the minister. It is impossible to describe the squalor of the purplish light on the imitation Oriental rug, dark furniture, dusty artificial flowers.

We were ready to start when the minister said, "The ring."

Aldous and I looked at each other, dismayed. We had planned to get one in Yuma, but we had not had a chance. Suddenly I remembered—I had one in my traveling bag. The year before, when traveling in Europe alone, I had bought a wedding ring in a five-and-ten. I used it only once or twice when I wanted to bring to a close a conversation with a too demonstrative train acquaintance; the appearance of a ring on my left-hand ring finger was the most effective symbol of a husband—possibly a dangerously jealous one. I was handed my large traveling bag.

How is it that a traveling bag is practically a woman's biography? How many objects can a traveling bag contain? Everything seemed to be in mine. I started to take things out one by one, and finally in desperation emptied the entire contents on the floor. Aldous and the others did not move from their positions but looked on—fascinated or flabbergasted?—I do not know. The ring was not there. After further exploration I felt it; it had slipped between the lining and the leather. It wasn't easy to work it out of the small hole through which it had slipped. When finally I recovered it, quickly and triumphantly I slipped it on my finger. Unanimously the trio protested.

"You are not married yet!" the minister said severely. "Give him the ring."

I gave it to our "witness" and then got in position again. Finally the minister read his bit. It would be impossible to imagine a more uninspiring, a more shallow scene. A small ant dutifully transporting a crumb of bread would have been infinitely more real, interesting, inspiring.

But rituals, even when reduced to their minimum, are a powerful force. The fact that a stranger (regularly licensed or ordained), witnessed by two other strangers, read aloud certain words changed our status and many important facts in our outer lives. We are part of a society that feels pacified when it can label people; now it could comfortably call us husband and wife. Aldous and I felt relieved, amused, and hungry.

We asked about a restaurant and left the Drive-in Chapel in a hurry —naïvely feeling light and free. But we had scarcely sat down at the restaurant when two sleuths from the local newspaper descended on us. Aldous was surprised and dismayed. He had no idea that his marriage would interest the press—or that the interest would be so immediate. Had we had the slightest idea of it, we could simply have driven out of town. Aldous gave little satisfaction to the newsmen, but, we heard later, the news was on the radio within an hour.

I was not worried about my family hearing the news. Aldous had written my father a month before and had received his answer. Ginny knew that we were getting married; she would call a few of my close friends. I had taken it for granted that Aldous had made a similar arrangement. I did not quite realize that it was in Aldous's nature to act first and speak later. Yesterday, just before leaving for Yuma, he had had lunch with his great friend, Gerald Heard. Surely, I thought, our marriage had been the principal subject of conversation. How egocentric and pedestrian was my logic! They had spoken of the exceptional good health and longevity of laboratory mice—those who were given massive doses of sexual pleasure through electronic devices; they had spoken of the prodigiously superior, strong, and ethereal nets spiders make under the influence of LSD; they had spoken of cockroaches and telepathy—but not of our marriage!

I thought Aldous seemed worried out of proportion by the sudden appearance of the journalists. As soon as they left, I understood why;

he had not told his son yet and was deeply distressed by the possibility that Matthew might hear the news first from the press.

We left Yuma and drove to a nearby resort. We took a large bungalow, and Aldous wrote immediately to his son and daughter-in-law.

Yuma, Arizona
19-III-56

Dearest Matthew and Ellen

As you have probably read already in the papers—for the press was on hand within two minutes of our signing the license—Laura Archera and I got married today at Yuma in a naïve hope of privacy that has turned into publicity all the same. You remember her, I am sure—a young woman who used to be a concert violinist, then turned movie cutter for Pascal. I have come to be very much attached to her in recent months and since it seemed to be reciprocal we decided to cross the Arizona border and call at the Drive-in Wedding Chapel (actual name). She is twenty years younger than I am, but doesn't seem to mind. Cocola[1] was fond of her and we saw her a lot in Rome that last summer abroad. I had a sense for a time that I was being unfaithful to that memory. But tenderness, I discover, is the best memorial to tenderness. You will be seeing her in April when we come East.

Ever your affectionate

Aldous

---

[1] Maria's nickname.

The Angel of Love, a detail from Bernini's Ecstasy of St. Theresa, a favorite of Aldous

Bocca Baciata

As I WRITE these notes I am faced with many stumbling blocks. One that recurs very often is the difficulty of describing a certain way Aldous smiled to me or at me—not all the time, but when something in me surprised or pleased him. Aldous had many kinds of smiles. Rarely was his smile ironical, and when it was, it was benevolently so. Often it was a sensuous smile. Although he was extremely polite, I rarely saw on him a perfunctory smile.

But the smile which—against all the rules of egolessness—I call *my* smile was different from all of these. It was one of his many unconscious gifts to me. It was a sudden smile, surprised, loving, and amused. The best way to describe it is to say that it was luminous. It was one of those little miracles with which more fortunate human beings enlighten each other's lives.

One of the first times I noticed it was the evening Aldous asked me to marry him. It must have been in January 1956. He had mentioned marriage before, in the fall of 1955, after our summer meeting in New York. It was not an easy matter for either of us. He had asked someone in marriage thirty-six years before, and the marriage had been one of the happiest, one of the most complete. For me it was not easy, either— I, who had never married, who had an almost compulsive attachment to freedom.

Now our lives had become very close. We had taken trips together; we knew and liked our design for living. Marriage would only be a confirmation of the closeness of our lives.

We were having dinner at his house. Christmas and the New Year had come and gone. Aldous was invited everywhere to give lectures—

there were to be several in the East in early spring. "It might be nice to be in Washington for the cherry blossoms," he had said nonchalantly earlier. And then, as if picking up an interrupted conversation, he said briskly, "Well, now, what about plans—shouldn't we decide the date we are going to marry?" The tone was light and gentle. Such an important question—but he was not going to make this heavy or momentous. I felt a trembling in the air, a suspension. As I was silently experiencing that timeless moment, Aldous continued, "Don't you think we should get married?"

His tone was now more pressing, but not *too* pressing—he was not going to force an answer if I were not ready for it. (I cannot remember Aldous's ever forcing me or anyone into anything. I think he was incapable of forcing.) Like a hummingbird miraculously suspended, seemingly motionless, his question hung in the air, sustained by our emotions—then it glided into my being. Passing to him the delicious veal Marie had cooked for us, and even more lightly and matter-of-fact than he had questioned, I answered, "I think it is very logical."

Then! How can I express that smile, that sudden light and warmth? From across the table he took my hand. "Thank you. You couldn't have said it any better." Ever since then, Aldous thought that logic was one of my strong points.

Men and women of outstanding achievement came to see Aldous. If he thought I would not be particularly interested in certain visitors, he would take a walk with them or converse in the garden. ("You don't have to be here, darling; you do something sensible, like swimming, while I talk with the philosophers.") Otherwise, we would usually ask the caller either for lunch on Saturday or for tea on Sunday. Many of the people who called on Aldous when they were passing through Los Angeles were outstanding scientists of various kinds: they were especially involved in the humanities, engaged in projects concerning education, the population explosion, and, generally speaking, the improvement of the human race, covering every phase, from the abolition of hunger to the correction of bad taste. Some of these projects were more worthwhile than others, but all of them, good or bad, had a feature in common which was to me disconcerting and discouraging. I can sum it up more or less like this: the scientists or educators would say, "We have a committee now," and then would ask Aldous to join the committee. "We are forming a non-profit foundation. When we have capital, say a million dollars, we will constitute another committee, buy a building, and engage some personnel. We will then start our work on an experimental basis to prove that our ideas are correct. After this is done, we can apply for greater funds and start to work with a group of individuals."

This was almost always the program. Aldous would give wonderful suggestions—at times so simple that they could be used the next day—but no, it always seemed necessary to have a committee, a million dollars, an experimental group, and many, many papers. I was becoming, at this time, more aware that the work I was doing personally with a handful of people could be useful to many.

I remember a particular Sunday—it must have been in 1959—when two brilliant English scientists had come for tea and discussed a very worthwhile project. But again, it was a question of large sums of money, committees, laboratories, and it seemed hopelessly long before any of this would have a practical application. I, being continuously involved in practical application, could hardly imagine a million dollars, or a million people, but I was very clear-minded about the individuals in question—quietly self-liquidating in streets, hospitals, and prisons, long before the project would even be out of the organizational stage.

After the two scientists left, Aldous and I were sitting in the living room, ending an interesting Sunday afternoon with a last cup of tea. Aldous said, "Those are bright young men."

I was seething with impatience. "Yes, they are bright—but it is going to be years before what they have planned will have any practical application." And even before I had time to coordinate my thinking, I heard myself suddenly announce, at breathless speed, "You know what I am going to do? I am going to write a book. I am going to make a book of my techniques—and everybody can use them right away, without a committee, and without a million dollars. And I am going to call these techniques 'Recipes for Living and Loving.' "

Then! The smile! Surprised. Delighted.

"A wonderful idea—and a very good title!"

I realize now, as I write these episodes, that *my* smile would light up when I said or did something completely unexpected—not only by Aldous, but by me as well. Once in the library we were looking something up in the encyclopedia but were thinking about something else. Aldous had found the volume and was reading aloud: "... 'stony sea lilies of the extinct *Uintacrinus Socialis* species were preserved in the crust of Kansas in Cretaceous times ninety million years ago, at which period . . .'"

I interrupted him and heard myself saying: "Wouldn't we rather go to bed?"

All the poems in that library could not have described his smile.

The last time I saw that smile was about two weeks before Aldous died. Two years before, getting ready to take a long trip, Aldous and I had spoken about making a will, and Aldous said we should go to a lawyer. I have an allergy to lawyers, so I kept postponing. The day before we left, we each wrote a will without a lawyer.

In that last summer of 1963, before going to Europe, we spoke again about wills. Aldous said that he had lost the will he had written previously. It irritated him to lose anything, and when he did, he generally looked until he found it—but not this time. When Aldous's son Matthew came for what was to be his last visit with his father in October, I told him about the lost will. He said that, lost or not, a will made without a lawyer would probably not be legal.

One morning, about two weeks before Aldous died, I found the lost will in a very unlikely place. When I told him that Matthew thought such a will made without a lawyer would probably not be legal, Aldous promptly said, "Then let's do it properly." Max Cutler, our doctor and friend, was just coming for his morning visit. He solved the problem easily by suggesting that Aldous put down the directions, and his lawyer would set them into legal language.

The next morning there were a few business items which I had to discuss with Aldous—taxes, insurances, a signature. Then I asked if he wanted to read the will I had found. He said no and gave me a few directions, as usual very simple and clear, about legalizing some papers. Then he said, "Let's divide the income from the literary property in this way: four-fifths to you and one-fifth ———"

"Four-fifths!" I exclaimed, bewildered. I was thinking only of the arithmetic involved. Dividing into fifths was not part of my habitual arithmetic. I remembered how easy it had always been to divide a cantalope into four portions, but how difficult to make five. "Four-fifths! That is too difficult. Isn't it much simpler to divide it by four?"

Then *my* smile came over his poor emaciated face and gave it light again; it was the same loving and amused smile, just as unexpected, just as surprised. Again he put his hand over mine with overwhelming tenderness—again the whole place was lighted with his immense capacity of loving. "Don't worry, darling, they will know how to divide by five."

Years ago, just before our marriage, we were driving in the hills near La Jolla. It was dusk, that magic hour of orange and gold. Aldous was speaking about the population explosion and a technique for birth control. A sudden memory surprised me and I interrupted: "Yes, yes, you are right, Aldous. I remember that time I decided to conceive...."

Again, *my* smile—it matched the luxuriant sunset. *"Cara cara,* you suddenly toss off these marvelous little snatches of your life. You hadn't told me about the time you decided to conceive," he said, tenderly and amused. And then, mockingly serious: "You know, darling, I love you in spite of all those lovers!"

"In spite!" I countercharged, and matching his mocking tone I said reproachfully, *"In spite!* Aldous, you are absolutely incapable of lying —you meant *because!"*

In answer, Aldous quoted an Italian song:

> Bocca baciata non perde ventura
> Ma si rinnova come fa la luna.
>
> A kissed mouth loses no fortune
> But is ever renewed, like the moon.

That Poor Fellow—
He Can Hardly See

I DO NOT KNOW how legends are made. I would think they spring from something which may once have been true and to which we cling because of our tendency to accept what is familiar. In Aldous's case, the legend of his blindness was based on the fact that forty years before he had been practically blind for eighteen months.

In 1958 we were in Rio de Janeiro as guests of the Brazilian government. We were flown to the Matto Grosso on an army plane and landed on an air strip in the middle of the jungle. Immediately, we were surrounded by a primitive tribe, literally neolithic, that had neither pottery nor agriculture and still lived mainly by shooting fish with bow and arrow.

Aldous was delighted by this diminutive people. All his antennas were out; he went from one group to another; tried to communicate with them, and looked twice as tall as our astonished hosts. They could not know how astonished we were! Three hours before, we had been in Brasilia, an ultramodern metropolis; now, swarming around us, excitedly shouting wild sounds, were almost a hundred dark-olive savages, stark naked.

We civilized people are so thoroughly conditioned that when we encounter large groups of human beings we expect them to have clothes on. After a few minutes, Aldous ran excitedly toward me. "Did you see, darling?"

"A lot I see," I answered.

"But, I mean," continued Aldous, "did you notice that these people all have vaccination marks on their arms?"

This was the man whom many persons thought nearly blind. Only two months after this episode, someone in Paris who supposedly knew Aldous well suggested to him that he should use the white cane of the blind!

When we moved, a few months after our marriage, to the hilltop, I completely redecorated the house. The floor had been covered with wall-to-wall carpeting. I was very keen on substituting for that carpet a marvelously shining, white floor. To throw out a new carpet would seem a needless extravagance to most husbands, but Aldous generously agreed. One evening a friend came to see us, elegant as always in her own style and good taste. Later she wrote me about that visit: "I remember once when I was up at the house, and wearing gold shoes, and Aldous was looking down at them, and I felt very uncomfortable. I am foot self-conscious and found myself, at that moment, being a little embarrassed that Aldous was looking at my feet ... when suddenly he said: 'How beautifully the golden light from your shoes shines over the floor!' I almost wept."

Aldous was fascinated by reflections of light, and that floor became an unending source of pleasure. Sometimes, coming home late at night, we would delight in finding the moonlight reflected on the living-room floor as on a pond.

One never had to worry about directions when driving with Aldous; he would always know the way if he had been there just once. He made mental note of landmarks—an empty lot, an unusual building, a tree, even a little fruit stand. Only if the landmark had been changed would we have to retrace our steps.

"We have gone a mile too far," he would say. "We should have turned where that Australian eucalyptus is—it has grown so much that for a moment I did not recognize it. Sorry, we must turn around."

In his book *The Art of Seeing,* Aldous recounts the story of his recovery from near-blindness, caused by a severe illness in 1910, when he was sixteen. By 1939, in spite of greatly strengthened glasses, he could hardly read.

... Just as I was wondering apprehensively what on earth I should do, if reading were to become impossible, I happened to hear of a method of visual re-education. . . . Education sounded harmless enough and since optical glass was no longer doing me any good, I decided to take the plunge. Within a couple of months I was reading without spectacles and, what was better still, without strain or fatigue. . . . My own case is in no way unique; thousands of other sufferers from defects of vision have been benefited by following the simple rules of *The Art of Seeing.* [1] ...

In the spring of 1957, Aldous was giving a series of lectures in the East. He was in a period of highest efficiency, creativity, and health. One morning I saw to my amazement a reference to Aldous by the celebrated Dr. Walter Alvarez in his widely read column in the *Los Angeles Times.* Nothing could have been more inaccurate or unjust. "Some readers," wrote Dr. Alvarez, "tell me of Huxley's book on the subject [eye re-education] and have read it. The only trouble with his argument is that, according to ophthalmologists who know him, in spite of his exercises the poor fellow can hardly see!"

Who were, we wondered, these ophthalmologists on whose opinion Dr. Alvarez based his assumption? I was incensed and answered with the following open letter to Dr. Alvarez, published in the *Los Angeles Times* on May 21:

I am the wife of the "poor fellow who can hardly see," Aldous Huxley. (I quote from your article published in the *Times,* May 12.)

The "poor fellow who can hardly see" is on a lecture tour in the East, traveling alone. At home, he writes and reads for seven or eight hours a day without the aid of lenses. Moreover, though blind in one eye and carrying scar tissue on the other, he can do his work without eye strain or fatigue—thanks to the "Art of Seeing" which he learned from Dr. Bates' gifted and resourceful pupil, Mrs. Margaret D. Corbett. [2]

That oculists should be the only doctors who totally ignore the findings of psychosomatic medicine is still a puzzle to my husband. Nor can he understand why they should so passionately object to the self-evident proposition that training in the proper use of an organ is likely to improve its function.

In this matter, it would seem, orthodox eye doctors are about half a century behind their colleagues in other branches of medicine.

> Laura Huxley
> (Mrs. Aldous Huxley)
> Hollywood

A few days later I received a long letter from Dr. Alvarez, which was destroyed with the rest of our possessions when our house burned down in 1961. However, its content is made clear by the open letter Aldous

[1] *The Art of Seeing* by Aldous Huxley (Harper & Row, 1942).

[2] Deceased.

wrote to Dr. Alvarez, which the *Los Angeles Times* did not see fit to publish.

Dear Dr. Alvarez:

I have been so extremely busy of late that it has been impossible for me to comment on the long letter you wrote last June to my wife. Today my attention has been called to another reference in your column to the matters under discussion, and, though still unconscionably busy, I feel impelled to send you these few paragraphs, in the hope of correcting some errors and clearing up some misconceptions.

It is quite obvious, first of all, that you have not read my book, or, if you have, that you have completely forgotten what it is about and entirely misunderstood its purport. I never said that the practice of the Bates Method relieved the inflammation (due to keratitis), which originally caused the opacities on my corneas. This inflammation had subsided thirty years before I ever heard of the Bates Method. But the opacities remained, along with very poor vision, to relieve which I was having to use ever more powerful lenses. What I wrote about in my book was precisely what its title so clearly formulated, namely *"The Art of Seeing"* —in other words, the technique of making the best possible use of the mind-body in relation to vision. What I claimed for the Bates Method was simply this . . . that it shows people how to make the best possible use of such visual powers as they possess. I also pointed out (and surely everyone will admit this) that organs function best when properly used, and that when they function well it often happens that organic defects are reduced or abolished.

Bates was never tired of insisting on a fact which is now a commonplace of psychology, namely that vision is at least fifty per cent a mental process and that improvement in the mental state of patients suffering from defective vision was apt to result in improvement in their seeing and ultimately, through the effect of good functioning upon organic defect, in their eyes. In this respect Bates Method differed radically from the methods of orthoptics, which ignore the mental side of seeing and seek to improve vision by the repetition of fatiguing exercises. Being based on unsound principles, orthoptics do little or no good. Being based on essentially sound principles, Bates Method is often very effective.

Bates worked on the minds of his patients in a variety of ways. First of all, he encouraged the systematic use of the memory and the imagination. It is a commonplace of psychology that we see best those things with which we are familiar, and of which we have a clear memory. Thus, teaching people to have a clear memory of lower case letters (many persons have surprisingly poor memories of them) may help to improve reading ability. And memory has other uses in relation to poor vision and the eyestrain which so often accompanies poor vision. It has been known for at least ninety years that the act of remembering pleasant scenes or episodes from the past is a highly relaxing procedure. Indeed it is so relaxing that, as early as the sixties of last century, Fahnestock of Chicago was making his patients intensively remember, in order to produce hypnotic trance. In our own day eminent hypnotherapists frequently make use of techniques involving memory or imagination in order to induce trance. Bates, of course, did not push his memory techniques to the point of sending people to sleep; he used them merely to promote relaxation and in this way to promote better seeing. There is nothing surprising in this; for everyone now knows that relaxed minds and organs tend to function better than tense ones.

Another point which Bates constantly stressed was the bad effect on vision of the habit of fixedly staring at things. He insisted—and recent research has fully confirmed his findings—that normal eyes are constantly making very small shifts. This shift is so rapid that (as a recent writer on the subject has put it) it would, if it were audible, make a buzzing, sound. Bates attributed many defects of vision to faulty habits of use—habits under whose influence the patient would do his best to immobilize the normal shifting of the eyes by fixedly staring. Many of his techniques were designed for the purpose of breaking these bad, vision-impairing habits and replacing them by new habits, more in accord with the eyes' true nature.

We come now to what, for most doctors, is the great stumbling block —Bates' insistence that accommodation is brought about by the extrinsic muscles of the eyeball, and not by the ciliary muscle working on the lens. Other people besides Bates have questioned the absolute correctness of Helmholtz's hypothesis. I myself take no stand in the matter, for the simple reason that I am not qualified to have an opinion. But what I would most strongly emphasize is the fact that, so far as Bates' method of psycho-physical education is concerned, the whole matter is entirely irrelevant. To the teacher of a psycho-physical skill, a correct knowledge of physiology is not necessary. Did Bach know how his muscles worked? No. But he played the organ very well and was a magnificent teacher. If proficiency in any psycho-physical skill depended on correct knowledge of physiology, there would have been no good singers, dancers, pianists, runners and so forth until the middle of the twentieth century. Proficiency in the psycho-physical skills (and seeing is one of the most fundamental of these skills) does not depend on a knowledge of physiology; it depends on a knowledge, unconscious or conscious, of the principles of good functioning and of the best ways to apply those principles to the learning of the skill which it is desired to acquire. Bates was a physician; but most of his life's work was in education. He understood the principle governing the acquisition of any psycho-physical skill . . . the principle to which I have given the name of "dynamic relaxation" . . . and he was extremely ingenious and resourceful in developing techniques for applying that principle to the teaching of the art of seeing.

Dynamic relaxation is that paradoxical combination of relaxation with activity, which is the secret of proficiency in all the psycho-physical skills from dancing to golf, from violin playing to mental prayer. The universality of the principle is the guarantee of its soundness. Bates was merely applying to the special case of poor vision the principles which are applied by teachers in every other field of human activity. To the poor seer he was saying, in effect, what the golf pro says to the poor golfer, what the spiritual director says to the novice: "Be active, and yet remain relaxed; don't strain and yet do your damndest; stop trying so hard and let the deep-seated intelligence of your body and the subconscious mind do the work as it ought to be done." Why you or any other doctor should object to the application of this universally valid principle to the problems of visual re-education simply passes my understanding. Let the doctors practice medicine and prescribe corrective lenses. For those whom optical glass and the current methods of medicine cannot help, let the teachers of the art of seeing do what they can by means of their techniques or re-education. This is all that I ask. And in the meantime please do not talk in this context about quack cancer cures or arthritis cures. The Bates Method is not a branch of medicine, either orthodox or unorthodox. It is a method of education, fundamentally similar to the methods of education devised and succesfully used by all the teachers of psycho-physical skills for the last several thousand years. Almost everything you wrote in your letter to Mrs. Huxley is entirely beside the point and has nothing whatever to do with the issues under discussion.

With apologies for the length of this letter and for my very bad typing, I remain

> Yours very truly,
> Aldous Huxley

New York
August 12, 1957

We have a tendency to forget that human beings are not static entities—in fact, change is inevitable; it is the direction of change which is, in part at least, a matter of choice. Eyesight is particularly subject to change because it is particularly sensitive and dependent on a variety of inner and outer stimuli for its functioning. Aldous kept improving his eyes by using them in the proper manner. Moreover, during most of the period between 1956 and 1960 his whole organism was improving. He was happy and well most of that time, very active, doing good work. His sight improved noticeably. Shortly after we married we moved from the dark villa on Kings Road to the top of a Hollywood hill in a house flooded with sun and light. I arranged the electric illumination so that the contrast between light and shadow was very strong. There was a good reading light every few feet, specially in his workroom.

In August 1961, we were in Gstaad and met Krishnamurti there. He and Aldous had not seen each other for over five years. They used to go for walks in the Ojai Valley—now they went for a morning walk in the Swiss meadows. Later that day, in that intense way of his, Krishnamurti asked me, "Tell me, Laura, what has happened to Aldous' eyes? He sees so much better! I used to help him when we would walk together, but when I did this morning I realized that I had made a mistake. He did not need help."

Krishnamurti was obviously pleased with Aldous' improvement, but I also detected in him an underlying feeling of self-annoyance. For a moment he had responded in the present with a reaction conditioned by the past. The difference between Krishnamurti and most other people is that Krishnamurti was almost immediately aware of the change in Aldous and therefore behaved differently toward him. Most other people were unaware of any change and therefore treated Aldous not as he was *now* but as he was *then,* thus denying his ability to accomplish an important and marvelous change.

I could quote many articles in which Aldous was referred to as practically a blind man. Such misrepresentation may be understandable when it comes from people who did not know him personally, but it is a grave injustice when it comes from people who did know him. Robert Craft, in an article in *Encounter,* spoke of Aldous as "alone and blind" and unable to find his fork on the dinner table!

However, most people closely associated with us noticed and marveled at the change in Aldous's eyes. Marie Le Put was one—Marie, who on the surface could not have been more different from Krishnamurti—of different race, culture, and circumstances—yet what a similarity in that freedom of mind and heart which is the essence of awareness! For these two, the mystic revolutionary and the gentle, exquisite culinary artist, Aldous had a similar affection, admiration, and gratefulness. The smile Aldous had for Marie was akin to what I called *my* smile. How many times, after we moved to our house on the hilltop, Marie said to me as well as to Ginny, "Monsieur is different. Monsieur can see quite well now!" Like Krishnamurti, she was not living in the past and did not frame others in it.

However, although I feel it was an injustice to treat Aldous as though he were blind, it is true there were many indications of his impaired vision. For instance, although Aldous did not wear glasses, he would quite often use a magnifying lens—to read a menu in a dark restaurant, to study an artist's stroke on a canvas. The use of a lens is much more noticeable than the wearing of glasses. Besides, paradoxically, no one thinks of "impaired vision" if one wears glasses.

One of Aldous's outstanding characteristics was the ability to listen. If the person talking to him was in good light, he would look at him intently, for he was fascinated by the expression of faces and bodies. However, if the light was poor, Aldous would listen with his eyes closed, as he always did when listening to music. Or, instead of closing his eyes, he would use one of the best techniques for eye relaxation, called "palming." In palming, light is completely excluded by closing the eyes and covering them with the palms of the hands. Ideally, one should be seated with the elbows resting on something—a table, or a cushion laid across the knees. The position—elbows on his knees, head buried in his hands—was one of Aldous's favorite positions. It was soothing to his eyes, conducive to receptivity and thinking. But to others—and, oddly enough, even to those who should have known better—that comfortable position looked like an attitude of pain or despair; it indicated a lacerating *Weltschmerz* or an excruciating headache. Actually, Aldous told me that he could hardly imagine a headache: he had one only once or twice with a high fever. And Aldous was not one to parade his *Weltschmerz* or his concern for humanity by a dejected posture. He always transformed it into activity, as is obvious from the staggering amount of work he did.

Aldous could not see in the dark. Most of us have some night vision, and our eyes quickly adjust to dimness. Aldous's night vision was practically nonexistent.

All these factors contributed to the impression that Aldous had almost no vision. It may seem of no consequence, now, whether he had or not. But I feel that this misconception about his vision is an injustice in that it invalidates one of the great achievements of his life: that of having gained his sight. How? By applying, and not merely intellectualizing, that "freedom from the known" of which Krishnamurti has spoken and written with such a passionate intensity for years. In 1939, what Aldous knew about his eyes was that he was approaching blindness and that the doctors told him there was nothing to do about it. Aldous, although not a scientist, had, according to scientists, an amazing scientific knowledge. In spite of it he was able to be objective about an unorthodox method such as the Bates Method. It is easy for someone without scientific knowledge to accept an unorthodox approach. But for the people learned in any field it is very difficult to accept a conclusion totally different from that which they have formulated through years of work and study. Aldous was exceptional in that although he had an enormous capital of knowledge he was not attached to it emotionally and was ready at any time to relinquish any part of it which seemed wrong—ready to explore not only new but also potential knowledge, even if it were in opposition to previous data. Aldous's freedom was not only intellectual: it was the emotional freedom from possessiveness, from the need of being a winner; the lack of these freedoms can obscure even the most brilliant intelligence.

Although Aldous was not interested in proving or disproving a theory, or his opinion of it, he was interested in finding whether a theory, when applied, gave the expected results. On the subject of theory-worship Aldous would quote his grandfather, T. H. Huxley: "The great tragedy of Science—the slaying of a beautiful hypothesis by an ugly fact."

Sir Kenneth Clark, in his memorial address[3] at Friends House in London a few weeks after Aldous's death, speaks about his "power of visual understanding" with deep perception and beauty. From reading Aldous's essays collected in *Art and Artist,*[4] one realizes how keenly he saw and what pleasure he derived from his sight. This was true even to his last week, when there was almost no sight left, almost no life. Aldous could hardly move his head then; the cancer had spread to his neck. On the right side of his chin a bandage covered the usurping intruder. The left part of his face remained unblemished; a nobly chiseled profile, extraordinarily beautiful, manifesting a rare achievement of racial evolution. His room, full of hospital equipment, was now only, and sadly, utilitarian; his favorite roses, grown and delivered throughout his illness by a friend, Mrs. K., the only deliverance. Now Aldous could not see more than two feet away. That morning I arranged the slant of his pillows and the spotlight behind them. Then I kept a rose very close to him, just where he could see it, feel it, without moving. First, I turned the rose slowly so he could see it from different angles. He looked at it for a while with the magnifying glass, then he let go of it and relaxed his hands. He lay in complete comfort with the rose

---

[3] *Aldous Huxley, 1891-1963.* A memorial volume edited by Julian Huxley (Chatto & Windus, 1965; Harper & Row, 1966).
[4] Harper & Row.

two inches away from his face, breathing it. Salmon pink, perfectly harmonious, luminously alive, the rose was looking at Aldous and Aldous was looking at the rose. There was perfect communication between the two—and complete silence. As Aldous opened himself to the rose his face became peaceful and smooth. Time stopped. We were motionless for a long while. Then I asked, "Is it enough?"

Almost inaudibly, but with the utmost clarity, he answered, "It is never enough. Never enough." It was the faintest whisper, but it had the intensity of a thousand voices. They were saying, "Never enough of beauty. Never enough of love. Never enough of life. . . ."

He died two days later.

This Wind . . . Tonight

MAY 12, 1961, began as a routine day. I had appointments for several therapy sessions. Aldous had no special commitments, which meant he would write in the morning (he was working on the last chapter of *Island*) and in the afternoon he would read, walk, and perhaps write some more.

My last appointment, at five-thirty, was with a woman who did not have a car. After the two-hour session I had planned to drive her to the bus at the bottom of the hill, then stop at Ginny Pfeiffer's, who was away for the weekend, to feed their cat, the illustrious Edgarallancat. This would take approximately fifteen or twenty minutes. On my return I would prepare dinner, we would dine at about eight-fifteen. A friend had asked us to see a very disturbed Hungarian scientist, and he was to come at nine o'clock and discuss his situation with us.

At about seven-thirty my client and I came down from the quiet room upstairs where these sessions took place. On our way out, we stopped a moment in the living room. It was almost dark now, a marvelous evening. A whimsical, boisterous wind had dissipated the last vestige of smog. Everything was supernaturally clear. The immense city below extended all the way to the Pacific, shimmering with millions of lights. The outline of the hills behind our house was dramatically black against the clear dark blue sky. Everything had a limpid, shining quality of newness and eternity. Again, as innumerable times before, I felt how lucky I was to be living surrounded by simplicity and beauty. It had been a good day.

Aldous was still upstairs working, so I left without disturbing him. On the way back I noticed the red car of a fire chief and wondered why

he was there. I stopped at the Pfeiffers' empty house, only five hundred
yards away from ours, and went out in the garden to call the cat. Then
for the first time I saw smoke and flames coming from the canyon
below. The wind was wilder now. I went into the house to make sure
that Edgarallancat was not locked in somewhere. From the living
room, high above the canyon, I saw the flames springing from one
hundred fifty feet below. Just as I started to call the fire department, I
heard a siren.

Then something unexplainable happened to me. From that moment
until the end of the evening I behaved in a way totally contrary to my
nature. In emergencies I have usually responded with immediate
action. When faced with adverse circumstances, I have hardly ever
accepted them; almost always I have tried—and sometimes succeeded
—in using them to my advantage, applying whatever intuition, determination, logic I could muster. Here, I was faced with the destruction
of the home and belongings of my best friend, and of the studio where,
since the war, I had lived some of the most momentous years of my life.
Dangerously near was my present home, where Aldous and I lived,
loved, and worked. When the fiery embrace began, destroying all that I
loved, normally I would have leaped into action. Instead, what did I
do? I stood immobile, fascinated by the wild grace of the flames, by the
ever changing voice of the wind.

Why did I not immediately take the hose and wet the roof and everything around the house? The full swimming pool was a source of power
against the flames. Why did I not call for help? Why did I not take
clothes and valuables away? I could easily have packed dozens of suitcases with necessary and some irreplaceable things. Instead, what did I
do? First, I went into the kitchen, still propelled by my initial purpose
of opening a can of cat food. As I realized that it was no longer necessary, I looked around the charming kitchen and then went downstairs
to the workroom, where, in the darkroom and in tin cans, were the
results of so many years of work in cinematography. In the typewriter
was a letter, half finished. I thought of other writings that were there—
a play Ginny had written. "But Ginny doesn't care anyway," I thought.
Maybe I should take some clothes for her. I didn't. I saw her beautiful
fur coat. "Too hot for that now." Fortunately, I took a box in which I
knew she had some important papers—the only thing I did for her. I
went to the children's room and looked at their toys. Which would
Paula want? And which was Juan's favorite?

At that moment our dear friend, the architect Raymond Johnson,
came in. He had built that perfectly proportioned, light, lovely house,
high in the then-solitary hills—built it with skill and love. He took the
heavy box from my hands and suggested something, but I did not pay

attention. I asked about his own house, which was nearby. Then I went out to the street. There were people there now, ready to help. Each could have carried away several suitcases; even furniture could have been saved.

I left, and drove home to tell Aldous. He was still upstairs writing.

"Ginny's house is burning."

We drove down the hill and parked the car somewhere between the two houses. There were many cars now, and television trucks all over—no room for fire engines. We walked down to Ginny's house, which was now ablaze. Like a mischievous goblin the wind was playing fires all over the hills. Aldous and I stood there speechless. Suddenly Aldous said, "We must go home. The fire might jump there; I must get the manuscript of *Island*."

The road was already swept by fire. We could not get to our car or walk home the usual way. A man—I do not know to this day who he was—offered to take us home in his car by a road around the hill.

Aldous was right. The fire was about to choose our home, beginning to burn the plants on the slope under the terrace. Aldous went upstairs and got his almost finished manuscript of *Island;* he had started it five years before, when we moved into the house, and had been working steadily on it for the last two years. When he came down he said, "Don't you think I should take some suits?"

I said, "Yes."

But I was looking—only looking. How beautiful everything was! The flames from the outside were giving to the white walls a soft rosy glow. That very day I had changed the flowers. In a large vase a triumphant bunch of "hot pokers" were illuminated from inside and out. The simplicity of the decorations, the shining liquid whiteness of the floors, the few objects—everything was given a glowing life by the dancing flames outside.

In decorating the house, the most difficult problem had been the lighting. We had solved it satisfactorily, but not perfectly. Now the mobile, changing light of the flames did what the static electric lights could never do.

"At last," I thought, "the perfect illumination."

I walked from one room to the other, touching the objects I loved. I can still feel the perfect weight, the roundness and coolness, of a Steuben glass owl I picked up from the round table in the living room—and put carefully back in the very center of the shining surface; certainly, I thought, its best background. The unknown man who had driven us followed me from room to room, asking if I did not want to save something.

"What a bore he is being," I ungratefully thought to myself.

The flames were approaching the French windows of the bedroom and the living room. I closed them, for the curtains were being sucked outside by the hot vacuum of the fire. The wind was playing with them—*les enfants terribles*—that is what the wind and the flames were.

"Don't you want to take anything?" the man repeated. Right there, carefully kept in a drawer, were the letters Aldous had written me over the years. I did not take them.

Aldous came down with three suits on hangers, and said, "You'd better take some clothes."

I took three or four hangers also. Then in the closet I saw my violin, a Guarnieri made in Cremona in 1705. "Joseph Guarnerius filius Andree fecit Cremone sub titulo S. Teresie 1705," says the original label. This work of art, this defenseless beauty, which had dominated most years of my life . . . it had been a tree once, singing in the wind, like this wind, tonight. Then, what destiny! The great master had chosen that tree among so many, and with infinite, now-lost skill, had created a new being, and given it a perfect body, a wondrous voice. I was twenty when my father had given me that violin. How many other vioninists had embraced it, as I did, the nobility of the instrument? It was now 256 years old. It had not sung in the past few years. . . . "Nobody has made love to him." Tonight the fire, only a few yards away, would conclude its destiny, in a matter of seconds. "Succumbed in Hollywood." It was insured for ten thousand dollars: what did that mean? It meant that ten thousand dollars would pay for its death and silence. The thought of insurance suddenly seized my attention and I started to look only for the things that *were* insured: a fur coat, a pin, and a few other items. Then I did take an object I cherished: a Chinese dancing lady of the T'ang Dynasty. Indescribably elegant, she was dancing, as she had been dancing for the last eleven centuries. She had a sister, who was in Ginny's house. "She is burning now"; that thought moved me to put my lady back, but the man had already taken her to the car. Aldous was near me, but I was unaware of anything except how beautiful everything was.

We left our home, never to see it again. Not a drop of water had been put upon it. But a lot of TV time had been filled with it.

So with manuscript, violin, lady from China, clothes on their hangers, and a few other items in the car trunk, the man drove us away. Aldous and I did not speak. Aldous had left all his books, each indexed and marked with his comments. There were cases of letters and diaries and notes for future writings; letters from Aldous and from Maria and· their son; famous letters and many of Aldous's manuscripts and notebooks—his whole past was there. All my reports of therapeutic and psychedelic sessions were there; the records of my debut in Carnegie Hall; irreplaceable photographs. . . .

It was usually Aldous and I who took the initiative. But in that moment we were stunned. If a friend had been there he could have awakened us to action. Cases and suitcases and drawers could have been put in the empty driveway, which remained untouched by the fire. Actually, the only items which were saved were the two stored by the driveway: one, a large case of books that Aldous had discarded from his library and was sending to a charitable organization; the other, devilishly avoided by the flames, was the firewood.

Passively we left everything and were driven back to Ginny's house. There was our car, scorched but usable. It had been saved by a young neighbor, a boy who, like so many restless adolescents in Hollywood, had gone through some episodes of delinquency. We thanked him—I remember Aldous speaking to him. But my attention was all on those flames, on that wind, now totally triumphant.

Below was the wide clear expanse of city lights; above, an immense crescent of fire. The sky was high and dark. Aldous and I were standing there, muted—one of the few times in our lives when we were not communicating. Around us flames, flames, flames, leaping and darting, capriciously choosing one house for burning, one for sparing.

"If I only knew how to talk to the wind . . ." I thought.

The Pfeiffer house was completely gone; the studio over the garage was now burning. How much life I had lived there! I saw a trunk full of letters go leaping lightly into the flames, and another full of sheet music I had brought from Italy.

For the first time I saw firemen. The man next door, an Italian sculptor, was pouring water on his house, which was adjacent to the studio. Two firemen were doing something around the house, slowly. The Italian man went in and returned shortly with two cans of beer, which he offered to the firemen. This penetrated some corner of my mind as something incongruous. Weren't the firemen supposed to extinguish the fire? Wouldn't the beer distract them from their job? Or was beer the conventional drink in fireman circles? Or had everybody given up?

Abruptly I realized that Aldous was not with me. For a while I looked for him and waited. Then suddenly I became very worried. Where could he have gone? And how? And why? I asked several persons; nobody had seen him. People looked at me with sympathy, but they had no idea how to help. He couldn't have gone far, yet he wasn't there. As my agitation increased, and I was wondering what to do, or where to go, suddenly Aldous appeared at my side. I must have shrieked, "Where have you been?"

Vaguely he said, "Well—with Johnny." This was the boy who had saved our car.

"With Johnny! What for?"

"Darling, the car almost burned a while ago. We thought it might be wise to drive it a little further away. Then we went on to see the fire. You see," he said, lowering his voice like a con man, "the roads are all blocked." Then he added, smiling: "But Johnny knows how to get around the police, so we could go *anywhere*."

"Anywhere! Where *did* you go?"

Aldous put his hand on my arm; he knew that I was at the breaking point. "Cara," he cleared his throat, "I noticed that the car was nearly out of gas." He hesitated, then he quickly plunged: "So I thought we had better go down to the gas station and fill up the tank."

"ALDOUS! But . . ."

"Darling," he interrupted quickly, "that is not what took so long; it was coming back—you have no idea of the jam there is down below—police cars, TV cameras, even fire trucks—they won't let *anybody* through. But," and the amused smile came over him again, "it is remarkable how many ways there are to avoid the police; we went through roads I never knew existed. Besides, that nice boy knows how to talk to the police—they wouldn't listen to me." And then, even more confidentially and pleased, as though he were suddenly a big shot by association: "His gang helped, too."

In my mind's eye I was seeing Aldous being driven by a teen-age gang in and out of fires, through the maze of policemen—our car filled to the brim with gas for a bigger and better explosion. I started to remonstrate but then I just laughed. This was the nearest Aldous had been to delinquency—of course he could not let such an opportunity slip by! Later, he often spoke with affection of his new friend, that nice juvenile delinquent—and rightly so. Not only was he the only person who had given actual help by saving the car, but he had also given Aldous an excursion into a world he had never known, while the world he knew so well was vanishing.

A few days later, the fire was reported in *Time* magazine.

Flames licked through dry grasses and gutted twenty-four luxury homes in Hollywood Hills. Destroyed were Author Aldous Huxley's two-story house, his manuscripts and mementos of a lifetime. While firemen restrained the nearly blind British author from running into the blaze, Huxley wept like a child.

This was in the May issue. Aldous's reply was printed in the June 16 issue:

Sir:

As an old hand at fiction, may I congratulate the write-up artist who penned the account of my actions on the night my house was burned down (May 12).

The facts are these. My wife and I started the evening at the house, a little way down the road, of an absent friend. Having rescued a box of her papers and tried in vain to locate the cat, we left this house in flames and were driven back to our own home by a friendly onlooker. Here we picked up a few clothes, my wife's Guarnieri violin, and the MS of the book on which I have been working for the past two years. By the time these had been taken to the car, the house was burning. There was nothing we could do, and all the local fire engines (though not the TV trucks) were somewhere else.

So we got into the car and drove away—sadly enough, goodness knows, but (ignoring those conventions of the romantic novelette to which your write-up artist so faithfully adhered) not crying like babies, nor requiring to be restrained from running back into the flames.

Santa Monica, Calif.

After the Fireworks

AROUND MIDNIGHT OF May 12 the fire, like a Dionysian revelry, burned itself out. Most people returned to their homes, happy still to have one; we did not see those who had lost theirs. Spent and silent we drove down the hill to Franklin Avenue where there is an unpretentious little hotel. We went in and the night clerk rented us two rooms. It was a clean, quiet place, and no reporter would have looked for Aldous there. We went next door and had a snack. It must have been almost two o'clock before we went to bed—without brushing our teeth; the toothbrushes were the first discovered loss, the first of a long list of inconveniences. Later, we had to make inventories, convince insurance companies of the obvious fact that *everything* in the house had gone, look for addresses and telephone numbers, reconstruct files, and so on.

Aldous took care of most of the letters and telegrams we received in the days following the fire. We both spoke to a great many people on the phone to reassure them that though we were homeless we were well. After three or four days Aldous resumed his working habits. He was finishing *Island*, writing the last chapter, perhaps the most important and beautiful in the book, in which so much happens: the protagonist has his first revelatory psychedelic experience; toward the end, this free Island is taken over by an army maneuvered by industrial tycoons, unquenchably thirsty for the rich oil wells, and by an omnivorous pseudo-spiritual mother, insatiably hungry for power. Aldous worked for two weeks in the hotel, then went for two weeks to Santa Monica as a guest of Margaret Gage; Gerald Heard was there too. When Aldous finished *Island,* he left for London on June 15. Six weeks later I joined him in Switzerland.

59

On May 14 Ginny and her children Paula and Juan returned home from their weekend in the desert, to find that they had no home at all. With all their possessions—two weekend bags—they came to stay in our hotel. Now our close friendship had another common ground; our pasts had been wiped out; we were without possessions. It was to be expected that three people who had suffered shock, who had grave responsibilities, who were no longer young, would not be too cheerful. And we were not. But neither were we as distraught and desperate as most people thought. Reverberations of the shock came later.

About a week or two after the fire, Aldous looked worried and depressed. Especially at meals, something would come over him, and although he ate with good appetite, he seemed to have some difficulty, as though he had a toothache. Yet the very day after the fire we had kept the appointment with our friend, Dr. Glick—described by Aldous as the Heifetz of dentists—who found no cause for toothache.

One day Ginny, Aldous and I lunched together at the cafeteria; he left early, saying that he was going to the Beverly Hills library.

"Something is wrong with Aldous, but I don't know what it is—he is so depressed," I said to Ginny.

"It isn't too surprising," she replied, "considering that he lost everything just two weeks ago."

Of course she had also—and so had I. However, I felt that Aldous's preoccupation had another source.

"No Ginny. What Aldous has on his mind is not the fire—not his writing—not money. It is something else—something that has happened just in these last few days.

I found out a few hours later. It was late afternoon and as I was relaxing in the bathtub, getting ready to go out for dinner, there was Aldous's characteristic knock at the door—a very light knock as though he were patting the door, but this time there was a note of impatience in it, a gay impatience.

"Come in, come in!"

Aldous knelt near the bathtub. He was light and smiling; the cloud had obviously lifted.

"Darling," he said with a smile and speaking more quickly than usual, "I didn't tell you, but in the last few days I had some pain in my gums when eating, and I thought it might be a recurrence of the cancer. I went to see Cutler, and he said that all is well! The discomfort is a normal reaction to last year's treatment with the radium needles, is easily taken care of, and will pass in a few weeks."

I listened breathless, mute, immobile. Then the reaction came—overwhelming and beautiful. After a while I asked Aldous, "Why didn't you tell me?"

"You have quite enough on your mind these days—I didn't want to worry you."

"But you did!" And I told him the conversation Ginny and I had had a few hours before.

"I can't have any secrets!"

We talked and laughed, and said how this wonderful news diminished the importance of the fire. If only we could tell it to those nice people who were sympathizing with us over our lost possessions.

Our financial situation and Aldous's state of mind were succinctly but clearly expressed in the following letter to his son, written a few days after the fire:

17.v.61

Dearest M,

Nothing much to report since our talk last Saturday.[1] Literally nothing remains of the house or its contents. I am now a man without possessions and without a past. This last I regret as much for you as for myself; for what has gone is a piece of your life and heart and mind as well as of mine. But there is nothing to do except try to start from scratch. Insurance formalities are a nuisance and although we were fairly well insured, as insurance goes, the amount we get won't approach the real loss. The difference between insurance payments and real loss can, however, be taken off one's taxes.

I expect to go to stay with Gerald tomorrow and shall try to get my book finished there.

All my love

Ever your affectionate
Aldous

Aldous was, until about August, thinner and paler than usual, and his mouth bothered him. But nothing in his actions or words justified, it seems to me, the way people treated him: not only as though he were a "historical monument" (as he would jokingly say) but as though he were a monument about to become a ruin. There must be some obscure reason why when a celebrity looks ill he becomes more interesting and newsworthy. "Poor Aldous—burned out, blind, and looking so thin, as though he did not get enough to eat—what is the good of all that brain power?"

All this time, Aldous was full of energy and plans and had an enormous interest in his work. He was happy to have finally finished

[1] The day after the fire.

Island, and he enjoyed a deserved and satisfying recognition from all over the world. Above all, he loved and was loved. I felt that even the best-intentioned people did him an injustice by treating him with insistent commiseration.

When Aldous arrived in London, the same lamenting chorus began. To make things worse, this commiseration was reflected in the newspapers, and a well-meaning French relative started to make a public collection of books for the "almost blind," destitute, bookless author. All this was echoed in the Italian newspapers. My father, then eighty-two, was upset by the rumors and cabled us from Italy asking if we had kept the real situation from him, and offering financial help.

There was really enough for me to take care of, in those weeks, without the added burden of these unnecessary worries, endless recountals and explanation—all the while being told how sick Aldous looked, and seeing him treated as though he were as fragile as an egg and should be kept in an incubator.

During the six weeks we were separated Aldous wrote me twenty-three letters, some postal cards, and one or two cables. Better than any comment of mine, Aldous's letters represent him and his feeling about our situation at that period. Most of his letters deal with the specific problems of those days. He responded promptly to anything I proposed or asked, dealt with problems immediately and with exceptional practical sense, had projects for the future, toward which he looked with unquenchable interest and enchanting verve. That people should think a man who reacted so youthfully and promptly was a depressed, sick old man was to us preposterous. Probably, such a misunderstanding stemmed from a natural wish to protect anyone we admire and was furthered by Aldous's physical appearance: delicately handsome, thin, and slightly bent—a posture often characteristic of very tall people.

Here are some of his letters of those six weeks:

4 Ennismore Gardens
London SW.
17.vi.61

Well, my darling, here I am in a fantastically quiet apartment overlooking a large garden full of trees where there is less noise than at Borrego. The journey was uneventful though I didn't sleep very much as we stopped at 3 a.m. at Toronto—after which we were served breakfast and (at about 8 a.m. our time) lunch. Julian and Juliette met me at the airport—both of them pretty well, though Juliette is rather tired for she is without a maid, and they are making alterations in their house. Today Julian had to attend a meeting at the Board of Directors of Prior's Field, my Mother's school, and I drove down with him and went for a long walk while he and the others were doing their business. There are trees in the school garden which I remember being planted and which are now 60 feet high with trunks 6 feet around. They look as if they had been there for 300 years. One of the oddest changes in the countryside is due to the extermination of the rabbits: what used to be smooth grassy slopes are now covered with bushes. The rabbits used to eat the young shoots as they came out of the ground. Now the shoots develop into wild rose bushes, elder trees, brambles—a real jungle. After California everything is extraordinarily green and luxuriant.

I couldn't sleep the other night. I practiced some of the exercises in self-awareness out of *Zen Flesh Zen Bones*[2]—which resulted in a kind of quiet ecstasy that modulated into an experience of love in which you were almost physically present. Such tenderness, my darling, such an intensity of desire and erotic pleasure.

My love to Ginny and the children

Your

A

4 Ennismore Gdns
London SW 7
19.vi.61

My darling, how are you? And how is Ginny getting on?[3] Let me have a line or two in the intervals between all your chores. Here all goes well. Pleasant weather, everything very green and the flowers exuberant in the parks and gardens. Spent the day yesterday with Julian and Juliette and their grandchildren—3 girls from 12 to 17, with whom and their mother and Anthony we had tea. . . . I dined with Eileen,[4] who invites us both to her conference at Le Piol near Nice from July 10 to 20. Doesn't tempt you? There will be some interesting people there including Servadio from Rome and other parapsychologists and LSD experimenters from Italy, Switzerland, France. Eileen herself seems completely recovered and is off to Rome in a few days. . . .

Goodbye, my precious one, I think very often of my favorite face and my favorite flower.

Yours

A

---

[2] Paul Reps, *Zen Flesh Zen Bones* (Vermont and Tokyo: Tuttle, 1957).
[3] The week following the fire, she had a minor but painful car accident.
[4] Eileen Garrett, the well-known medium and eminent researcher in parapsychology.

4 Ennismore Gardens
London S.W. 7
20.vi.61

I went this morning, my sweetheart, to see Sir S.C., the surgeon to whom
Max Cutler recommended me. He confirmed Cutler's diagnosis,
admired the excellent job Cutler did and prescribed Vitamin B$_{12}$ in a
liquid form which he says is particularly effective. So this is all very satisfactory. He told me that, over the last 30 years, he had treated more than
700 cases of tongue cancer with the radium needles and that this method
is definitely more effective and gives less chance of recurrence than the
drastic cutting recommended by the — — Hospital boys. This hospital
had a great man at its head in the 20's and 30's, Dr. — —, who taught the
use of the needles. Then he died and they imported a man from Chicago
whose one idea was to undo everything that — — had done. So in came
"radical surgery" and the mangling of patients—with worse results, so
far as recurrence is concerned, than the needles. What a squalid little
story of personal vanity—for which thousands of unfortunate victims
have had to pay. I go tonight to see the *Devils*. Will write and tell you my
impressions.

Goodbye, my darling. Be well and don't do too much.

Your   ∶

A

This letter refers to an episode that had occurred a little over a year
before. Aldous had gone to a hospital in Los Angeles to have a biopsy of
his tongue. It was a minor operation, but a light, general anesthetic was
given.

I waited in the corridor for Aldous to be brought back from the opera-
ting room. What is there more distressing than a hospital corridor? Pain
and fear, unavoidable and avoidable suffering impregnate the air more
thickly than the disinfectants. Rarely—not as the rule but as the excep-
tion—one finds compassion, which might be expected to be one of the
essentials of a hospital.

Aldous was wheeled back, still unconscious, to his room. I was told
that the tissue was being examined, that I should wait for the doctor in
his office.

"It is malignant," the doctor told me. He was an intelligent man,
quite young, with ice-blue eyes. "We have a very good surgeon here; he is
a specialist in this type of operation."

"What operation?"

"The best thing to do for this malignancy is to cut out one third of the
tongue."

Aldous's speech, that perfection of each sound, his love for words, his pleasure in reading poetry aloud! . . . I wanted to strike the man, to shout defiantly . . . but I only murmured: "But he is a public speaker . . ."

"Yes, yes, his speech will be a little impaired, but there are exercises . . ."

"Don't say anything to my husband. I will speak to him."

"No—*I* must speak to him; it is my duty."

I was against the procedure of speaking to patients when they were still partly under the effects of anesthesia; I did not want Aldous to make a decision in this weakened condition.

"All right, then, speak to him, but will you wait until tomorrow?"

He agreed. And added: "The best thing is for him to remain here, so we can operate soon."

Later that day I spoke to Aldous, who was by then feeling almost well. I told him that some degree of malignancy had been detected but that I was more worried about the people who were supposed to take care of it than about the illness; that they suggested an operation and wanted to talk about it tomorrow. "Let's listen to what they have to say. In any case, we will leave the hospital—then decide."

The next day the surgeon, supposedly an eminent man, came to talk to Aldous. He was muddled and inarticulate; to make himself clear, he took a large writing tablet, made a drawing of the tongue, and showed Aldous how much he intended to cut off. His hands were trembling so intensely that Aldous remarked about them as soon as he left. As we usually did when dealing with anyone in an extreme emotional state (and this surgeon had all the symptoms), we let him speak without interruption or questions. When he finished, there was a long silence, which obviously perplexed him.

"We will let you know," Aldous said after a while.

As soon as the doctor was out of the door, I gave Aldous his clothes. "Let's get out."

Aldous smiled at my concentrated fury.

"You mean escape?"

Aldous was now feeling completely normal. In five minutes he was dressed and we were ready with our weekend bag. As we started for the door, the little plastic nurse came in, with the plastic lunch. When she saw her patient fully dressed, a comic look of astonished disapproval came over her face. We left quickly. In the corridor we had to pass by the nurses' desk—it was impossible for Aldous to be unnoticed under any circumstance, and here they knew that he was a patient.

Seeing him dressed, and his wife carrying the overnight bag, the head nurse had the same flabbergasted look, almost of shock. "He has not been dismissed! The papers, signatures . . ."

"Send us the bill at home," I said. Providentially the elevator came and we disappeared in it. Before the staff could decide what to do with escaping patients, we were at home, where Aldous ate a good lunch. An hour later we were at Dr. Cutler's, not only one of the great cancerologists of our time but also one of the gentlest and kindest men I ever have known. He reassured us and spoke about the operation in exactly the same terms as Sir S.C. that Aldous had described in his letter. Later that summer Aldous was in another hospital, under an assumed name, for eight days; then he convalesced at home for several weeks. He recovered completely by the end of August and in the beginning of September of that year (1960) he was able to participate in the Dartmouth convention on "the great issues of conscience in modern medicine." There, eminent surgeons and doctors, philosophers and humanists spoke about the ethics of science and medicine and their use for the improvement of human welfare. Aldous gave an unforgettable talk on "medicine's moral issue." His tongue was permanently healed and his speech remained perfect until the last days of his life.

4 Ennismore Gdns
SW7
22.vi.61

No news from you, my darling. I hope everything is all right with you and that Ginny progresses satisfactorily.

I went to see the *Devils* on Tuesday night and found that play and the acting excellent except at one or two points. . . .

So many of my old friends are either dead or ill or out of town that I am finding London rather sad. Not all the time, however, for the colouring is so beautiful when the sun comes out, and the foliage and flowers are so rich that I find myself at moments almost in an LSD state. And I have met some very nice people; so don't let me complain.

Goodbye, my darling. Write to me when you have the time—even a postcard.

Your

A.

4 Ennismore Gdns
London SW7
23.vi.61

My darling, your cable wasn't given to me yesterday, and I have only just got it. I can't imagine why you haven't received my letters. I have written 3 or 4 times. Meanwhile no news of *you*. How are you? And what are your plans? I have to go out now. I lunch with Andrew and his wife. This evening I see S. Will write again tomorrow. *Intanto* I love you.

Your
A

4 Ennismore Gdns
London SW 7
24.vi.61

I was happy to get your letter, my darling, but sad that the news about Ginny is still so gloomy. Over and above the break in the bone, there is always the shock. It took me two months to get over that fall from the edge of our road[5] and I didn't really hurt myself. So she will probably be feeling very low even if the bone mends quickly—which I hope to goodness it will. . . .

Saw —— yesterday. She looks well, but suffers (she told me) from obsessive fears of accidents and misfortunes of all kinds. She needs some of your treatments to take her back over that terrible accident she had two years ago and abreact it—for I imagine that this is the immediate trouble, though the roots of the fear probably go deeper into her past. London is bright and positively hot—hotter than LA when I left. The parks all look like pictures by Monet. Give my love to Ginny.

Ti voglio bene

A.

4 Ennismore Gdns
London S.W. 7
26.vi.61

I have been thinking of you all day, my darling, with a strange kind of intensity—thinking how extraordinary you are in your power and your vulnerability, your capacity for loving and your "noli me tangere" passion for being left alone; thinking with so much tenderness and desire, such a sense of not being really complete without your lovely, incalculable presence moving in and out of my life, without those exalting ecstasies of your lips. . . . Can I ever complete you in the way that you complete me? I would like to feel that I could—would like to feel that I can love you with so much understanding tenderness that I shall always know what to do, or what to refrain from doing in order to help you in your strength and support you in your vulnerability. . . .

---

[5] A year before, Aldous had taken a walk in the dark and had stumbled over a foot-high curb. He fell eight feet to the terrace below; it was a minor miracle, due, probably to his saving state of relaxation, that he didn't really hurt himself.

I listened to my tape yesterday and shall now be able to reconstruct my notes for the Copenhagen conference. I am also working on my speech for India, which they want a copy of in advance—I do a broadcast tomorrow with John Whiting—about *The Devils,* will report on that in my next letter; also on my dinner with Dr. William Sargant, the man who wrote "Battle for the Mind."

Be well, my sweetheart, and let us try to be happy and peaceful malgré tout[6]—because of one another.

Your

A

4 Ennismore Gdns
London S.W.7
29.vi.61

My darling, thank you for your letters and the plan of the house.[7] My only doubts about this plan arise from my memories of the width of our property. Is the lot wide enough to permit the two wings of the house to spread out at a reasonable angle? . . . One could, of course, have a sort of bridge hanging over the edge of the slope leading from the front to the kitchen door. In fact I think this would be a good idea, in any case; for it would permit us to use the whole of the flat ground for the house without wasting any on paths. Did P. ever suggest anyone who might do the job? If so, or if you think K. ——— could do it, why don't you ask what he would charge to make a preliminary rough plan? On the basis of such a rough plan one could really start thinking concretely. It would be a very good thing to get one—even in very rough form—before you come to Europe. London is boiling hot—exhaustingly so, though much less exhausting than New York, since there are so many parks and gardens. I shall go down to Le Piol on July 15 for a week, after which I might go for some bracing air to Saint-Lud in Switzerland, then come back to Paris. . . . My mouth is about the same and of course haven't talked about it, merely said I'd had some dentist work done.

A

4 Ennismore Gdns
S.W.7
2.vii.61

My darling, I stupidly forgot to mail my letter to you in London before coming down to the country yesterday. So it and this one will go out

---

[6] In spite of everything, one of the rare allusions to our fire loss.
[7] I had sent him my sketch; facetiously he responded with the plan illustrated on the following page.

My apartment

Draw-bridge

Your apartment

River

Not shown — under-
ground passage for my
use when the draw-
bridge has been raised
to the top.

H/

together. The heat yesterday was incredible for England and this season—93° in the shade. Today it is a little cooler and it feels as though there might be a thunderstorm later on. This is pleasant country about 50 miles SE of London—fruit trees, pastures, hop gardens (the flowers of the hops are used for flavoring beer). The R.'s live in a 15th century house, well modernized and very comfortable except that one has to be very careful not to bump one's head on the low doorways. The garden has a pond in it with ducks and there are lots of tall grass, buttercups, campions, cow parsley, wild geraniums in immense profusion. Very mescalinish at the near point.

I hope Ginny is getting on normally and without complications of any kind. Give her my love. And what about you, my sweetheart? Don't let yourself get too tired. It will be very good for you and Ginny to get to the beach as soon as the children are out of school and at camp.

Good night, my darling, and sleep well.

Your

A

4 Ennismore Gdns
London SW7
4.vii.61

I hope, my darling, that you're feeling better—for your report of yourself in your last letter was far from good. Do try to get away somewhere for a rest even though rents *are* monstrously high.

Several things to report from this end. First, I went yesterday to see young Dr. — — —, with whom I have been in correspondence for some time. He is an acupuncture expert—quite young, but with a good practice, based on the fact that he cures people who can't be cured by other doctors (mostly chronic cases). The state health service pays him to spend a day each week acupuncturing difficult patients in a public hospital—a good mark in favour of official medicine in England. He felt my pulse, found general health good, but detected a certain weakness in kidneys and liver, which he tonified with needles in the foot and knee. I shall go back to him once or twice before I leave and report on results.

In the evening I went to — — —, where I met Professor Tolstoy, son of the novelist Alexy (a distant relative of the great Tolstoy). He tells me that I am very popular in Russia among people of his generation and urged me to visit the country. So what about going on to Russia after Copenhagen for ten days or so. We would see everything we wanted under the best possible circumstances—for Tolstoy is an important man and knows everybody. Let me know at once what you think of this idea. I have a feeling that it is a very good opportunity and should not be missed.

Your

A

4 Ennismore Gdns
S.W.7
4.vii.61

My Darling, just got your letter about the Stampa quotation from the Daily Mail. What is one to do? The man asked me if it was true that we had lost $300,000. I said of course it wasn't. Then he talked very sensibly about my work and we got on to psychology and I mentioned that you were working in that field—but evidently that didn't get into the interview (which I didn't see), whereas some sensational nonsense about money did get in. And the man who did the interview seemed very decent and intelligent—but he had to earn his living as a journalist. In future I shall avoid all interviews if possible. I have had 2 broadcasts—one with John Whiting about *The Devils* and one about my book. Both harmless since I was doing the talking. But really this press sensationalism is too disgusting, and it makes trouble and causes distress. I'm very sorry that this should have happened. . . . Meanwhile, what do you think about the Russia plan? Would you like to go there after Copenhagen?

Then there is the house problem. As I said, I think you should pay some architect to make a rough plan about which we can think concretely.

Goodbye, my darling. Keep well and tell me what your plans are.

Your

A.

4 Ennismore Gdns
London SW7
July 5, 1961

My darling, I received your two letters this morning, and along with them that nauseous article in the Daily Mail, which I hadn't seen before. One should never put any trust in journalists. This man was recommended as a decent fellow, and turned out in many ways to be pleasant and intelligent. The part about the money arose when he asked me if I were a rich man, saying that I must have made a million pounds in the course of my life. I said that about a quarter of that sum would be more like the figure. Needless to say, I never said I was broke, and I made a joke about the necessity of reading any important books again from start to finish instead of consulting my private index of marked passages. And the whole thing is placed between quotation marks, as though it were direct quotation! As for waiting for something to turn up, I said that the fire seemed like a broad hint from the higher powers that books weren't the solution to the problems of life and that perhaps some other hint would be vouchsafed. And I mentioned the possibility that I might do something in the way of direct relationship with people, and in this context I mentioned your work in this field. All this part of the conversation was quite brief, and most of the time was spent in talking about literary matters, in which the man was very well informed, and about the new book—whose title he got wrong! And of course there is no redress. One must merely avoid these people—as I would have avoided this man, if I hadn't been given a good account of him. I thought I had put a stop to his sensation-mongering about money by telling him that his wild estimate of my having lost three hundred thousand pounds worth of possessions was completely ridiculous, as well as his estimate of the amount I had earned in the course of my life. But he managed to make a lurid story out of the money business all the same. It is a lesson. Give as few interviews as possible and don't let the interviewer touch personal matters. Meanwhile I am distressed at the thought of the way this disgusting article has upset you and given a totally false impression to our friends. As I say, I hadn't read the piece—they didn't even send me a copy. And since nobody I knows reads the Daily Mail I had had no reactions to the article at this end.

And now Hemingway's death. Where, you ask, is the All Rightness? Certainly not on the level where he lived and killed himself. That was the Buddha's world of Sorrow; but there is also the ending of Sorrow—only it's very difficult to achieve. Somebody asked Ignatius Loyola what would be his feelings if the Pope (as seemed possible at the moment) were to dissolve the Company of Jesus. It would be a shock, he admitted; but 'fifteen minutes of mental prayer, and I should think no more about it.'—no more about the destruction of his entire life's work. Obviously, it isn't easy. But some people have managed to do it. And some people don't have to work at it very much; they are born capable of living in the All Rightness inherent even in the most monstrous circumstances. Would it be good for Ginny[8] to remember all the good and the bad of the past times in the light of another LSD or psilocybin experience? It might be.

[8] Ginny had had a close friendship with Ernest Hemingway, her brother-in-law.

And now for the plans. First, the house. . . .

Now for projects at this end. I leave London for Le Piol next Saturday, the fifteenth (address, Le Piol, Saint Paul de Vence, Alpes Maritimes, France). I expect to stay there for about a week. After that I shall probably go for a few days to Vaison la Romaine. . . . I may come back here, spend a day or two with Julian and Juliette, whose house will then be clear of the workmen now making alterations, and then shall go for a motor tour with S. All this, of course, if you don't decide to come over to Europe and suggest doing something else. We are supposed to be in Copenhagen by the thirteenth of August and are to be there until the end of the week. After that would you like to go to Russia for a week or two? As I wrote yesterday, I know we could go under the best possible circumstances, thanks to Professor Tolstoy who is anxious to do everything possible to make our stay interesting and arrange for us to see whatever we like. I told him that you and I were particularly interested in the preventive medicine and mental health side of Russian life, and he would undoubtedly be able to get us into hospitals, rest homes, clinics etc. Let me know as soon as possible what you feel about this project, so that I may start making arrangements with Tolstoy, before I leave London on the fifteenth. (He is to be here for several weeks in charge of a Russian scientific exhibition of optical equipment, shortly to be opened here.) My own feeling is that we should go to Russia. I have never been anxious to go; but Tolstoy's extreme cordiality and obvious desire to be helpful have changed my feelings, and I think we ought to take the opportunity that is being presented to us. (Maybe this is one of the hints for which I have been waiting!) If we go to Russia, it will be about the end of August before we can rejoin your sister and her family in Italy. Let me know very soon, I repeat, how you feel about all this. Good bye, my darling. I don't imagine that either of us will ever be able to do what St. Ignatius said he could do. But even if the final All Rightness of the world may never be vouchsafed to us as a permanent experience (only perhaps in flashes), I believe we can do quite a lot—you complementing me, I complementing you—to achieve a relative all rightness for ourselves and a few other people in the midst of the awful all wrongness of what Keats called 'the giant misery of the world'. Ti voglio bene.

A

Oaksey
Wilts
8.vii.61

Here I am, my darling, in the country staying with Gervas and Elspeth Huxley. It is an amazingly quiet region, off the main stream of traffic and solidly agricultural, with big stone farmhouses and barns—16th and 17th century buildings—in the midst of pasture land, wheat and barley fields fenced with stone walls. Gervas and I went for a long walk —partly along the old Roman road which is at this point just a track across the fields with a profusion of wild flowers in the hedges, partly along narrow lanes, and met nobody but one small child and three or four cars. Twenty miles away there is an inferno of cars and motorbikes and parking problems—but here only farming, highly mechanized of course—but that means that very few people are needed to do the work. The others have all moved into the towns and are working in factories.

I wrote postcards to both sets of children and will send more next week.

How are you, carissima? Keep well.

Your

A

The Athenaeum
Pall Mall SW1
11-7-61

My Darling, just got back from the country and found your 2 letters— very hard to read the handwriting, I fear. Am trying to get Krishna- murti writings, but no answer so far. The hot weather is over and London is gray and cool, so I'm not tired. I propose to go to Le Piol on Saturday the 15th and stay about a week, then go for 3 or 4 days to Vaison in Provence. . . . After that I might come back to England or else go to Switzerland and listen to Krishnaji. *When are you coming over?* My movements will depend on your dates.

I will start the business of getting a Russian visa tomorrow. *You will haved to do the same,* as soon as possible. Our date for Russia will be about August 20th. I hope we shall get in and out before Mr. K. brings on a serious crisis which he now seems quite determined to do. How unspeakably boring as well as horrible.

I'm sorry to hear of Ginny's flu. What bad luck she's having!

Will write or cable tomorrow when I have heard more about Krish- naji. (I *can't read* the name of the place you say he's speaking at.)

I love you, my darling. Be well.

Your

A

4 Ennismore Gdns
London SW7
July 12, 1961 (A.M.)

My darling, I discovered another fragment of your last letter typed, almost invisibly, on the back of a letter. . . .

Today I must go to the Russian consulate, to get my visa. After that shall have to see what can be done about hotels, both in Leningrad and in Switzerland. There may be great difficulty in securing accommodation at this late date. This is now the curse of travel—not finding room, unless one reserves months in advance. I will let you know as soon as I get reservations at Gstaad, where Krishnaji will be staying. He came yesterday to see me for a few minutes—looked well, but also curiously different from what he used to be; for he is now a small bright old man, with a bald head ringed by white hair. But I was very glad to see him, and look forward to being in his neighbourhood for a few days. Good bye, my darling. There is such a lot to do before I go; but will keep you posted by letter or cable as I get things done. About the earthquake[9]— the seismologists have been telling us to expect it for the last three or four years. Are they more urgent about it than in the past? I suppose the event becomes more probable as time goes on; for it depends upon the building up of pressures. However, the pressures can be released by shocks whose centre is far from inhabited areas, as it was by the big Tehachapi quake of four years ago.

Your

A

12.vii.61 P.M.

Yet another letter, my darling, to say that I have reserved rooms for us at Gstaad from July 28th for 10 days. I expect to have the confirmation on Friday—*Intanto* I thought I'd better let you know that we shall have accommodations, all paid in advance (they demand it), half pension (they demand that too) from the 28th, with Krishnaji round the corner and the Bernese Oberland in the background.

Bring your flower and rainbow tapes with you; many people will like to hear them and it may be worth while to pop over to England for a few days so as to talk with this man who has a recording studio and who is

---

[9] I was repeatedly told that the burning of our home was a sign of Providence, warning us to move away from Los Angeles, which was to be destroyed by an enormous earthquake. I had asked Aldous what he felt about this news.

interested in trying new ideas and embarking on novel projects. I doubt very much if our Russian plan will go through—in fact am rather off the whole thing after the realization at the consulate this morning, that one is supposed to be officially sponsored—unless one goes through the official tourist agency.

But for the present let's concentrate on Gstaad and a holiday in the mountains. It might be very good for Ginny too. Will send you the name of the hotel as soon as I know it.

Your

A

4 Ennismore Gdns
London SW7
13.vii.61

My Darling, I wrote you a long letter this morning, but forgot to put it in my pocket when I went out—so it will be mailed after this later note. In the interval I have been to the Soviet consulate. What a mess! First of all half an hour's wait, because the consul hadn't turned up. When he did turn up, he was single-handed and had no secretary; so everything took a very long time. Finally I asked for my visa: but it seems that unless one is travelling in one of the Intourist Groups, one has to have an official invitation to go. Of course I *could* get such an invitation from the Writers' Group there: but (a) there is not much time for this and (b) I don't want to go officially. A letter from Professor Tolstoy would also get me a visa; but I hesitate to ask him—and anyhow it would be impossible to get it and bring it back to the consulate in time to get my passport back by Saturday, when I leave. We *could* go with his letter to the consulate in Copenhagen, but meanwhile there is the problem of hotels, about which the consul was gloomy. So it really looks as though our Russian trip was off. Do you mind very much? Another year we will make the necessary arrangement 6 months in advance. Last minute plans are unworkable these days. Now I must go and see if we can get rooms at Gstaad.

Goodbye, my love.

Aldous

4 Ennismore Gdns
SW7
15.vii.61

My darling, one last word from London which I shall be leaving in an hour or so.

We have rooms at The Palace Hotel, Gstaad from July 27th for 10 days. Our neighbors will be Krishnaji and Yehudi Menuhin, who comes to his chalet at Gstaad on August 1st (I dined with him and his wife last night). So we shall have pleasant company and even enlightening company. I will write you from Le Piol. Be well, my sweetheart, Ti voglio bene.

A

Le Piol
Saint Paul de Venice
(A.M.) France
16.vii.61

. . . I left London in a terrific rainstorm and arrived in Nice two hours later in the hot sun. The whole coast has been built up with hotels and huge apartment houses, and there are thousands of parked cars and millions of people. Le Piol lies a little inland, and here the country is still pretty unspoiled. Today the mistral is blowing and everything is very bright and clear. Will write again soon. Meanwhile remember that we have rooms at the Palace Hotel Gstaad from July 27th for 10 days. So it won't be so long, I hope, before I see you again, my sweetheart.

Your

A

Le Piol
Saint Paul de Venice
(A.M.)
17.vii.61

I have the impression, my darling, that the mails here are very erratic, and I don't know when my previous letter went off. However, sooner or later what I write will reach you—so here I go.

The conference has started. Quite interesting group. Two Italians—Servadio, a psychiatrist, and Cavanna, a neurologist—a Dutchman, a Swiss or two, the Englishman, Gray Walter (whom you saw, I think, at the Brains Trust broadcast in 1958)—very bright and well informed. And of course Eileen in the midst of it—mostly silent, but sometimes describing her experiences very well, and making her comments, generally very sensible. We discussed ESP experiences under LSD today—and the conclusion seems to be that LSD and psylocybin do not improve ESP except perhaps in the field of travelling clairvoyance. The Russians have been repeating the experiments performed 70 years ago by Janet and much earlier by Esdaile and Puységur inducing hypnosis at a distance. The same thing is being done by Hoffer in Saskatchewan. This seems to be very promising.

Meanwhile how are you, my sweetheart? and when am I going to see you?

Your

A

Le Piol
Saint Paul de Venice
(A.M.)
21.vii.61

Just received your letter forwarded by Juliette, my darling. What a disappointment about the publisher![1]

Most of the participants at the parapsychology congress have now left and there will only be a handful at the final meeting tomorrow . . . —then Palace Hotel, Gstaad, Switzerland, where I am looking forward —how eagerly—to see you. The conference has been interesting on the whole. . . . Today we had a holiday, and I went for a long drive into the mountains behind Venie. Strange, barren country that turns into woods and meadows at 4000 feet. . . .

Goodbye, my love, I will write again from Vaison. . . .

Your

A

Vaison la Romaine
23.vii.61

Here I am, my darling, in a little room at the top of a medieval house near the castle that dominates this little town, where the Romans built a huge theatre that can still be used. . . .

I had forgotten how beautiful Aix is—a town with fountains and very sober, noble 17th century houses. It was a pleasure to see A again. And it was another pleasure to visit the palace of the Popes at Avignon— though not so pleasant to have to do so in a group of at least a hundred tourists. Europe is fairly swarming with people on the move—millions of people eager to see beautiful things and, in the process, making the beautiful things invisible, or actually (when it comes to natural scenes) destroying them. The countryside is very beautiful—vineyards,

[1] The MS. of my book (*You Are Not the Target*) had been returned.

orchards, wind-breaks of cypress trees. But the agriculture is becoming completely mechanized, industrialized, chemically controlled as in America. They have now reached a point at which they can make a half a dozen different types of wine out of the same batch of grape juice. It is just a question of extracting water, (by freezing), or adding chemicals or of aging the wine artificially—you get everything from vin ordinaire to port. And now there is a new industry—extracting oil from the seeds of the grapes after pressing, or of tomatoes after extracting the juice. Very fine unsaturated fatty acid, as good as saffoil—and it's a brand new French and Italian industry, dating back only to 1955.

Our Italian maid, Rina, who came to us in 1924 when she was 13, turned up at Vaison to see me. Such a wonderful example of the most civilized and noble kind of peasant of the old school. She is now a woman of 50, married to a younger man (very happily) who has worked his way up to the head of a transport company. They have 16 10-ton trucks based on Marseille, and Rina organizes the whole business and at the same time retains all her old qualities of simplicity, kindness, native common sense and goodness. One has a sad feeling that people of this kind are becoming rarer and rarer. . . .

I am so eagerly looking forward to seeing you again—very soon now, my sweetheart.

Your

A

Brightness

"SERAI GENEVE lundi avec voiture tendresses."

After all the tentative planning, this cable from Aldous made our rendezvous in Geneva definite. And there Aldous was at the airport, tall and smiling, in the bright Swiss morning. Aldous also was looking bright, much better than six weeks before in Hollywood. He had planned, and it turned out to be, one of the best summers we ever had.

Aldous had rented a car for the day; on our way to Gstaad we stopped for lunch—it is so easy to eat simply and well in those little restaurants, full of bright geraniums. My strongest impression of that week in Switzerland is brightness: Aldous was bright, the geraniums were bright, the sky was bright, the air was bright, our friends were bright. We arrived in Gstaad in the early afternoon. Aldous had rooms for us in one of the big old-fashioned hotels. In my room there was a basket of strawberries, also bright, a welcome gift from Iris Tree. She was a long-time friend of Aldous, from that period in his young life, in Bloomsbury, of which I know nothing and about which so much has been written. Iris and I had become friends recently in Hollywood; I found her fascinating and was happy she was there.

The day after our arrival in this resort town was a memorable one. It is unusual to meet, within one hour, as I did, three persons of such diversity and prominence: the former Queen of Italy, Krishnamurti, and Yehudi Menuhin. Krishnamurti gave a talk, that morning, of unique intensity. Aldous's comment on this in his notebook was: ". . . the impression of intrinsic authority that he gives, the enormous reserve of power." I had met Krishnamurti, superficially, years before when he was in California. This morning after his talk I met him again, with Aldous, and we planned to see each other the next day.

Among Krishnamurti's listeners were Yehudi Menuhin and Marie José of Belgium, former Queen of Italy. Years before, when I was studying with his teacher, Georges Enesco, I had met Yehudi briefly; Aldous had dined with him and Diana, his wife, just a few days before in London. Aldous had great warmth and admiration for Yehudi. He felt in him an extraordinary inner power and peace over and above his artistic excellence. I have the impression Yehudi was not thinking of music that morning but was under the impact of Krishnamurti's intense talk. We met Diana and Yehudi later in the week. What a marvelous fusion of talent, kindness, and brilliance! What a pleasure, Aldous and I agreed, to view the world through their bright humor and compassion!

After the talk Aldous and I were walking leisurely in the vast expanse of green in front of our hotel, waiting for lunch. A gentleman, leaving a nearby group of four or five people, came to Aldous and introduced himself; he was the personal ambassador of Marie José of Belgium. She was there, a few yards away, and was inviting us for lunch. It was an unexpected honor and pleasure.

It was a lively, interesting lunch. There were many similarities between Marie José and Aldous. Both were tall and slender; both had had difficulty with their eyesight; there was, in both, a strange aura of defenselessness that made people want to take care of them; and both had that peculiar kind of shyness which arises not from preoccupation with the self but rather from a concern for causing others to be shy. Perhaps the basic quality Marie José and Aldous had in common was an inner, intrinsic aristocracy, regardless of rank or position or place; it would be evident in the Royal Palace or in the fish market, in the most sophisticated library or in the Brazilian jungle—or even on Hollywood Boulevard.

Marie José was an admirer of Aldous; he had known her mother, the Queen of Belgium. There was much talk about *The Art of Seeing,* about Krishnamurti, ESP, and life after death. Then the Queen, who was practicing with a new camera, took pictures of us all.

Years before, as a girl of fourteen, I had played one of my first concerts in Turin in the presence of Her Highness, then Princess of Piedmont. As we took leave I told her what a great honor and emotional experience that occasion had been for me. Between that concert and today's lunch Marie José had participated in history in the making: she had become queen and had been dethroned; her native country, Belgium, had been invaded and its Royal Family exiled. But noblesse oblige: the Queen, of course, said that she remembered with pleasure my performance.

The next day we were invited for lunch by Signora S., a Florentine woman who was Krishnamurti's friend and hostess. A year and a half later, when Aldous went to Rome for a few days to attend a congress, Signora S. and Krishnamurti were living there. Aldous wrote me, "Signora S. looks after Krishnamurti with enormous devotion—but does it without being a holy woman which is not easy in the circumstances. She is really a very remarkable woman." I knew exactly what Aldous meant by holy woman. He had had to develop ways to evade the eager solicitude of holy women, for though it sometimes amused and touched him, it also usually embarrassed him. It arose naturally enough from his being famous and pale and handsome, from us having written cynical novels as well as *The Perennial Philosophy,* [1] and from his having been, years before a vegetarian. Aldous had gone on a vegetarian diet to improve his digestion, but most people interpreted his action as evidence of spirituality. I think that what especially disturbed Aldous about holy women (and men, too, who had the same approach) was that they tended to make their idol into a symbol and in so doing diminish his humanness.

At the Signora S.'s we had a delicious luncheon—the regime was completely vegetarian. Anyone can successfully prepare the good classic American dinner in fifteen minutes—salad, steak, frozen peas, and ice cream; it is nutritious, unimaginative, and satisfying. But a completely vegetarian dinner is very often a failure—understandably so—for to achieve variety and nutrition without meat, fish, eggs, and milk products requires imagination and knowledge, patience, and above all a really Epicurean perception of Nature's gifts.

At Signora S.'s the food was natural, alive, and varied. Aldous and I praised it and were told that the order and combination of the courses had been made according to the famous Dr. Bircher-Benner of a nearby clinic in Zurich. From recipes for food, we went on to speak of my "Recipes for Living and Loving." I had been very active in psychotherapy that year and had almost finished my book. Aldous spoke about the origin of the word "recipes"—it is the imperative of the Latin word *recipere,* to receive—and told our hosts how my recipes had succeeded with some people for whom the orthodox methods had failed. Krishnamurti asked a few questions and listened intently. We spoke about vitamins and imagination, solitary confinement, LSD, alcoholism, and the congress on extrasensory perception that Aldous had recently attended in the South of France.

After lunch Signora S. tactfully suggested that I might want to speak alone with Krishnamurti. She and Aldous went into the living room. A

[1] Harper & Row, 1944.

large French window opened onto the terrace, where Krishnamurti and I were left alone. The French window was closed, but, as I realized later, Aldous could see us silhouetted against the sweeping view of the Alps. An hour or two later, when we left our hosts, Aldous could not wait to ask, "What in the world happened between you and Krishnaji? You two were gesticulating with such animation and excitement—it almost looked as though you were having a fight. What happened?"

The silent pantomime Aldous had seen through the French window must have been descriptive of our conversation—an extraordinary conversation against an extraordinary panorama. Krishnamurti and I had stood, walked, and sat on the terrace of the Swiss chalet, enveloped by high peaked mountains and pine woods of all gradations of green, light exhilarating green, and the deeper green of the vast mountain pastures. Brightness again, in luminous sky and in shining flowers, in sensuous undulating valleys, in Krishnamurti.

Brightness everywhere.

The first thing I asked Krishnamurti, continuing our table conversation about psychotherapy, was how he dealt with the problem of alcoholism. He said nonchalantly that it had happened quite often that people, after one or two interviews with him, stopped drinking. When I asked how this came about, he said he did not know. He dismissed the subject and asked me whether LSD, mescaline, and the psychedelic substances in general were really of any benefit or just gave a temporary illusion. I told him of the medical research done in Canada in the field of alcoholism—of unexpected and successful results reported by Canadian doctors with a number of hopeless alcoholics who stopped drinking after only one or two administrations of LSD, and without further therapy. Krishnamurti seemed surprised.

He was silent for a few moments. There was something that he was going to say; also I had the feeling that his inner intensity was too powerful for the medium of words. I had no idea what was coming, but I knew something was about to happen. Silently he was holding my eyes with his dark burning look. Then with an extremely tense voice, he exploded, "You know, I think that those people who go about helping other people . . ." He stopped—then, with an even more piercing gaze, he spat out the next words like bullets of contempt: "those people . . . they are a *curse!*"

After the conversation at the table I had no doubt that "those people" included me. The accusation and the fire with which he flung it at me were for an instant paralyzing. Then, almost without thinking, I asked, "What about you? What do you think *you* are doing? You go about helping other people."

As though he had never thought of himself as belonging to that cursed category, Krishnamurti was taken aback for a moment, totally surprised and perplexed. Then, with disarming simplicity and directness, he said, "But *I* don't do it on purpose!"

It was the most extraordinary of statements. Aldous was enormously impressed by it, and also very touched and amused. Of course he understood it. But I must have looked bewildered, for Krishnamurti, in a softer, calmer way, said, "It just happens, do you see?" Alas, I did not see very well. Krishnamurti continued, "I am not a healer, or a psychologist, or therapist, or any of those things." The words "healer," "psychologist," "therapist" burst from him like projectiles ejected by compressed power. "I am only a religious man. Alcoholics or neurotics or addicts—it doesn't matter what the trouble is—they get better quite often—but that is not important; that is not the point—it is only a consequence."

"What is wrong with such a consequence?" I asked. "I only give people techniques or recipes or tools to help them to do what they need to do—what is wrong in using the transformation of energy to change those miserable feelings into constructive behavior?" That had been what we had discussed at lunch. I knew that Krishnamurti was violently opposed to dogmas, rites, gurus, and Ascended Masters—to all the gadgetry of those organized powers whose aim is to impress the masses with keeping the godhead and its graces as their supreme and private monopoly. But I had no idea that he also objected to psychophysical exercises, such as my recipes. Unaware of this fact, I had innocently exposed myself and my work. Now I realized that he had restrained himself during lunch, tactfully waiting until we were alone. He did not restrain himself now; vehemently, with unspeakable intensity, he spoke.

"No! No! Techniques—transformation—no—rubbish! One must destroy—*destroy . . . everything!*"

Fleetingly a thought crossed my mind: how easily such a man can be misunderstood, misinterpreted! I wanted to understand—I knew that he wanted me to understand, but *how* to ask—that was the question. "But what do *you* do?" I repeated.

And he repeated: "Nothing—I am only a religious man."

It had the sound of a final statement, a baffling one to me. Six words, I thought, but hundreds of different meanings, according to each person's conditioning. Perhaps he was simply restating what Christ had said:

But rather seek ye the kingdom of God; and all these things shall be added unto you.

But I was not thinking about Christ—I wanted to know what Krishnamurti meant by "a religious man."

"What *is* a religious man?"

Krishnamurti changed his tone and rhythm. He spoke now calmly, with incisiveness. "I will tell you what a religious man is. First of all, a religious man is a man who is alone—not lonely, you understand, but alone—with no theories or dogmas, no opinion, no background. He is alone and loves it—free of conditioning and alone—and enjoying it. Second, a religious man must be both man and woman—I don't mean sexually—but he must know the dual nature of everything; a religious man must feel and be both masculine and feminine. Third," and now his manner intensified again, "to be a religious man, one must destroy everything—destroy the past, destroy one's convictions, interpretations, deceptions—destroy *all* self-hypnosis—destroy until there is no center; you understand, *no center.*" He stopped.

No center?

After a silence Krishnamurti said quietly, "Then you are a religious person. Then stillness comes. Completely still."

Still were the immense mountains around us.

Infinitely still.

One Never Loves Enough

"ONE NEVER LOVES enough: How can I love you more?

As the years passed, Aldous's theme song increased in intensity. I had heard it in 1955 the first time he had taken mescaline with me; he said it then while he was in an ecstatic state.

"One never loves enough"—that feeling was now in his everyday state of mind, increasingly present in him. He would express it again and again, not only to me, but also when speaking publicly. Not long before he died he said in a public talk, "It is a little embarrassing that, after forty-five years of research and study, the best advice I can give to people is to be a little kinder to each other."

With me he was always selfless and giving, and he continued to be so, even through the discomfort and depression of his exhausting illness.

He was equally patient and tender during my difficult moments. I have had, throughout my life, periods of restlessness and discontent. While such moods may appear irrational, and sometimes may be so, they often have within them a creative potential. (It was in the process of trying to make sense and utilize the irrationality of these periods of depression that I developed some of the techniques of *You Are Not the Target.*) Fortunately, these periods have never lasted very long and, either by psychophysical means or by initiating something new, I have been able to handle them, and often profit by them. Aldous felt that my "miseries" were caused by a disequilibrium between physical strength and emotional and mental drive.

"You see, sweetheart," he would say, "you have the motor of a Thunderbird and the body of a Topolino." (Topolino, meaning Little Mouse, is the name of the smallest Italian car.)

I knew I was difficult to live with at such times, and I would try to stay, as much as possible, alone. On one particular day, I think in the autumn of 1958, I felt miserable. It was a beautiful sunny morning and Aldous and I were driving Ginny's children to school. In the car I had a burst of anger. Aldous tried his best to turn it into a joke, but I was in no mood for jokes. Driving with set jaw I said, "It is serious—we'll speak about it later."

We left the children at school and returned home, Aldous carefully silent, I broodingly so. More upsetting than anything else was the fact that I knew no one was responsible for my misery; certainly not Aldous. As soon as we entered our house Aldous quickly went upstairs to his quiet workroom. As on every other morning of his life, he was going to work: he knew that in such moods I always preferred to be alone. I went to my room, smoldering because he had done exactly what I wanted him to do. No, I had nobody to blame—and the garden was blooming, my room full of peaceful spaces. . . .

After a while the inner pressure became too great—I had to do something about it. I went upstairs and stood near Aldous, who was seated at his typewriter. I knew what I wanted to say but I was so afraid of hurting him, although part of me must have wanted to hurt him.

"Aldous, something is wrong, I don't know what, certainly not you. It must be that I am not the type to be married." I took a deep breath. "I believe we should divorce." What pain in pronouncing that word!

Aldous looked at me with such deep love, with such dissolving tenderness. He took my hand and kissed it. "I caught a nymph," he said. "I must let her go," and released my hand.

My breath stopped; I burst into tears and fell into his arms.

"But I don't want to go! I don't want to leave you—it is just this peculiar married life. . . ." I was trying to understand myself—crying—wondering.

Aldous consoled me, teased and caressed me, and said that I was only half a creature of this world—the other half belonged to some other world; that it was difficult to be both human and a nymph. Maybe I should go away alone for a few days. . . .

I went up to the Sequoia forest. Those millenary trees, the earth fragrance, the animal grace of chipmunks and deer, the inescapable divinity of the place, brought me quickly back to harmony. I called Aldous to tell him that everything was marvelous.

He sounded happy and excited on the phone "I found your picture!" I did not understand. "I found your picture in a book; you are Queen

Dedes as Prajnaparamita!" I understood even less.

"Who is she?"

Aldous had been looking at one of his favorite art books, Zimmer's *The Art of Indian Asia.* He had come upon the reproduction of a Javanese statue of the late thirteenth century. The resemblance between the statue of Queen Dedes as Prajnaparamita and me is remarkable. Aldous was delighted and amused. "Prajnaparamita means 'the transcendental Wisdom of the far shore'; maybe that is why you are sometimes a little impatient with home life."

He made fun of me with such a light, affectionate touch. My sister never forgot the time we were visiting her in Italy. We were sitting on her flowering terrace overlooking the Ligurian Sea. I was complaining that I had so much to do; no one to help me with my work—it was not a secretary that I needed; I just wanted someone who could do my therapy work with the techniques I had written—carry them out. Aldous was listening attentively. Then, "Laura ha solo bisogno di qualche apostolo [Laura only needs a few apostles]," he said, smiling at my sister.

Often in his letters Aldous joked in that same unique, charming way. The nymph theme was a favorite of his. The last time he mentioned it was in a letter seven months before he died.

In May 1963, I was scheduled to go to New York for a series of public appearances, synchronized with the publication of my book. Never was the duality of life more evident. On one side I was having every satisfaction that a new writer could wish for; on the other, Aldous, ghostly-looking, was declining every day. No one except Ginny and me knew his real condition. I asked Dr. Cutler if I should cancel my trip.

"How long are you going to stay?"

"One week." He suggested I change nothing.

Our routine, on the surface, remained normal. Aldous came down to breakfast every morning at eight, ate a good-sized meal, went to his room to work, took a walk in the afternoon—but he was different. He did not complain, but he would not talk. There was a sense of separation in him which I had never seen before. Even later, when the illness was much more advanced, he did not exude such depression. And he was remote. He would participate with animation and interest in discussions about my book, which was for us the great news of those days. Otherwise he was silent—silent in a different way than he had been before. He would sit with his elbows on his knees, his face buried in his hands. I had seen him in that position throughout the years when he was thinking, listening, palming, or doing some mental exercise. Now the position was the same—but what was he thinking? I did not know; I only knew that it was not good—the same position from the outside, but the feeling within was totally different. I felt inadequate, and of very little comfort, but I did not want to go away even for a week. Yet my New York appearances had been carefully scheduled. They would acquaint a large audience with my book. If I cancelled my trip, I certainly would have to give a valid reason for upsetting so many plans, and the real tragic reason I did not want to give.

I left Los Angeles with a heavy heart. I was reassured by the fact that Aldous was with Ginny. She is particularly helpful when someone is depressed, and Aldous felt more comfortable with her, I think, than with any other friend. "She has no Bovaristic angle," he would say—meaning that she never put on a show, never tried to be what she was not.

In the plane I kept wondering: what was Aldous thinking? He never said anything to make one think he was expecting death soon. Was he? What would I say to his son in New York? How could I give him this tragic news? And when? I would be staying in New York as short a time as possible, and every hour was scheduled—it was a week of public life. "The show must go on," came mockingly to my mind. But what *was* the show? I did not know—except that I was expected to be the woman who had solved life's problems pretty well. I realized that if I looked worried I would defeat the very purpose of my book: to give hope and courage to those who are troubled, to tell people how my "recipes" would help them. Fortunately they *are* helpful—not theoretically, but operationally and practically; yet one day they almost failed me. It was my second day in New York.

As I was leaving the hotel room a special delivery from Aldous arrived. I was on my way to the lobby to join a charming young woman, in charge of public relations, who was going to take me to a television interview. Where television is involved, punctuality is a point of honor. I wanted to read Aldous's letter at once but I could not take the time to go back to my room. I had written to him from the plane two days ago; I had written about his present difficult moment and about my inadequacy and clumsiness in dealing with it. This letter was his immediate answer. I read it in the gray corridor waiting for the elevator.

My darling,

Thank you for your sweet letter.

You don't have to do any apologizing; it is I who am the clumsy one. Being sick makes me very inarticulate. I tend to just creep into a corner and lie down, like a dog, until the thing is over. The little infection is about over now—as for the other thing, let's hope we'll get the better of that, at least for a few years. There are plenty of things I would still like to have time to do—and things which perhaps I still have capacity to achieve. But I wouldn't like to drag on in a diminished way as a caricature of myself and a burden to you and to everyone else. Meanwhile I am happy that things are going as well as they are—that you are feeling not too rushed and tired, and that the book promises to become a booming best seller. I knew that I had trapped a nymph—but had no idea that the nymph would also turn out to be a Cosmic Phenomenon!

A Respectable Literary Gentleman

WHEN THE FIRE destroyed our home, only one of Aldous's letters to me was saved—and only because I always kept it in my purse. It was written at the end of the summer of 1958 in Turin. It had been a particularly active summer of traveling on three continents: a triumphant summer, in the sense that never before had either Aldous or I realized how widely celebrated and loved he was.

Traveling was one of Aldous's greatest pleasures. However, "It is pleasant to be back here in the sun, able to do some honest work for a change . . ." he wrote to Humphry Osmond after returning to our hilltop from South America and Europe. "I was simultaneously touched and appalled to discover that I am now, as the result of having been around for so many years, a kind of historical monument, which sightseers will come quite a long way to inspect, and which radio and press reporters find newsworthy. In Brazil it was as though the leaning Tower of Pisa had just come to town, wherever I blew in; and even in Italy I found myself talking to full houses in large theatres. It was really very odd and embarrassing."

On this subject the most touching episode for me was one that took place in the immense and largely unexplored Brazilian jungle, the Matto Grosso. We were visiting Brazil at the invitation of President Kubitschek. On our flight to Brasilia, the new capital then being built, we stopped in the middle of the jungle in a place inhabited by a primitive tribe. Excited and naked, some with red paint dripping from their hair, the natives surrounded us. Our pilot was surprised not to see the head of the Indian Protection Service on hand with them for the welcome. We heard later that he had not expected us, because his radio had been out of order for the past three months.

Being paler and taller than any other person in our group, Aldous attracted particular attention from these unusual people, who were some two feet shorter than he. As we were trying to communicate, a frail-looking white man, the type one expects to meet in a library, came out of the jungle. He looked at Aldous as though he had seen an apparition. Since his visit was unannounced, Aldous—long, white, and cool—might indeed have seemed an apparition. As if mesmerized, the man stopped dead for a moment—then he recognized Aldous. With tears streaming down his cheeks, he approached him, saying, "Uxley—Uxley . . . *Contrapunto.* . . ." The two men embraced. Aldous, too, was moved. Tears were in my eyes, then and now. No praise, no honor given to Aldous ever moved me as the homage of this gentle solitary man, isolated from the world of literature and civilization, dedicated to the protection of a group of human beings who did not even know that literature existed—this man shedding tears at the implausible, maybe fantasied, encounter with "Uxley . . . *Contrapunto.* . . ."

Later that summer we stopped in Turin, my home town, to see my family. Turin is one of the fashion centers of Europe, and I always do much of my shopping while I am there. It is a city of a million inhabitants, but the center where most of the shopping is done is not large, and it is pleasant to walk there. There are miles of porticoes, and reinvigorating cafés; the stores are quite small and extremely elegant. If you wish to buy a blouse, you will not be confronted with two thousand blouses, as you might be in a large department store; you see probably a dozen at the most—but each is original and in good taste. What makes shopping fun, however, is the courteous and interested behavior of the sales people. As a young and pretty salesgirl explained to me, their salary is rather small, "so we have to compensate by making our client happy!" Only people with inborn self-respect (or is it called ego-strength?) take such pride and pleasure in serving others.

Aldous also enjoyed shopping with me in the afternoons; in the mornings he worked and answered letters in the very room, large and somber, in which I had spent thousands of hours—years and years of my life—practicing the violin. In that same room there were, in several large drawers, letters and letters—most adolescent love letters I had received years before.

One morning, before going out to shop, I said, jokingly, to Aldous, "If you don't feel like working today, open those drawers and read some of the letters; they might amuse you and give you some ideas," Aldous would sometimes say, half teasingly, that he was thinking of writing my biography, "but the best parts would be unprintable." So I returned his joke by offering him some material. I certainly was never concerned about Aldous's being jealous; jealousy has a thousand overt and hidden faces—not one had I ever seen in Aldous.

Later that day Aldous and I did some shopping together. Then I had to go to my dressmaker, and he to his tailor for a fitting. It was a little early for Aldous's appointment, so I left him in a sidewalk café under those lovely porticoes. (It was remarkable what he would notice when he was just sitting in an outdoor café. "In Turin one man out of ten smokes in the street," he told me once after I had left him in the same café, "and in a half hour I haven't seen a single woman smoke in the street.")

After our fittings we were to meet at my sister's for dinner. He was there first, and met me at the door. Smilingly and almost shyly he handed me a folded paper: "I don't really know why, but I had to write you this letter. . . ."

Since that day I have kept that letter in my purse. It is written on a scrap of paper:

. . . the only piece of paper I found in my pocket. So I scratch this out and write you a letter, my darling, while I drink my coffee in Corso Vittorio Emanuele.

A letter to tell you that you really must be a *strega*[1]—otherwise why should I keep falling more and more in love with you? Why should I start being jealous of the people who loved you in the past? No, not jealous, really—rather sad because I wasn't there, because I wasn't ten other poeple loving you in ten other ways, at ten different times of your life and mine . . . being made one with you in tenderness and passion and sensuality and understanding. Well, I am not ten other people and I am here and now, not then and there. But here and now I love you very much and only wish I could love you more and better—could love you so that you would be well always, and strong and happy; so that there would never be that discrepancy between a tragic suffering face and the serenity of the nymph's lovely body with its little breasts and the flat belly, the long legs . . . that I love so tenderly, so violently.

Well, I must go to mail my letters and try on my suit and act the part of a respectable literary gentleman who doesn't sit in cafés writing love letters, of all people!—to his wife.

A.

[1] Sorceress.

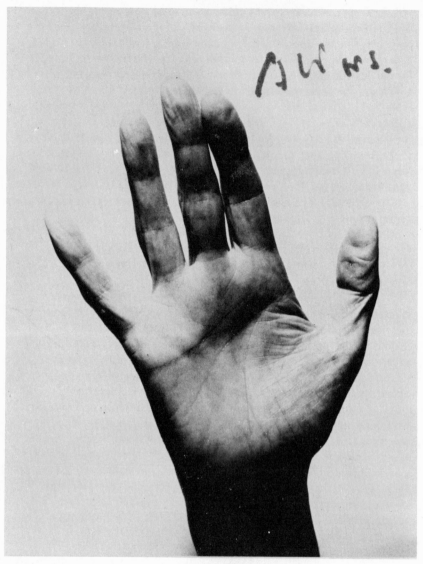

Aldous wrote his name on this photograph of one of his hands shortly before his death

A Gratuitous Grace

THERE ARE SEVERAL means by which the psychedelic experience is induced: one of them is through chemical substances. In the years between 1953 and 1963, Aldous had about ten or twelve chemically induced psychedelic experiences: *the total amount of chemical taken during those ten years was not as much as many people take today in a single week, sometimes in a single dose.*

The public abuse of these chemicals, the sensationalism and frequent misinformation of press reports are such that Aldous's position in relation to psychedelic substances should be clearly understood. In this chapter, extracts from letters and other writings of Aldous will, I hope, clarify his point of view on this subject. Along with many scientists, he considered the discovery of psychedelics one of the three major scientific breakthroughs of the twentieth century, the other two being the splitting of the atom and the manipulation of genetic structures.

In *The Doors of Perception,* Aldous describes his first experience with psychedelics, in 1953, under the guidance of Dr. Humphry Osmond and Maria. In *Heaven and Hell,* he speaks about the visionary experience and how it is produced by different means, such as meditation, vitamin deficiency, ascetic practices, chemicals, flagellation, deep hypnosis, or vision-inducing objects and works of art. In *Island,* he develops the social meaning of the psychedelic experience, which, through understanding, love, and compassion, can bring about a better world. Always Aldous emphasizes how delicately and respectfully these chemicals should be used; and that they are only one of many means through which it is possible to increase good will among men. He reminds them that the "real world is very different from the misshapen universe they have created for themselves by means of their culture-conditioned prejudices. 'HAVING FUN WITH FUNGI'—that was how one waggish reviewer dismissed the matter. But which is better: to have Fun with Fungi or to have Idiocy with Ideology, to have Wars because of Words, to have Tomorrow's Misdeeds out of Yesterday's Miscreeds? How should the psychedelics be administered? Under which circumstances, with what kind of preparation and follow-up? These are questions that must be answered empirically, by large-scale experiments. Man's collective mind has a high degree of viscosity and flows from one position to another with the reluctant deliberation of an ebbing tide of sludge. But in a world of explosive population increase, of headlong technological advance and of militant nationalism, the time at our disposal is strictly limited. We must discover, and discover very soon, new energy sources for overcoming our society's psychological inertia, better solvents for liquefying the sludgy stickiness of an anachronistic state of mind."[1]

Since Aldous's death in 1963, the psychedelic explosion has taken place. The very word *psychedelic* has become common currency, mainly because the younger generation is the champion of this explosion. Not only university students are involved: teenagers also are influenced by frightening or enticing LSD reports. The amount of misinformation is staggering. In the United States the original psychedelic drugs have been declared illegal and the result of this legislation is of thought-provoking significance: every few weeks we hear that the young experimenters have discovered still another source, directly from nature, of psychedelic elixirs.

One must ask, among other questions, what are the sociological stimuli of this quest, as well as what are to be the sociological effects. In *Island,* such abuses were avoided because young people were given the *moksha*-medicine as part of their education, once a year and under supervision, beginning at adolescence. Now, finally, many doctors and educators admit that education of young people in the use of psychedelics, rather than prohibition, is called for. As early as April 1953 Aldous wrote:

The basic problem of education is, How to make the best of both worlds—the world of biological utility and common sense, and the world of unlimited experience underlying it. I suspect that the complete solution of the problem can come only to those who have learned to establish themselves in the third and ultimate world of "the spirit," the

[1] *Playboy,* November 1963.

world which subtends and interpenetrates both of the other worlds. But short of this ultimate solution, there may be partial solutions, by means of which the growing child may be taught to preserve his "intimations of immortality" into adult life. Under the current dispensation the vast majority of individuals lose, in the course of education, all the openness to inspiration, all the capacity to be aware of other things than those enumerated in the Sears-Roebuck catalogue which constitutes the conventionally "real" world. That this is not the necessary and inevitable price extorted for biological survival and civilized efficiency is demonstrated by the existence of the few men and women who retain their contact with the other world, even while going about their business in this. Is it too much to hope that a system of education may some day be devised, which shall give results, in terms of human development, commensurate with the time, money, energy and devotion expended? In such a system of education it may be that mescaline or some other chemical substance may play a part by making it possible for young people to "taste and see" what they have learned about at second hand, or directly but at a lower level of intensity, in the writings of the religious, or the works of poets, painters and musicians.

This letter, as well as the others in this chapter, was written to Dr. Osmond,[2] who with Aldous in 1957 coined the word *psychedelic,*

[2] Several superficial observers wrote of Aldous that he was overly susceptible to quacks, spiritual confidence men, and experimenters. It is amusing, in this regard, to see the background of Dr. Osmond, the experimenter who introduced him to psychedelics. This open letter was drawn in response to a request from Aldous to help a man booked on a charge of addiction:

[November 1955]

To Whom It May Concern:

I, Humphry Osmond, Member of the Royal College of Surgeons, England: Diplomat in Psychological Medicine of the Royal College of Physicians, London, England; Certified Specialist in Psychiatry by the Royal College of Physicians and Surgeons, Canada; Member of the Royal Medico Psychological Association, London: Member of the Canadian Psychiatric Association; Member of the Group for the Advancement of Psychiatry; Consultant to the Federal Department of Health and Welfare, Ottawa, on the Training of Psychiatric Nurses; Clinical Associate in the Department of Psychiatry, the University of Saskatchewan; declare that I am presently Physician Superintendent of the Saskatchewan Hospital, Weyburn, Saskatchewan.

After training for medicine at Guys Hospital, London, England, I was licensed by the General Medical Council, London, England, in 1942. Following my internship and a period spent at sea as a Surgeon Lieutenant, Royal Navy, I have spent the last eleven years in the practice of psychiatry (psychological medicine) . . .

meaning mind-revealing or mind-opening. Under this name he refers to three chemicals, similar in many ways: mescaline, extracted from the peyote cactus; LSD, extracted from rye; and psilocybin, extracted from a mushroom. While these chemicals have great similarities, the experiences they produce are of an infinite variety. They might be aesthetic, psychological, philosophical insights, or emotional releases. They might be heavenly or infernal or in between. The highest is the mystical experience. Being beyond heaven or hell, the mystical experience is the reconciliation of the opposites, the consciousness of the "living primordial cosmic fact of Love." Aldous often referred to the mystical experience as "THE GRATUITOUS GRACE." Quoting Catholic theologians, he would explain that THE GRATUITOUS GRACE is just that: A Free Gift which might come unsought and while in the state of mortal sin, and, Aldous would greatly emphasize, is "neither necessary to, nor sufficient for, salvation." It is up to the recipient of this gift to apply in "the dreary intercourse of daily life" the enlightenment which he has received at the time of the experience, or, in Aldous's words, "to co-operate with grace—not so much by will but by awareness."

From the happenings of the last few years it is obvious that having mystical experiences is not enough, and that the greatest number of those who were given THE GRATUITOUS GRACE did not cooperate with it. Moreover, there are increasing indications that the *frequent use* and *high dosage* of psychedelic chemicals, often combined with a fribbling approach, are producing undesirable consequences.

The voluminous correspondence between Dr. Osmond and Aldous on psychedelics is a fascinating and valuable record of two mutually stimulating, brilliant minds. Aldous freely wrote about an incredible variety of subjects to Humphry Osmond, reported to him his own psychedelic experiences, and discussed guidelines for the administration of these chemicals.

Following are excerpts of letters from Aldous to Humphry on psychedelics. About research Aldous proposes:

[February 2, 1958]
. . . a project that would test the efficacy of graded doses of LSD in affecting the performance of a group of professional artists. Another important project would be to give the drug to a group carefully selected to include representatives of the Sheldonian extreme and of the commoner specimen in the middle. Yet another project should be to find out whether people belonging to Galton's non-visualizing variety of human being ever see visions under average doses of LSD, whether they can be made to see visions by larger doses, and whether they can be made to see visions by suitable suggestions.

. . . it would be interesting to try it [mescaline] out on a logical positiv-
ist. Would he, like Thomas Aquinas towards the end of his life, when
he had been vouchsafed an experience of "infused contemplation," say
that all his philosophy was as straw and chaff, and refuse to go on with
his intellectualizing?

[February 22, 1958]

. . . Yet another project—the administration of LSD to terminal cancer
cases, in the hope that it would make dying a more spiritual, less
strictly physiological process.

On writing about LSD research being used for polemic purposes,
Aldous stated:

I feel that this is something we don't have to worry about. Anything can
be misused. The Sermon on the Mount is treated [both] as an instrument of Western Nationalism and a rallying cry against Russian
nationalism—nevertheless it remains a good thing.

As one of several guidelines for people under the influence of LSD,
Aldous suggests listening to poetry or to religious utterances; also that
questions such as these be asked: "In spite of all appearances to the
contrary, God is Love—what about it?" "Do you understand now what
Blake meant when he said, 'Gratitude is heaven itself'?" He suggested
giving short quotations such as this, from the thirteenth-century mystic
Eckhart: "The meanest flea as it is in God, is superior to the highest
angel, as he is in himself."

Reporting on one of his own experiences, Aldous wrote:

[January 23, 1955]

. . . Bach was a revelation. The tempo of the pieces did not change;
nevertheless they went on for centuries, and they were a manifestation,
on the plane of art, of perpetual creation, a demonstration of the
necessity of death and the self-evidence of immortality, an expression of
the essential all-rightness of the universe—for the music was far beyond
tragedy, but included death and suffering with everything else in the
divine impartiality which is the One, which is Love, which is Being. . . .

Meanwhile let me advise you, if ever you use mescaline or LSD in
therapy, to try the effect of the B minor suite. More than anything, I
believe, it will serve to lead the patient's mind (wordlessly, without any
suggestion or covert bullying by doctor or person) to the central,

primordial Fact, the understanding of which is perfect health during the time of the experience, and the memory of the understanding of which may serve as an antidote to mental sickness in the future.

At a later date (January 1963) Aldous was asked to accept the presidency of a foundation for research in LSD. He refused as follows:

January 25—63

Dear Mr. T.

Thank you for your letter and the enclosed draft. Your suggestion that I send out copies of this draft as a personal communication has revived all the doubts, about which I spoke to you on the phone a few days back. The last thing I want is to create an image of myself as "Mr. LSD"; nor have I the least desire (being without any talent for this kind of thing) to get involved in the politics of psychedelics. But this is precisely what the procedure you suggest would accomplish. I am not a medical man, nor a psycho-therapist, nor a research worker, nor an evangelist; and I am neither an organizer, nor a sitter on committees, nor a forensic orator. I am a man of letters who can work only in solitude, a writer on a great diversity of themes, of which LSD is only one. This being so, it would be foolish of me to accept the presidency of your group.

Aldous's first experience was with Dr. Osmond and Maria, in 1952. Following that experience, he had three or four others in very small groups, with a scientific experimenter supervising the session. In October 1955, Aldous had a psychedelic session with me—his first one, as far as I know, alone with an individual, and one which was not a planned scientific experiment. A detailed account of that day, which I wrote at the time, was lost in the fire. Now, twelve years later, I have reconstructed my impressions of that experience, in the chapter that follows. When I wrote it I was unaware of a letter Aldous had written at the time to Dr. Humphry Osmond, in which he gave a detailed account of his experience. I read it recently and was very moved—and also impressed by the similarity in the atmosphere, and the enormous difference in the description, of that distant, luminous day. This is the letter.

740 North Kings Road
Los Angeles 45, Cal.

October 24th 1955

Dear Humphry,

I had another most extraordinary experience with mescaline the other day. . . . I decided it might be interesting to find out why so much of my childhood is hidden from me so that I can not remember large areas of early life. So I sat down to a session with a woman who has had a good deal of experience with eliciting recalls and working off abreactions. . . . I took half the contents of a 400 mg. capsule at ten and the other half about forty minutes later, and the effects began to be strong about an hour and a half after the first dose. There was little vision with the eyes closed, as was the case during my experiment under your auspices, but much transfiguration of the outer world. . . . There was absolutely no recall. Instead there was something of incomparably greater importance; for what came through the opened door was the realization—not the knowledge, for this wasn't verbal or abstract—but the direct, total awareness, from the inside, so to say, of Love as the primary and fundamental cosmic fact. The words, of course, have a kind of indecency and must necessarily ring false, seem like twaddle. But the fact remains. (It was the same fact, evidently, as that which the Indians discover in their peyote ceremonies.) I was this fact; or perhaps it would be more accurate to say that this fact occupied the place where I had been. The result was that I did not, as in the first experience, feel cut off from the human world. I was intensely aware of it, but from the standpoint of the living primordial cosmic fact of Love. And the things which had entirely filled my attention on that first occasion, I now perceived to be false, or at least imperfect and partial Nirvanas of beauty and mere knowledge. I talked a good deal about these temptations; commentated on the light this realization threw on the legend of St. Anthony, on the Zen statement that, for a Bodhisattva, the Samadhi of Emptiness, Nirvana apart from the world, love, compassion and sentient beings is as terrible as the pains of hell. And I remember that I quoted the remark by Pascal, that the worship of truth without charity is idolatry, for truth is merely God's idol, which we have no right to worship. And of course the same is true in regard to beauty. (Actually the Platonic trinity of the good, the true and the beautiful is a faulty expression of the facts. Good implies bad and so perpetuates dualism. Love reconciles all the opposites and is the ONE.)

I also spoke a good deal, to my own subsequent enlightenment about objects and subjects. How easy, I kept saying, to turn whatever one looked at, even a human face, into a pure object—an object of the most magical beauty, strangeness, intensity of thereness, of pure existence! Do you remember that account given by Blake of seeing a fold of lambs in the corner of a field, and how he approached and suddenly saw that the lambs were pieces of the most exquisite sculpture? This is a good description of the process of objectification. It is a kind of Gorgon's-head effect—you look at the things solely with a view to seeing truth and beauty, and it turns into stone—living, changing, self-luminous stone, but still stone, still sculpture. Love de-objectifies the perceived thing or person. At the same time it de-subjectifies the per-ceiver, who no longer views the outside world with desire or aversion, no longer judges automatically and irrevocably, is no longer an emotionally charged ego, but finds himself an element in the given reality, which is not an affair of objects and subjects, but a cosmic unity of love. I also looked at a volume of photographs of nudes—a lot of them very tricky, bits of bodies taken from odd angles and under queer conditions of lights. Objects again. Lust is sexual relations with an object for the benefit of a subject—who may also enjoy as a kind of bonus, the manifestations of subjective enjoyment proceeding from the object. Love de-objectifies and de-subjectivizes, substitutes the primor-dial fact of unity and the awareness of mutual immanence for a frenzy heightened to despair by the impossibility of that total possession of the object, at which the subject mistakenly aims.

Among the by-products of this state of being in the given fact of love was a kind of intuitive understanding of other people, a "discernment of spirits" in the language of Christian spirituality. I found myself saying things about my operator, which I didn't know but which, when I said them, turned out to be true. Which, I suppose, is what one would expect if one happens to be manifesting the primordial fact of unity through love and the knowledge of mutual immanence.

Another thing I remember saying was that I now understood such previously incomprehensible events as St. Francis's kissing of the leper. Explanations in terms of masochistic perversion etc. are merely ridicu-lous. This sort of thing is merely the overflow of a cosmic fact too large, so to speak, for the receptacle, fashioned by the subjective ego in its life-long relations with objects and not yet completely melted away, so that the new fact finds itself constricted by the old confining habits, with the result that it boils over, so to speak, under pressure and has to express itself in ways which, though not particularly desirable, are completely understandable and even, in the particular context, logical.

Another thing I remember saying and feeling was that I didn't think I should mind dying; for dying must be like this passage from the known (constituted by life-long habits of subject-object existence) to the unknown cosmic fact.

I have not retained the intensity of my experience of the state of love; but something certainly remains and I hope I shall not allow myself to eclipse it by succumbing to old bad habits. I hope and think that by awareness of what one is doing from moment to moment, one may be able to remain out of one's own light.

What emerges as a general conclusion is the confirmation of the fact that mescaline does genuinely open the door, and that everything including the Unknown in its purest, most comprehensive form can come through. After the theophany it is up to the momentarily enlightened individual to "co-operate with grace"—not so much by will as by awareness.

Yours affectionately, Aldous

Aldous liked this photograph which I took on a train in Switzerland with a dollar camera in the summer of 1961

Disregarded in the Darkness

i

Now, IN 1967, when LSD has become a household word, I realize how lucky those of us were who ten years ago approached LSD before it had either the demoniacal or the paradisaical vibrations it has now—when it had no echoes of gurus and heroes, doctors or delinquents. We went into the experience not knowing what would happen, not expecting that it would be like the experience of someone at last Saturday night's party, or like that of Mary Jones, whose hallucinated, frightened eyes stare at me from the pages of a magazine, LSD—those three now-famous letters were free of association with scientific righteousness and beatnik conformity, with earthly paradise and parental loving concern—also free from closed-mindedness, obscurantism, and bigotry. The unconscious identification with those ideas, feelings, and fears inevitably occurs now, with disastrous consequences.

What was my own initiation to LSD? It was very simple: Aldous asked me to keep him company one whole day when he was going to take LSD.

"I would love to stay with you all day," I answered. "Is there anything I should know or do?"

Aldous smiled, "Nothing—just be as you are."

Was it naïveté rather than wisdom that made me pass over that statement so lightly?

I arrived at Aldous's home about nine o'clock. Aldous took the pills and gave me a paper on which he had written his main purpose for this session. I cannot quote his words exactly—however, their essence was this: "I want to know, and constantly be, in the state of love."

I wondered. To me Aldous seemed always to be in the state of love! However, my opinion was not the point; his feelings and his search only were important.

This was October 1955. Except for reading *The Doors of Perception,* I had no idea then what a psychedelic session was. However, I had had five years of experience in giving therapy. The best attitude, in these sessions, is to cancel out for that period one's opinions and to put aside one's tendency to judge others—just to be there, very attentive and free. Not that this free state is always reached or even reachable—but it is one of the goals. That state of attention would be appropriate, I thought, for the LSD day.

The levels on which we exist are probably infinite—though there are certain levels on which in everyday life, more or less, we meet. But a person in the psychedelic state is on completely different levels. I saw an example of this right at the beginning of our LSD day: Aldous was looking at my hair very closely and smiling that smile which later I recognized almost every time he was in the psychedelic state. With a voice lower and rounder than usual, he said, very slowly, "If you could only *see* your hair." And after a long silence: "You cannot imagine ..."

I said nothing but remembered the new rinse I had put on my hair the day before. Did it show? Was it the right color? This is typical of the different levels of consciousness. Aldous was looking at hair, seeing in it the very mystery and wonder of life. He was on a cosmic level, while I, on the cosmetic one, was worrying about the new rinse. I remained silent but was glad when he stopped looking.

Aldous said that day things which I began to understand only later. At the beginning of the day we tried to enter that period of Aldous's childhood of which he remembered very little. Our attempts failed completely. Very soon I gave up trying as I became aware that something awesome was taking place. I did not know what it was, but I felt that one had no right to disturb what was happening with the usual recall techniques of psychotherapy. I felt it would be like trying to find a faded photograph of a great cathedral while being in the cathedral itself.

The first psychedelic day as a companion to Aldous flowed easily and quietly. There is so much mystery in a psychedelic day, so much happens in the person who is having the experience that he cannot express. That day, as on many others when I was a companion to a "voyager," I became slightly affected by the drug, although I did not take it and never do when I am a companion. It is one of the many un-accountable qualities of these chemicals. Perhaps the breath of a person who has taken LSD has some trace of it; maybe it comes out from the skin pores. Or is this phenomenon due to hypnosis, imagination, energy-transfer, telepathy? Or to a yet unexplained osmotic process? I do not know. It is a fact, however, of LSD when in the presence of a person who has taken it. In slang, this is called "having a free ride." It is desirable that it should happen, for then the companion is not too separated from the voyager—the companion may participate, even though in a minute way, in the voyage. This natural participation is basic to psychedelic companionship.

The first trip with Aldous I remember as a timeless roundness. I was not this timeless roundness; Aldous was. My surface mind was still going at its petty pace, but I was aware enough of the timeless round-ness not to disturb it. In Aldous's case it could hardly have been dis-turbed, but in people not as prepared as he was, feelings, revelation, and reaction can be of a different nature. So are states of conscious-ness. The companion should not interfere with these states or judge them by word, gesture, or feeling—for it is important that the voyager accept all of them, whether blissful or hellish, intellectual or emotional, or unqualifiable—and relate them to his life, for they are all different aspects of himself and of his history.

As Aldous wrote to Dr. Albert Hoffman, the discoverer of LSD, "in *Island* the account of individual [psychedelic] experiences is first-hand knowledge." But I had not the slightest idea that day, and for a long time afterwards, that these experiences were to be the raw material for Aldous's writing. I was so totally unaware of anything connected with the process of writing that it was an enormous surprise for me to find much of our lives in *Island*.

That first LSD day was filled with aesthetic revelations. We listened to Bach's Fourth Brandenberg Concerto:

It was the same, of course, as the Fourth Brandenburg he had listened to so often in the past—the same and yet completely different. This Allegro—he knew it by heart. Which meant that he was in the best possible position to realize that he had never really heard it before. . . . The Allegro was revealing itself as an element in the great present Event, a manifestation at one remove of the luminous bliss. Or perhaps that was putting it too mildly. In another modality this Allegro *was* the luminous bliss; it was the knowledgeless understanding of everything apprehended through a particular piece of knowledge; it was undiffer-entiated awareness broken up into notes and phrases and yet still all-comprehendingly itself. And of course all this belonged to nobody. It was at once in here, out there, and nowhere . . . Which was why he was now hearing it for the first time. Unowned, the Fourth Brandenburg had an intensity of beauty, a depth of intrinsic meaning, incomparably greater than anything he had ever found in the same music when it was his private property.

. . . And tonight's Fourth Brandenburg was not merely an unowned Thing in Itself; it was also, in some impossible way, a Present Event with an infinite duration. Or rather (and still more impossibly, seeing that it had three movements and was being played at its usual speed) it was without duration. The metronome presided over each of its phrases; but the sum of its phrases was not a span of seconds and minutes. There was a *tempo,* but no time. So what was there?

"Eternity." . . . He began to laugh.

"What's so funny?" she asked.

"Eternity," he answered. "Believe it or not, it's as real as shit."[1]

I could follow Aldous in the world of music and colors; but when he spoke about the fusion of subject and object I did not understand. I did not understand, but I knew that he knew, and that, sometime, I would also know. "Subject and object," he said quietly and lovingly many times. "No separation between subject and object." In the silence of the large house, in the roundness of that day, there was his knowing, there was my ignorance. I was aware of both, and of the absence of conflict between the two. His whole person was emanating love and his voice was full of wonder—"Subject and object—they are one."

That day, partly due to my experience in psychotherapy, I had expected—in spite, alas, of trying not to expect anything—that Aldous might speak about Maria. I had hoped he would, and that he would express emotionally his pain. I had not realized yet that Aldous had his own and best way of directing the unfathomable alchemy by which we continuously transform our feelings and ideas into something else. Aldous transformed his love for Maria, and the pain of her loss, into the death of Lakshmi, an unforgettable passage in *Island.*

During that first LSD day the thought of Maria was often present. We were in her house, where nothing had been changed since her death. We had been silent for a long while, listening to music. Now the record came to an end—I wanted to stop the machine to avoid the forthcoming shocking click of the automatic stop. To do this I had to walk a few steps away from Aldous toward the record player. As I took the first step I felt suddenly that Maria was present. Present, but not outside of me—present in me. Amazed and fascinated, I knew that I was walking as Maria—that she, not I, was walking. It must have been at the third or fourth step toward the record player and away from Aldous that his voice reached and touched my shoulder. Extremely firm and gentle, the voice said, "Don't ever be anyone else but yourself."

Aldous did not have to remind me of that again.

[1]Unless otherwise indicated, all quotations are from *Island.*

Now that I have experience in LSD, this episode—which lasted two or three seconds at the most—is less surprising, though no less mysterious. I cannot explain what it was that made me feel, for a second to two, that I was Maria—and what on earth made Aldous realize my fleeting impression? Certainly not his seeing me take two or three steps in a dimly lighted room.

Since that first day as a psychedelic companion I have learned to be prepared to have no secrets from the voyager. A person in a psychedelic state can perceive much more in other human beings than he can when he is in his everyday mind. The voyager may see his companion at different ages of life, at different periods of history, and as different persons, sometimes conflicting with each other. At one time or another, during the psychedelic session, the voyager looks at his companion. Often it is an overwhelming discovery. Anyone who is a companion must give up any attempt at self-hiding. Not only is it useless, but it creates a fatiguing and distracting tension for both. "Who are you?" Spoken or not, the question is loudly asked in almost every voyage. Silent and naked, the companion must know that he cannot answer—for the essence of the answer lies as much in the questioner as in himself.

Will opened his eyes and, for the first time since he had taken the *moksha*-medicine, found himself looking her squarely in the face.[2]

"Dear God," he whispered at last.

. . . The eye sockets were mysterious with shadow and, except for a little crescent of illumination on the checkbone, so was all the right side of her face. The left side glowed with a living, golden radiance—preternaturally bright, but with a brightness that was neither the vulgar and sinister glare of darkness visible nor yet that blissful incadescence revealed, in the far-off dawn of his eternity, behind his closed lids and, when he had opened his eyes, in the book-jewels, the compositions of the mystical Cubists, the transfigured landscape. What he was seeing now was the paradox of opposites indissolubly wedded, of light shining out of darkness, of darkness at the very heart of light.

"It isn't the sun," he said at last, "and it isn't Chartres. Nor the infernal bargain basement, thank God. It's all of them together, and you're recognizably you, and I'm recognizably me—though, needless to say, we're both completely different. You and me by Rembrandt, but Rembrandt about five thousand times more so." He was silent for a moment; then, nodding his head in confirmation of what he had just said, "Yes, that's it," he went on. "Sun into Chartres, and then stained-

[2] In Sanskrit, *moksha* means liberation.

glass windows into bargain basement. And the bargain basement is also the torture chamber, the concentration camp, the charnel house with Christmas-tree decorations. And now the bargain basement goes into reverse, picks up Chartres and a slice of the sun, and backs out into this—into you and me by Rembrandt. . . ."

"You're so incredibly beautiful," he said at last. "But it wouldn't matter if you were incredibly ugly; you'd still be a Rembrandt-but-five-thousand-times-more-so. Beautiful, beautiful," he repeated. "And yet I don't want to sleep with you. No, that isn't true. I would like to sleep with you. Very much indeed. But it won't make any difference if I never do. I shall go on loving you—loving you in the way one's supposed to love people if one's a Christian. Love," he repeated, "*love*. It's another of those dirty words. 'In love,' 'make love'—those are all right. But plain 'love'—that's an obscenity I couldn't pronounce. But now, now..."
He smiled and shook his head. "Believe it or not, now I can understand what it means when they say 'God is love.' What manifest nonsense. And yet it happens to be true. Meanwhile there's this extraordinary face of yours." He leaned forward to look into it more closely. "As though one were looking into a crystal ball," he added incredulously. "Something new all the time. You can't imagine . . ."

But she *could* imagine. "Don't forget," she said, "I've been there myself." . . .

She broke off, and suddenly Will found himself looking at Incarnate Bereavement with seven swords in her heart. Reading the signs of pain in the dark eyes, about the corners of the full-lipped mouth, he knew that the wound had been very nearly mortal and, with a pang in his own heart, that it was still open, still bleeding. He pressed her hands. There was nothing, of course, that one could say, no words, nor consolations of philosophy—only this shared mystery of touch, only this communication from skin to skin of a flowing infinity.

"One slips back so easily," she said at last. "Much too easily. And much too often." She drew a deep breath and squared her shoulders.

Before his eyes the face, the whole body, underwent another change. There was strength enough, he could see, in that small frame to make head against any suffering; a will that would be more than a match for all the swords that fate might stab her with. Almost menacing in her determined serenity, a dark Circean goddess had taken the place of the Mater Dolorosa. Memories of that quiet voice talking so irresistibly about the swans and the cathedral, about the clouds and the smooth water, came rushing up. And as he remembered, the face before him seemed to glow with the consciousness of triumph. Power, intrinsic power—he saw the expression of it, he sensed its formidable presence and shrank away from it.

"Who *are* you?" he whispered.

She looked at him for a moment without speaking; then, gaily smiling, "Don't be so scared," she said. "I'm *not* the female mantis."

He smiled back at her—smiled back at a laughing girl with a weakness for kisses and the frankness to invite them.

"Thank the Lord!" he said, and the love which had shrunk away in fear came flowing back in a tide of happiness.

"Thank Him for what?"

"For having given you the grace of sensuality."

She smiled again, "So *that* cat's out of the bag."

"All that power," he said, "all that admirable, terrible will! You might have been Lucifer. But fortunately, providentially . . ." He disengaged his right hand and with a tip of its stretched forefinger touched her lips. "The blessed gift of sensuality—it's been your salvation. *Half* your salvation," he qualified, remembering the gruesomely loveless frenzies in the pink alcove, "*one* of your salvations. Because, of course, there's this other thing, "Mary with the swords in her heart," he went on, "and Circe, and Ninon de Lenclos and now—who? Somebody like Juliana of Norwich or Catherine of Genoa. Are you really all these people?" . . .

Half in mysterious darkness, half mysteriously glowing with golden light, her face had turned once again into a mask of suffering. Within their shadowy orbits the eyes, he could see, were closed. She had retreated into another time and was alone, somewhere else, with the swords and her open wound. Outside, the cocks were crowing again, and a second mynah bird had begun to call, half a tone higher than the first, for compassion.

"Karuna."

"Attention. Attention."

"Karuna."

ii

Not long after that day we decided that it was my turn to have a psychedelic session. I was driven to Aldous's home at about nine o'clock in the morning. I could feel how happy he was in being able to give me something so extraordinary. I saw Aldous in the following years in that same mood, youthful and excited, every time he gave a present with which he was especially pleased. He derived pleasure from giving presents. He once came from London with the most marvelous necklace of amber, each oval piece of a deep living color, a joy to look at and to feel.

"They are like angel balls," he said. "You deserve them, my darling."

The morning of my first LSD day, more than my own state of mind, I remember Aldous's delighted anticipation. He gave me a glass of water containing the mescaline. After a while—maybe half an hour—I became a little nauseated.

"You are on your way," he said smiling.

Nausea is usually expected from mescaline. It lasts only a short time, after which the experience begins. I was "on my way."

I was lying on the sofa in the living room. Suddenly another human being, also lying down, came into my consciousness—*became* my consciousness: a baby I had seen a few days before. It was a recent experience, fresh in my memory—only now it was not a memory, it was the experience itself, perceived and felt with an intensity a thousand times greater than when it happened. Before, I had only been moved by the event; now, the event and I were almost one.

The previous week Ginny and I had visited an orphanage in Tijuana: eighty-six infants left there by women unable to keep them—six nuns to care for them all. The nuns were magnificent. With the most meager financial resources they had the daily care of eighty-six infants— washing diapers, preparing food, cleaning and bathing. I see them now doing their work in a happy, spirited manner, running from one end of the hall to the other. But there is no time left for the nuns to take the children in their arms. Imagine the time required just to wash and fill eighty-six bottles six times a day. . . .

The children were left hours and hours lying in their cribs, small, alone, and undergiven—alone and undergiven before they were born. Lying there, untouched. Some cried, others had already given up crying and had receded into an echoless silence, without light. A few were sleeping peacefully; many were staring, staring. One child had made a deeper impression on us than all the others; Ginny had baptized him "the violinist." He was about ten months old. Silent, the wide dark eyes open and unblinking, set in pale blue skin, he seemed more than the others alone. He kept his left hand up in the air as though he were holding a violin; the long fingers incessantly moving as though search- ing the notes on the string. In comparison to the small emaciated body, his hand was big, ideally formed to play an instrument. The fingers, moving in solitary space, were searching, searching, it seemed, for a contact with somebody, a human contact which could have come, at this time in life, only through touch. There was no one to touch. He had been given life, but no contact with life. Immersed in a sea of loneliness the little boy kept his arm up high, moving his fingers, hoping—vainly hoping. Would the little fingers ever find someone to touch? Would they find someone *in time,* before they would accept the present separation as life's essence? Or would death lift the oversized incubus imposed on the little creature?

As I entered the psychedelic state these feelings—thoughts invaded me with an indescribable intensity. I broke into a desperate sobbing. Simultaneously present with the loveless destiny of the little violinist, my own childhood, filled with love and care, seemed an offense to the unlamenting infant. Why? Why such injustice? Why so much love showered on one and none on that other equally guiltless creature? His little, long, white fingers incessantly moving in emptiness, vainly searching for a human note, became to me the essence of humanity's loneliness and despair. I don't know how long I sobbed. Aldous was very near and very quiet. I sobbed until I could not breathe. I had to sit up to take some air. But my breath was practically stopped by what I saw—what a spectacle! Framed in the Spanish window, which gave it a powerful perspective, there was a new country—the garden. And right by the window a rich climbing bush of a rose of Portugal. Tenderly sensual, generous, and unafraid, the roses were smiling at me. But among the roses was an object, an everyday object suddenly now so powerful and magnificent and dangerous—dangerous, not for me, but for the roses! It was a ladder, the metal ladder, obviously forgotten by the gardener. Inconceivably brilliant and clear, it leaped at me like a virtuoso's *arpeggio* of a wind instrument; all the while, unaware and perfect, the roses were exuding their fragrant melody on strings. The ladder was beautiful, but hard and piercingly cruel. One should not let it be so near the roses—how could they coexist? Undulating, triumphant, and free, the roses did not realize, did not fear, the cruel object on which someone will climb with garden shears . . . The roses know better—they live in this timeless moment.

In the psychedelic session, thoughts-feelings occur with such rapidity as to appear simultaneous; the conflict of the rose of Portugal and the metal ladder brought feelings and thoughts of all kinds and degrees, but the conflict remained for me unsolved. I was not able yet, as Aldous was, to reconcile the opposites:

"Beauty and horror, beauty," he repeated, "and horror. And then suddenly, as you come down from one of your expeditions in the mountains, suddenly you know that there's a reconciliation. . . . A fusion, an identity. Beauty made one with horror in the yoga of the jungle. Life reconciled with the perpetual imminence of death in the yoga of danger. Emptiness identified with selfhood in the Sabbath yoga of the summit."

Another image of that day is still marvelously vivid in my mind: a dirty soup dish. After a few hours—or centuries?—Aldous had given me a bowl of vegetable soup, beautiful and delicious. When I finished it, Aldous made a move to take the bowl and wash it. I held on to it as though he were taking my most precious possession.

"Please don't, Aldous."

The round, white bowl with little pieces of vegetable was to me the cosmos, round and infinite, punctuated by light exuding planets and stars of fiery orange and translucent green. Aldous smiled; he knew what one can see in a dirty dish when the doors of perception are cleansed.

At the end of the day Ginny fetched me and drove me home. I was wide awake the greater part of the night—pleasantly awake. I had a few very clear images with my eyes closed. One of these images came back again and again. It was this image that gave me, several months later, the style and color for the house we bought and decorated after our marriage. The strange part of it is that only years after did I realize that my decoration had been inspired by that image.

The next day I passed quietly at home. I spoke to Aldous several times on the phone. I had kept the day absolutely free, but in the late afternoon I was supposed to attend the funeral of the sister of a dear friend. Aldous and Ginny and I discussed whether I should go or not; although the intensity of the previous day had diminished, I still felt unusually open to outer stimuli. I began to wonder what going to a funeral would do to me, in this sensitive state. Would I start to cry uncontrollably? Not because the woman who had died meant much to me—but in the psychedelic state one is particularly vulnerable to the pain of others. Besides, I had attended several funerals in my lifetime—two of which had been almost unbearable. Would the emotional memory of these old griefs come back? We decided to sit in the back of the chapel near the exit. If necessary we could easily leave.

As we drove to Forest Lawn Cemetery, colors were still very vivid. Forest Lawn was a new experience for me—I had never been to a funeral in America.

As the ceremony started I did not feel any pain. All my feelings were, somehow, taken up by amazement. What kind of barbarous custom was this? A party over disintegrating matter? I looked around. I was struck by the obvious attention people had given to their choice of clothes for that afternoon—but that attention should be given to the woman who had died, and died so tragically, at the height of moral suffering. What was going on in the little chapel had nothing to do with her. Why were we not thinking of her? Why were we not giving her courage, instead of indulging in these mindless words and gestures? The speech of the pastor—it had nothing to do with the desperate, lonely creature who had killed herself and had been found, seven days later, in an apartment on Sunset Strip. One should be loving and strong—give her courage—not listen to a speech for which this man in uniform had been paid.

Then he said something that surprised me: the woman had already been cremated. I sighed with relief; for years and years I had gone with my father, once a week, to put flowers on my little brother's tomb—later, on my mother's. In Italy, a Catholic country, cremation is unusual.

"What a novel idea," I thought. "How good and practical. Instead of those heavy caskets, that pitiless lid which closed in, suffocatingly, on those I loved. Instead of that—fire—and then clean, clean ashes—practically nothing."

And then an extraordinary thing happened. I understood the pastor to say: "The ashes will be sent to Seattle by air, to be put in the family pot." Surely, he must have said *plot*—but I heard *pot*. The word *plot* never came to my mind—although later I was told repeatedly and definitely that the word was *plot,* to me it was *pot.* It still is.

Words, whether we see them or hear them, bring to us not only meaning, sensations, and emotions, but also images. As that moment the word *plot* had no images for me—but *pot!* What a variety of chamber pots and tea pots I had seen during my life in Europe! And now all these different pots began a spirited dance. With the speed and precision that only the mind possesses, a complete picture was presented to me: a light comedy, playing, singing, and dancing for my benefit in a clear, cosmic, Offenbachian rhythm:

> The pot
> The pot
> The family pot.
> The tea pot?
> Or the chamber pot?
> Why . . . .
> THE FAMILY POT!

Cosmic orchestration, lively rhythm, singing chorus—all there, free and gay, making fun of the pastoral speech, of the stereotyped ceremony—a thousand cherubs had been sent to me to shake out, out of me, the powerful impact death had had on me, to shake out the past, to show me another side of the view. And now the cherubs, pink and white and red, started a chorus with bassoon and piccolo accompaniment:

> To Seattle by air
> The ashes will fare
> And find their peace
> In the family's pot.

An immense cosmic laughter exploded throughout my trillions of cells. Again and again it shook me like an earthquake.

Ginny looked at me incredulously: was I mad? Anyone else would have panicked—not she. Instead, she gave me a handkerchief; tears were streaming down my cheeks. The unending, immeasurable laughter could, thank heaven, be interpreted as uncontrollable sobbing. How long did this explosion last? I do not know. Blowing my nose, and with my face bathed in tears, I let Ginny lead me from the chapel. The ceremony was almost finished; we could leave now and people would attribute the sobbing to my Italian emotionality.

Crying and laughing are branches of the same tree—the tree of emotions. Not two of the leaves are the same, yet all have the same roots: the capacity to feel and the need to express those feelings. Whether I was crying or laughing was really not to important, except on the conventional level. The important point was that the tree of my emotions was being vigorously shaken and liberated of some withered leaves which had hung on it too long.

When we were a little way from the chapel I started to explain to Ginny what had happened. I wanted her to know. I started to tell her about the family pot, but laughter overtook me again.

Ginny carefully and gently asked, "What family pot?"

"Where the ashes will find peace," I attempted to say, but the double meaning the sound of the word "peace" conjured brought about another shower of tears and laughter, making it impossible for me to articulate the words. We were by now at the parking lot. Ginny felt safer when I was inside the car.

"Let's call Aldous," she said.

"Yes, he will love it!" I answered with enthusiasm.

"Love what?"

"The musical comedy," I attempted again, this time a little more successfully, to tell here what had happened.

Ginny's approach to death had always been totally opposite to mine. Besides, through long years of friendship she knew the role death had played in my life. When I was able to tell her what had happened at the funeral, she understood the liberating trigger my mind had put in motion: by using the uncunningly simple device of taking the "l" from the word *plot*, it had started a beneficent chain of images which swept away, shook away, some of the heaviness of past tragedies. The long crying of the previous day had prepared the way—I had felt the pain of the world. Later, in spite of death and the preposterous way it was approached, I could know and participate in a cosmic laughter—as I had in a cosmic despair. Experiencing the extremes of human emotion leads to a better understanding of what there is in between, a wider acceptance of feelings and actions which would otherwise be unacceptable and inexplicable. To some poeple, looking only at the surface, the sequence of events of my first psychedelic experience might seem to border on madness; others will see in it a profound logic and wisdom.

As soon as I arrived home I called Aldous. It was difficult to tell him of my musical comedy, for the exploding laughter occurred again. Aldous was delighted and said, what I heard him say so often in the following years: "This drug seems to do for each person what the person needs."

Would Aldous still say this if he knew that many people now take LSD either alone or with a companion chosen with no more discrimination than a drinker choosing a companion at a bar in the small hours of the morning? The importance of a companion has been for years so obvious to us that we concluded that almost more important than the question "Who should *have* LSD?" is "Who should *give* LSD?"

Aldous and I were once taking LSD in a group. We became aware that a young woman, the wife of a psychiatrist, was sinking into terror. Aldous moved near the sofa on which she was reclining; he did not say a word, only took her foot into his hands and quietly held it. The woman looked at Aldous, astonished. In a few seconds the anguish which was lining her face gave place to a smile of relief, a deep sense of gratefulness. Aldous had not said a word; it was not his brilliant intellect, or his eloquence or knowledge, which had in the space of seconds changed this woman's terror into serenity. It was the warm human touch of his hand on her foot and the feeling of friendliness and compassion which had inspired it. And she knew that, whoever or whatever she was, she was not alone. Had she been taken into a hospital and treated as a psychotic, she would have, in all probability, broken into a psychotic episode.

On another occasion, a strong young man who was taking LSD for the first time suddenly had the feeling that his heart was going to give way. I put my hand over his heart.

"Your heart," I said quietly. "Listen to it." I took his hand and put it over his heart. "Listen to your heart beat. It is life, *your* life—*all* life pulsating through you."

There was no longer fear—only wonder.

Would Aldous still say: "This drug seems to do for each person what the person needs," if he knew that most people take it now, not only without preparation but also without follow-up? It is certainly not

enough to have psychedelic ecstasies. In fact, they have meant nothing
to many individuals, and have harmed some. But those who have
approached the experience with a receptive mind have often found
meaning and liberation, even in the most prosaic everyday life.

"Liberation" Dr. Robert began again, "the ending of sorrow, ceasing
to be what you ignorantly think you are and becoming what you are in
fact. For a while, thanks to the *moksha*-medicine, you will know what
it's like to be what in fact you always have been. What a timeless bliss!
But, like everything else . . . it will pass. And when it has passed, what
will you do with the experience? What will you do with all the other
similar experiences that the *moksha*-medicine will bring you in the
years to come? Will you merely enjoy them as you would enjoy an
evening at the puppet show, and then go back to business as usual,
back behaving like the silly little delinquents you imagine yourselves to
be? Or, having glimpsed, will you devote your lives to the business, not
at all as usual, of being what you are in fact? All that we older people
can do with our teachings, all that Pala can do for you with its social
arrangements, is to provide you with techniques and opportunities.
And all that the *moksha*-medicine can do is to give you a succession of
beatific glimpses, an hour or two, every now and then, of enlightening
and liberating grace. It remains for you to decide whether you'll co-
operate with the grace and take those opportunities."

Love and Work

THE FOLLOWING IS a report of a psychedelic session with Aldous. It is the only one of which I have a tape recording, not of the entire session but of the major portion.

A few months after Aldous's death, when I found this tape, I was deeply moved by it. I had forgotten it, and now, after his death, these words were more than ever meaningful if, at times, equivocal. And how nice it was to swing from "life after death" to "soup here and now," from the Sermon on the Mount to running noses! And again I realized the constant consideration and encouragement Aldous gave to my current project, even on that extraordinary day.

I first thought of publishing his recorded words as they are, without comment. But when the tape was transcribed on paper I began to see that they would not be as clear to a reader as they were to me, a participant in the dialogue. There is a world of difference between reading a conversation and hearing it. In reading, two important elements are missing: the voice, so significant particularly in Aldous's case, for he had such a variety of inflections, of color and moods and rhythm; and the pauses, always important but more so in this kind of dialogue. I could have edited this conversation, but I prefer to leave it as it is on the tape. Aldous's phrases are not as well rounded and clear as in his writings and lectures—but he was not giving a lecture; he was speaking to me. I feel that the content and the authenticity of his words outweigh the consideration of literary elegance.

Another reason for commenting on this taped conversation is that Aldous is referring to subjects unfamiliar to many people. The experiencing of the Clear Light of the Void, of the Bardo or after-death state, of the fighting hero of the Bhagavad-Gita these are not everyday topics; yet they are of the greatest importance for us all. In this conversation Aldous refers to two books: The Bhagavad-Gita and the Tibetan Book of the Dead. I had not read these books at the time, but Aldous had told me a great deal about them. To anyone who has read them, what Aldous says is intellectually clear. But while familiarity with these books throws a light on our dialogue, Aldous's conversation—the atmosphere, the aura of it—is in no way a discussion of them. The extraordinary part of this conversation is the feeling that Aldous is experiencing that which he has known for a long time. But, as he wrote in *Knowledge and Understanding,*[1] there is a world of difference: "Understanding is primarily direct awareness of raw material." On the other hand, knowledge is acquired and "can be passed on and shared by means of words and other symbols. Understanding is an immediate experience and can only be talked about (very inadequately), never shared." Knowledge is "public." Understanding is "private." In *Island* the children are given an illustration of this difference in the lower fifth grade, at about the age of ten.

"Words are public; they belong to all the speakers of a given language; they are listed in dictionaries. And now let's look at the things that happen out there." He pointed through the open window. Gaudy against a white cloud, half a dozen parrots came sailing into view, passed behind a tree and were gone. . . . "What happens out there is public—or at least fairly public," he qualified. "And what happens when someone speaks or writes words—that's also public. But the things that go on inside . . . are private. Private." He laid a hand on his chest. "Private." He rubbed his forehead. "Private."

The words Aldous spoke in this psychedelic experience can be looked up in the dictionary; they are public. The understanding of his experience is a private matter for each of us.

This session was different from others in many ways. Usually, when we had a psychedelic session, the evening before and the day of the session were kept absolutely and rigorously empty. This time we went out to dinner the night preceding the session. I further notice from my calendar that on the day of the session, January 22, 1962—a Monday—there were three other entries: a house guest arriving at the airport, the maid's birthday, and a tentative visit to a family whose three members were all mentally ill, but at large.

[1]*Collected Essays* (Bantam, 1960).

It was because the day was not to be entirely free that we changed from LSD to psilocybin. Unlike LSD, which lingers on for many hours even after the high point is passed, psilocybin usually shuts off completely. In fact, this session lasted only from 10:40 a.m. to 3:00 p.m. Considering that Aldous had taken such a small dose, we wondered later, that it had such a marked effect.

That morning after breakfast we went to my studio apartment, where we would not be disturbed. The studio is practically empty of furniture. The floor is covered by a shaggy white rug—it looks like white grass and is soft and pleasant to sit on. As usual, but especially for a psychedelic session, there were fresh flowers and fruits. Here and there, punctuating the white emptiness, there were fresh bamboo, shells, art books, records, and a few branches of golden acacia that had just burst into bloom in our half-burned garden. In the nook off the living room there were unpainted bookshelves, a large piece of unpainted wood which serves as a desk, a tape recorder, and two small armchairs.

At 10:40 a.m., Aldous took four mg. of psilocybin.

There is a period of half an hour to about two hours between the ingestion of psilocybin and the beginning of its effect. Usually during this period we talked or looked at pictures; more often we listened to music—or did nothing at all. One never knows in which direction these experiences may move. Sometimes the "doors of perception" are cleansed suddenly with a jolt; sometimes the cleansing comes gradually with ever increasing discoveries. These discoveries may be psychological insights, or may be made through any of the senses—it is usually from the eyes that the scales first flake off.

In the psychedelic session the role of a companion is to be there, fully attentive, and with no preconceived opinion of what might happen. A companion must be, at the same time, completely there and completely out of the way. Sometimes one feels that one should be there in the most intense and alert passivity one can master—but, paradoxically, be there invisibly. However, this was never the case with Aldous. Sessions with him had always been easy, and I knew he wanted me there, visible and tangible.

A companion to the psychedelic experience should not have a preconceived idea—but to have *no* opinion is very hard to achieve. As it happens, this morning I found myself thinking that this session would be very light, since the dosage was so small, and that it would be similar to the others I had with Aldous—that it would modulate from beauty and the intense presence of life to love on all levels, the human as well as the mystical.

Surprisingly Aldous asked me to stop the music. It was Bach, probably the *Musical Offering* or a cantata.

I turned off the record player, and as I was wondering whether Aldous would want to hear something else, he got up from the floor where he was sitting and began pacing the corridor joining the living room to the bedroom. This also had never happened before. Aldous, like most people in a psychedelic experience, would move very little, generally staying in the same place most of the day.

I paced with him a few times, trying to feel what he was feeling. He looked preoccupied, and there was a feeling of agitation in him, and—again most unusual—he was muttering something in a low, unclear voice. I could not at first make out what he was saying. Then I understood the words "Confusion—terrible confusion." I paced the floor with him again—there was an unusual agitation in his movements, in his expression, in the half phrases he was saying. After a while, to my question, "Where is this confusion?" he said it was in life after death; I think he mentioned the word *limbo*. He was contacting, or being, or feeling, a bodiless world in which there was a terrifying confusion.

In psychedelic sessions there are often long periods, sometimes hours, when not a single word is uttered. Music, or sometimes silence, is the least inadequate way to express the unspeakable, the best way not to name the unnamable. But I knew those ecstatic moments, for they are reflected in Aldous's face—and even in those moments Aldous would say a word or two. But this was a different situation. Aldous was not having an ecstatic experience—he was going through something very intense, of great importance, but not pleasant. He did not seem to be willing or able to put it into words. This state lasted perhaps half an hour. Then quite suddenly he said, "It is all right now—it is all right." His face changed; he sat in the armchair near the tape recorder; that other world had suddenly dissolved. He looked well and I could feel he was now ready to speak about his experience. His mind was at a high pitch of activity.

Aldous's first words on tape:

YOU SEE, THIS IS—I WAS THINKING OF ONE OF YOUR TITLES—THIS IS ONE OF THE WAYS OF TRYING TO MAKE ICE CUBES OUT OF RUNNING WATER, ISN'T IT? TO FIX SOMETHING AND TRY TO KEEP IT—OF COURSE, IT IS ALWAYS WRONG.

I thought he meant it was wrong to fix his impression on tape.

Laura: WELL, LET'S STOP THE RECORDER.

Aldous (immediately and with emphasis): NO, NO—I DON'T MEAN
THAT. I MEAN THE PURE LIGHT IS THE GREATEST ICE CUBE OF ALL,
THE ULTIMATE ICE CUBE.

Aldous was referring to one of my "Recipes for Living and Loving,"
which had required a lot of rewriting. The title of the recipe is: "Don't
Try to Make Ice Cubes Out of a Flowing River." Its concept is that our
organisms are continuously changing in a continuously changing
world; that the essence of life is its fluidity, its ability to change, to flow
and to take a new course; that the trouble is that sometimes, usually
unconsciously and unwillingly, we freeze a piece of this flowing life into
an "ice cube." In the recipe, examples are given illustrating how harm-
ful this can be; then there are directions on how to unfreeze these "ice
cubes" that imprison our life and energy. Briefly, "ice cube" refers to
the enduring, chilling effect of an unexpressed overemotional experience of grief, anger, or fear in their varied and numerous
manifestations.[2] Aldous had helped me with the recipe, and the phrase
"ice cubes in a flowing river" was a current phrase with us.

Aldous: THE PURE LIGHT. THIS IS THE GREATEST ICE CUBE OF ALL—
IT'S THE ULTIMATE ICE CUBE.

The Pure Light. The Clear Light of the Void. The experience of
Godliness. Mystical experience. The peak experience. . . . How many
names, throughout the centuries and in all different cultures, have
been given to that state for which the most sophisticated of word
virtuosos say there are no words! I remember Aldous's saying that Saint
Augustine, who wrote volumes of treatises basic to Catholic theology,
toward the end of his life had the experience of Pure Light—and never
wrote a word again. In *Island* Aldous describes that experience as
"knowledgeless understanding, luminous bliss."

Laura: YOU THOUGHT YOU WERE GOING TO HAVE <u>THAT</u> [the Pure
Light] TODAY?
Aldous: WELL NOW, I CAN IF I WANT TO! BUT I MEAN IT IS VERY GOOD
TO REALIZE THAT IT IS JUST THE—SO TO SAY—THE MIRROR IMAGE
OF THIS OTHER THING. IT IS JUST THIS TOTAL DISTRACTION—I
MEAN, IF YOU CAN IMMOBILIZE THE TOTAL DISTRACTION LONG
ENOUGH, THEN IT BECOMES THE PURE, ONE-POINTED DISTRACTION
—PURE LIGHT.

[2] *You Are Not the Target* (New York: Farrar, Straus and Giroux, 1963),
Chapter 23.

Laura: IF YOU CAN IMMOBILIZE IT? WHAT DO YOU MEAN?

Aldous: YOU <u>CAN</u> IMMOBILIZE IT, BUT IT ISN'T THE REAL THING—YOU
  CAN REMAIN FOR ETERNITY IN THIS THING <u>AT THE EXCLUSION OF</u>
  <u>LOVE AND WORK.</u>

Laura: BUT <u>THAT THING SHOULD</u> BE LOVE, AND WORK.

Aldous: (with emphasis): <u>EXACTLY!</u> I MEAN THIS IS WHY IT IS WRONG.
  AS I WAS SAYING, THIS ILLUSTRATES THAT YOU MUSTN'T MAKE ICE
  CUBES OUT OF A FLOWING RIVER. YOU MAY <u>SUCCEED</u> IN MAKING ICE
  CUBES . . . THIS IS THE GREATEST ICE CUBE IN THE WORLD. BUT YOU
  CAN PROBABLY GO ON FOR—OH, YOU CAN'T GO ON FOREVER—BUT
  FOR ENORMOUS EONS—FOR WHAT <u>APPEARS</u> [this word is greatly
  emphasized] TO BE ETERNITY, BEING IN THE LIGHT.

In his later years Aldous put more and more emphasis on the danger
of being addicted to meditation *only*, to knowledge *only*, to wisdom
only—without love. Just now he had experienced the temptation to an
addiction of an even higher order: the addiction of being in the light
and staying there. "Now, I can if I want to," he had said. Staying in
this ecstatic consciousness and cutting oneself off from participation
and commitment to the rest of the world—this is perfectly expressed
today, in powerful slang, in the phrase "dropping out."

Aldous (continuing): IT COMPLETELY DENIES THE FACTS: IT IS
  MORALLY WRONG; AND FINALLY, OF COURSE, ABSOLUTELY CATA-
  STROPHIC.

"Absolutely catastrophic." These two words are said with the most
earnest and profound conviction. The voice is not raised, but each
letter is as if sculptured on a shining block of Carrara marble—and
remains sculptured on the soul of anyone who hears it. It is a definitive
statement: one cannot isolate oneself from one's fellows and environ-
ment, for there is no private salvation; one might "get stuck" even in
the Pure Light instead of infusing it in "Love and Work," which is the
direct solution for everyone's life, right here and now. Love and Work
—if I should put in a nutshell the essence of Aldous's life, I could not
find a more precise way of saying it.

After the words "absolutely catastrophic," the tape runs for a while
in silence. And then there is a complete change of mood. A tender,
enveloping smile is in Aldous's voice, *my* smile. It comes through the
voice, creating an atmosphere of love and amused surprise, but, above
all, of tenderness.

Aldous: I DON'T KNOW HOW YOU GOT ALL THESE THINGS, DARLING.
  (Laughter.) WHAT CAME INTO THIS HARD, HARD SKULL OF YOURS—
  HOW DO ALL THESE EXTRAORDINARY IDEAS COME IN?

He was so pleased when I invented something, and he was now going back to the ice-cube recipe.

Laura: AT LEAST THE ONE OF THE ICE CUBES I REMEMBER VERY WELL. I WAS GIVING LSD TO — — — AND I HAD THIS FEELING . . . I JUST PRACTICALLY WAS SEEING A TORRENT OF WATER—YOU KNOW, A RIVER—AND HE WAS TRYING TO MAKE SUCH LOGIC OUT OF IT—SO THAT HE WOULD SHOW THAT ALL THOSE PEOPLE LIED, YOU SEE. . . .
Aldous (interrupting with hearty laughter): OF COURSE THEY LIE!
Laura: AND I HAD THE IMPRESSION THAT HE WAS RATIONALIZING WATER, OR EVEN TRYING TO FREEZE A PIECE OF THIS FLOWING RIVER AND MAKE ICE CUBES OF IT. . . .
Aldous (still laughing, and touching my head): BUT YOU HAVE SO MANY IDEAS. OBVIOUSLY, THIS TERRIBLY HARD SKULL HAS A HOLE IN IT SOMEWHERE. (A great deal of chuckling and laughter.)
Laura: I HOPE SO.
Aldous (after a silence): IT IS CERTAINLY VERY REMARKABLE.

Having "a hole in one's skull" has different meaning for different people. Aldous meant here that these ideas must have flowed *into* my head, not *out* of it. Especially after his psychedelic experiences, Aldous often mentioned the Bergson theory—that our brain and nervous system are not the source of our ideas, but rather a reducing valve through which Mind-at-Large trickles only the kind of information that is necessary for us to survive on this planet. A temporary widening of the valve, or "a hole in the head," permits a fragment of Mind-at-Large to flow in—that is what we usually call inspiration. In *The Doors of Perception,* where Aldous reports his first psychedelic experience, he speaks at length of this theory of Bergson's and says that it should be seriously considered.

There is a silence on the tape and then the dialogue continues in a thoughtful, serious mood.

Laura: I DON'T REMEMBER IF I TOLD YOU, OR I DREAMED I TOLD YOU —DID I TELL YOU OF THE PHRASE RUNNING IN MY MIND THESE DAYS, "I AM A THOUSAND PEOPLE"?
Aldous: NO, YOU DIDN'T TELL ME.
Laura: BUT THAT ALSO DOESN'T MAKE ANYTHING EASY.
Aldous: NO, OBVIOUSLY. AND WHEN THERE IS NO ANCHORAGE ANY-WHERE—WHEN, TO COME BACK TO AFTER DEATH, I MEAN. THERE WILL BE NO ANCHORAGE. . . .
Laura: OH, YES. I SEE.

Aldous was thinking about, and putting in words, the experience he had had a while before, when he was walking up and down the corridor. He had experienced the bodiless state of After-Death, where there is a survival of consciousness, but not of the body as we know it.

Aldous: SO, WHEN THERE WILL BE A THOUSAND PEOPLE RUSHING IN DIFFERENT DIRECTIONS—I MEAN, ANYHOW . . . (then in a very low aside) YOUR HAIR SMELLS THE SAME AS ACACIAS . . . YOUR HEAD IS VERY SOLID (touching my head) BECAUSE THE POINT IS: WHEN THERE ISN'T ANYTHING LIKE THIS. . . .

This—a tangible body, something to see, to hear, to smell, to *touch* —in contrast to that other state of being, which he had experienced before, where there were feelings and thoughts, but no perceptions, senses, or solid forms as we are used to them.

Laura: WHEN THERE IS NOTHING TO HOLD ON. . . .
Aldous: THERE ARE A THOUSAND DIFFERENT PEOPLE GOING IN A THOUSAND DIFFERENT DIRECTIONS: AND THIS IS WHAT YOU HAVE A HINT OF NOW. AND THIS, OF COURSE, IS WHAT IS SO TERRIBLE, BUT I THINK THAT I KNOW— (And after a pause, with deep conviction) BUT I <u>KNOW</u> THAT THERE WILL ALWAYS BE—AND I MEAN <u>THIS</u> IS THE EXTRAORDINARY EXPERIENCE—AT LEAST THERE IS <u>SOMEBODY</u> THERE WHO <u>KNOWS</u> THERE ARE A THOUSAND OTHER PEOPLE GOING IN DIFFERENT DIRECTIONS—THAT THERE IS A FUNDAMENTAL SANITY OF THE WORLD, WHICH IS ALWAYS THERE <u>IN SPITE</u> OF THE THOUSAND PEOPLE GOING IN A THOUSAND DIFFERENT DIRECTIONS. AND WHILE WE ARE IN SPACE AND TIME, SURROUNDED BY GRAVITY, WE ARE CONTROLLED TO A CONSIDERABLE EXTENT. (I wish I could convey the depth of Aldous's voice here, the feeling of wonder.) BUT TO HAVE AN INSIGHT INTO WHAT IT IS WHEN THERE ISN'T ANY CONTROL EXCEPT THIS FUNDAMENTAL KNOWLEDGE—I MEAN THIS IS WHERE THE BARDO IS RIGHT.

Aldous is referring to the Tibetan Book of the Dead, or the *After-Death Experience on the Bardo Plane.* I had first heard of this book from Aldous a few days after Maria's death. In answer to a note from me he had asked me for lunch and a walk. He knew innumerable country lanes right in the middle of Los Angeles and not far from his home, so after lunch we went walking in Laurel Canyon. I had many questions in my mind about Maria and he answered them without my asking, telling me all that had happened after our summer meeting in Rome.

He said that for the last few hours of her life he had spoken to her, encouraging her to go forward, as in the Bardo. "What is that?" I asked. He told me then about the Bardo—or the intermediate plane following bodily death, as described in the Tibetan Book of the Dead, explaining that in these ancient teachings the dying person is encouraged to go on—to go further—not to be preoccupied or encumbered with this present body, or with relatives or friends or unfinished business, but to go into a wider state of consciousness.

He went on to say that the Tibetan Book of the Dead is as much a manual of the Art of Living as it is of the Art of Dying. The survivors are advised to think of the loved one and of his need and destiny in his new state of consciousness rather than to be completely and egocentrically involved in their own grief. "Go on. Go Forward"—to both consciousnesses, the one who is still using the body and the one whose body is being discarded—that is sound and compassionate advice. "Go on. Go forward."

How many of us are walking around, now wholly alive because part of us did *not* go forward but died with Mother or Father or some other beloved person—even, at times, a pet? The terrifying, incomprehensible fact of death is difficult enough to accept and assimilate even with the most illumined teaching, even with the warmest, most tangible encouragement—let alone when there is no help in understanding, in accepting, in speaking about death. How can one even begin to understand death when it is hardly a permissible subject in good society? Sex is now an acceptable topic of conversation; death is still swept under the carpet, still locked in the dungeon, as the insane were, not too long ago.

That first walk after Maria's death remained impressed on me. I had vaguely heard of this wise, noble way of dealing with death, as an esoteric doctrine. Now Aldous, stricken and pale, yet fully alive, was telling me how he had applied this knowledge; how he had encouraged Maria to go on without worry or regrets. As he spoke during that walk I compared my own acquaintance with death: the lugubrious services, tragically chanting of sin, hellfire, and eternal damnation; the piteous begging for mercy from a distant deity, alternately irate and forgiving; while we, the survivors, enmeshed in grief and completely centered in it, hardly gave thought to the dead person except in relation to our anguish. It is distressing to think that the concern and money lavished on cadavers in America would be enough to feed millions of children, enough to divert lives of delinquency and despair into lives of human dignity and happiness.

Aldous continued to tell me, during that first walk after Maria's death, how he had carried her over as far as he could. He was as crushed as any human being who has lost a beloved companion of a lifetime; and yet, at the time of her death, he had been able to divert his own attention from the pain of losing her and focus both her mind and his on that most important fact—on that *fundamental sanity* of which he speaks in every psychedelic experience—and throughout this one.

The tape continues.

Aldous: THE BARDO IS RIGHT. YOU SEE, YOU HAVE TO BE AWARE OF THIS THING, AND HANG ONTO IT FOR DEAR LIFE—OTHERWISE YOU ARE JUST COMPLETELY IN A WHIRLWIND.

Laura: YES, BUT HOW MANY PEOPLE DO KNOW THIS?

Aldous (with great emphasis): EXACTLY! BUT THIS IS WHY THEY SAY WE REALLY OUGHT TO START PREPARING FOR THIS. (Aldous was speaking about preparation for death.) AND I MUST SAY I THINK IT IS TERRIBLY IMPORTANT THAT THROUGH THIS KNOWLEDGE THAT WE GET THROUGH THESE MUSHROOMS OR WHATEVER IT IS,[3] YOU UNDERSTAND A LITTLE BIT OF WHAT IT IS ALL ABOUT. I THINK THE MOST EXTRAORDINARY EXPERIENCE IS TO KNOW THAT THERE IS ALL THIS INSANITY WHICH IS JUST THE MULTIPLICATION . . . THE CARICATURE OF THE NORMAL INSANITY THAT GOES ON. BUT THAT THERE IS A FUNDAMENTAL SANITY WHICH YOU CAN REMAIN ONE WITH AND BE AWARE OF. THIS, OF COURSE, IS THE WHOLE DOCTRINE OF THE BARDO—HELPING PEOPLE TO BE AWARE OF THE FUNDAMENTAL SANITY WHICH IS THERE IN SPITE OF ALL THE TERRIFYING THINGS— AND ALSO NOT REALLY TERRIFYING, BUT SOMETIMES ECSTATIC, WONDERFUL THINGS. YOU MUSTN'T GO TO HEAVEN, AS THEY CONTINUALLY SAY.

Again and again! No dropping out from Love and Work, even from an unsatisfactory society, into the personal isolated security of Pure Light with or without psychedelics. "As they continuously say"— Aldous is referring to the Mahayana Buddhists, for whom the Bodhisattva is the highest form of man: such a man does not wallow in private salvation but lives and participates in the world's activities out of compassion for those who have not yet achieved enlightenment.

I wanted to know more about not going to heaven.

Laura: YOU MUSTN'T GO TO HEAVEN?

[3] "The sacred mushrooms" (*psilocybe mexicana*), of which psilocybin is the chemical synthesis—"or whatever it is," meaning psychedelic materials in general.

Aldous: YOU <u>MUSTN'T GO TO HEAVEN</u>. IT IS JUST AS DANGEROUS. IT IS TEMPORARY—AND SOMEHOW YOU WANT TO HOLD ON TO THE ULTIMATE TRUTH OF THINGS.

Laura: THE ULTIMATE TRUTH OF THINGS?

Aldous: WELL, I MEAN . . . THE TOTAL LIGHT OF THE WORLD, I SUPPOSE, WHICH IS IN THE HERE AND NOW WE EXPERIENCE. IT'S OF COURSE THE MIND-BODY. BUT WHEN YOU ARE RELEASED FROM THE BODY THERE HAS TO BE SOME EXPERIMENTAL EQUIVALENT OF THE BODY, SOMETHING HAS TO BE HELD ON TO . . . I DON'T KNOW.

Laura: WHAT DOES ONE HOLD TO THEN?

Aldous: ALL YOU CAN SAY IS ONE HOLDS TO THIS FUNDAMENTAL SANITY, WHICH AS I SAY IS <u>GUARANTEED</u>, AS LONG AS ONE IS IN THE BODY, BY THE FACT OF SPACE AND TIME AND GRAVITY, AND THREE DIMENSIONS AND ALL THE REST OF IT. SOMEHOW, WHEN YOU GET RID OF THESE ANCHORS—

In the Tibetan Book of the Dead, we are often warned of this danger of going to a phantasmagoric, illusionary hell or heaven. The guide (or *guru*) explains that in this bodiless state all our thoughts and feelings seem to take concrete form. Thoughts are things. The dead person sees these things and, unless helped, he gets trapped in them. So he is continuously told that these apparitions are only hallucinations—are only a projection of his consciousness—and that he must go forward without being involved in them, without repulsion or attraction; that he must realize that they are only distractions which he himself has created. Continuously repeated is the admonition: "Oh, Nobly Born! Let not thy mind be distracted." Similarly, the first and last word in *Island* is "Attention." It is the first word the distracted, wounded traveler from the West—the man who would not take *yes* for an answer—hears on that Island, sung by the mynah bird; a charming way the novelist synthesizes in a single word an ancient vital message to all: Attention.

Aldous (continuing): BUT THERE IS AN EQUIVALENT OF SOME KIND WHICH HAS TO BE CAUGHT HOLD OF. OTHERWISE, THE WORLD ABOUT YOU IS THIN AND BECOMES—WHAT IS THE WORD—<u>PRETAS</u>, THE WORLD OF THE RESTLESS GHOSTS. ONE GOES TO HELL AND THEN IN DESPERATION ONE HAS TO RUSH BACK AND GET ANOTHER BODY.

Laura: TO HOLD ON AGAIN?

Aldous: TO HOLD ON AGAIN, WELL, THIS IS OBVIOUSLY THE BEST THING, IF ONE HASN'T GOT THE ULTIMATE BEST. BUT CLEARLY THEY ALL HAVE SAID THAT THERE IS SOMETHING WHICH IS THE EQUIVALENT—AGAIN IN THIS EXTRAORDINARY DOCTRINE OF CHRISTIANITY, THE RESURRECTION OF THE BODY, AND ULTIMATELY IMMORTALITY

WILL HAVE SOMETHING LIKE THE BODY ATTACHED TO IT. I DON'T KNOW WHAT IT MEANS, BUT OBVIOUSLY ONE CAN'T ATTACH ANY ORDINARY MEANING TO IT. BUT ONE SEES EXACTLY WHAT THEY ARE AFTER—SOME IDEA THAT SOMEHOW WE HAVE TO GET AN EQUIVALENT ON A HIGHER LEVEL OF THIS ANCHORAGE WHICH SPACE AND TIME AND GRAVITATION GIVE US. AND WHICH CAN BE ACHIEVED. ONE HAS, AS I SAY, IN THIS STRANGE EXPERIENCE, ONE HAS THE SENSE THAT THERE IS THIS FUNDAMENTAL SANITY IN SPITE OF ALL THE DISTRACTION AND PREPOSTEROUS NONSENSE WHICH IS GOING ON—AND WHICH IS IRRELEVANT TO ONESELF—WHICH HAS NOTHING TO DO, IN A STRANGE WAY, ALTHOUGH IT MAY SEEM VERY, VERY IMPORTANT. (Silence, then:)

IT IS VERY IMPORTANT IF ONE CAN, WHILE IT IS HAPPENING, IF ONE CAN SEE THE OUTER-APPEARANCE OF IT. IT IS OBVIOUSLY IMPORTANT TO LOOK AFTER ONE'S AFFAIRS IN A SENSIBLE WAY AND SEE THEIR IMPORTANCE, IN A SILLY WAY, BUT IF ONE CAN, THROUGH ALL THIS, SEE THIS OTHER LEVEL OF IMPORTANCE, IN THE LIGHT OF WHICH A LOT OF ACTIVITIES WILL HAVE TO BE CUT DOWN. THERE WILL SEEM TO BE ABSOLUTELY NO POINT IN UNDERTAKING THEM—ALTHOUGH A GREAT MANY HAVE TO BE UNDERTAKEN, BUT THEY WILL BE UNDERTAKEN IN A NEW KIND OF WAY—WITH A KIND OF DETACHMENT, AND YET WITH A DOING THINGS TO ONE'S LIMIT. THIS IS AGAIN ONE OF THE PARADOXES: TO WORK TO THE LIMIT TO SUCCEED IN WHAT YOU ARE DOING, AND AT THE SAME TIME TO BE DETACHED FROM IT—IF YOU DON'T SUCCEED, WELL, THAT'S TOO BAD—IF YOU DO SUCCEED—TANT MIEUX—YOU DON'T HAVE TO GLOAT OVER IT. THIS IS THE WHOLE STORY OF THE BHAGAVAD-GITA: SOMEHOW TO DO EVERYTHING WITH PASSION BUT WITH DETACHMENT.
Laura: PASSION AND DETACHMENT . . .

Passion and detachment. Years ago, before I had ever heard of these philosophies, with what passion I had longed for detachment! That was the ideal I had set for myself as a musician; to play with all I had, to burn with passion, yet maintain a crystalline purity and detachment in technical and stylistical perfection. And in these recent years of psychological work and exploration, I had seen, in my everyday life and work, in me and outside of me, all kinds and degrees of passion only or of detachment only—but how rarely the fusion of the two!

In the Bhagavad-Gita the hero Arjuna is a great warrior, and Krishna, or Incarnation of the Supreme Spirit, is his guide. Arjuna is told that he must fight with all his strength and valor—and yet must be detached from the fight.

If we look inside and around, we can see many ways in which this battle is carried on, three of which are the most conspicuous. One is the way of the fighter, who, being inwardly discontented, resentful, and punitive, is chemically and psychologically *compelled* to fight. He *has* to be contrary; he must give and take *no* for an answer even if—sometimes especially if—*yes* is to his advantage. He is fighting an outer enemy who often is only a reflected shadow of the inner one; even when the outer enemy is conquered, the inner one is only temporarily appeased. Then there is another kind of fighter: the man who is easily discouraged, who remains passive, rather than risk the possibility of defeat; overcautious and suspicious, he deceives himself rather than face problems and decisions. There is still another kind of fighter, the one of which Krishna speaks. We encounter this type also—but how rarely! He is one that fights only after an ethical evaluation of the issue and of his own original motives. Regardless of victory or defeat, an inner peace is there. This warrior, liberated from subconscious demons, clear-minded and controlled, may appear on the outside relentless, determined, even furious; inwardly, he is invulnerably harmonious.

In the Gita these three types of men are so described:

> The doer without desire,
> Who does not boast of his deed,
> Who is ardent, enduring,
> Untouched by triumph,
> In failure untroubled:
> He is a man of *sattwa* [the energy of inspiration].

> The doer with desire,
> Hot for the prize of vainglory,
> Brutal, greedy and foul
> In triumph too quick to rejoice,
> In failure despairing:
> He is a man of *rajas* [the energy of action].

> The indifferent doer
> Whose heart is not in his deed,
> Stupid and stubborn,
> A cheat, and malicious,
> The idle lover of delay,
> Easily dejected:
> He is a man of *tamas*[4] [the energy of inertia].

[4] *The Song of God: Bhagavad-Gita.* Translated by Swami Prabhavananda and Christopher Isherwood, with an introduction by Aldous Huxley (New York: New American Library, 1954).

Aldous was speaking of the man who fights with the energy of inspiration (*sattwa*).

Aldous: ONE CAN SEE WHAT IT IS—HE IS NOT INVOLVED EVEN THOUGH
   HE IS INVOLVED UP TO THE LIMIT. WHAT PART OF HIM IS NOT IN-
   VOLVED? BUT IT'S NO GOOD TRYING TO MAKE AN ANALYSIS BE-
   CAUSE, AS USUAL, IT IS A PARADOX AND A MYSTERY.
Laura: BUT EVEN IF . . .
Aldous: ONE BEGINS TO UNDERSTAND IT, THAT THAT IS THE MAIN
   PROBLEM.

There were many pauses in this conversation. Most of the words
were formulated slowly, in an effort to clarify realities to which most of
us are unaccustomed. Aldous had been speaking quietly and thoughtfully. In spite of the poor recording, which is often blurred by noises of
cars and static, one can feel that the atmosphere is impregnated with
thought and discoveries. Now there is a pause, then a few noises—we
are taking Kleenex out of a box. Then:

Aldous: MY NOSE IS RUNNING. (Now the mood and the voice change
   completely, become light, and there is amused laughter in Aldous's
   voice.) A VERY GOOD REMINDER THAT THE GREATEST PHILOSOPHY IS
   CONNECTED <u>INEXTRICABLY</u> WITH RUNNING NOSES. ONE OF THE
   THINGS THEY SHOULD HAVE TALKED ABOUT IN THE GOSPEL.
   OBVIOUSLY HE WAS ON A MOUNTAIN—THE SERMON OF THE MOUNT
   —IT MUST HAVE BEEN VERY BREEZY AND COLD UP THERE.
   PROBABLY HIS NOSE DID RUN.

There is no iconoclastic intention in the voice—only a chuckling and
a reaffirmation of Aldous's conviction that everything is connected with
everything else and that we should not forget it; that no matter on what
high plane of spirituality we dwell we are still bound by the laws of
nature. I am sure also that Aldous realized at that moment that he had
been speaking gravely for quite a while—it was natural for him, thank
heavens, to lighten gravity with charm and humor.

Laura (after a silence): BUT IT IS VERY DIFFICULT. HOW DOES ONE PRE-
   PARE FOR DEATH? ALL OF THIS SEEMS, AS YOU SAY, TO MAKE IT
   VERY . . .
Aldous: I THINK THAT THE ONLY WAY ONE CAN PREPARE FOR DEATH . . .
   YOU REALIZE THAT, WELL, AFTER ALL, ALL YOUR PSYCHOTHERAPY IS
   IN A SENSE A PREPARATION FOR DEATH INASMUCH AS YOU <u>DIE</u> TO
   THESE MEMORIES WHICH ARE ALLOWED TO HAUNT YOU AS THOUGH

THEY WERE IN THE PRESENT: "LET THE DEAD BURY THEIR DEAD."
OBVIOUSLY, THE COMPLETELY HEALTHY WAY TO LIVE IS "SUF-
FICIENT UNTO THE DAY IS THE EVIL THEREOF."

Aldous often quoted these words, which were Christ's way of saying,
"Live here and now." He suggested I put this quotation in my recipe,
"Lay the Ghost," which deals with the problem of haunting emotional
memories that interfere with our present. He felt that Christ's saying to
the man who wanted to bury his father, "Follow me, and let the dead
bury him," was about as strong a way as there was to say, "Live here
and now." One should not worry about the past or the future, since
each day has enough problems. That principle he also lived—either he
could do something here and now about a problem or he would not
permit it to interfere with here and now.

Aldous: YOU ACCEPT THIS WITHOUT BEING OBSESSED BY WHAT IS IN THE
PAST—YOU DIE TO IT. PREPARATION FOR ULTIMATE DEATH IS TO BE
AWARE THAT YOUR HIGHEST AND MOST INTENSE FORM OF LIFE IS
ACCOMPANIED BY, AND CONDITIONAL UPON, A SERIES OF SMALL
DEATHS ALL THE TIME. WE HAVE TO BE DYING TO THESE OBSESSIVE
MEMORIES. I MEAN, AGAIN THE PARADOX IS TO BE ABLE TO
REMEMBER WITH EXTREME CLARITY, BUT NOT TO BE HAUNTED.

Aldous is speaking here of the difference between the two memories,
the informational memory and the emotional memory. The informational memory is essential to us, to carry on our daily life. The
emotional memory has a more subtle, powerful, and, at times, all-
pervading quality; especially when unconscious, it can haunt us with
ghosts of our emotional past, robbing us of the energy and attention we
need here and now.

Laura: BUT EVEN WITHOUT THE MEMORIES THERE IS THIS COMPOSITE
FIGURE THAT WE ARE—THE COMPOSITION OF SO MANY CHARACTERS
—AND IF THEY DON'T HAVE SOMETHING TO MEET ON, A COMMON
GROUND, WHICH IS THE BODY, WHERE DO THEY MEET?
Aldous: WELL, THEY HAVE TO MEET, I SUPPOSE, IN SOME—WHAT IS
CALLED QUOTE "THE SPIRIT," AS WE MEET NORMALLY ON THIS
UNCONSCIOUS-SUBCONSCIOUS LEVEL. AND THEN THEY ALSO MEET
ON THE SUPERCONSCIOUS LEVEL, WHICH, OF COURSE, COMPLETELY
CONTAINS THE UNCONSCIOUS. (Pause.) AND THIS WOULD BE CER-
TAINLY THE TEACHING OF THE BARDOS—THESE THOUSAND FIGURES
—THEY CAN EITHER MEET IN THE WRONG WAY WHICH IS BY . . . TO
THE POINT OF DISTRACTION THROUGH THE ICE CUBE OR THEY CAN

MEET THROUGH THE RECOGNITION OF THE ULTIMATE IN THE SPIRIT,
ON THAT LEVEL.

This is a repetition of what Aldous said in the beginning: either
there is a meeting in that terrifying confusion of thoughts and emotions
whirling around without the safety of a common ground which is the
body; or there is meeting in awareness of that fundamental sanity-of-
the-world which he felt so strongly.

Aldous: AND THIS IS WHY THEY ALL SAY YOU HAVE TO WORK RATHER
HARD, AND TRY AND REALIZE THIS FACT—AND ONE OF THE WAYS OF
REALIZING IT IS—AFTER ALL, IN THAT LITTLE "ZEN FLESH ZEN
BONES"[5]—THE PREPARATION IS THROUGH THESE EXERCISES IN
CONSCIOUSNESS. THIS SORT OF LEADS ON TO THE THIRD LAYER OF
CONSCIOUSNESS.
Laura: BUT THEN IN BETWEEN THE TWO EXTREMES THERE IS SO MUCH
LEEWAY . . .
Aldous: THERE ARE TOO MANY WAYS OF GOING WRONG. I MEAN, THE
BEST-INTENTIONED PEOPLE GO WRONG. (Long silence.) I WILL LOOK
AT THIS REMBRANDT—

On the tape, one hears confused noises. Aldous was looking at art
books—Rembrandt was to him the greatest of all painters. My voice is
heard, from the other room, speaking on the phone to Paula, Ginny's
daughter, then eleven years old, who was not in school that day. Then
we again hear Aldous's voice. Since the fire we had been living with
Ginny and her two children, and this close association made the
problem of education very concrete to Aldous. He was seeing every day
the difficulty of educating two children in a large city like Los Angeles.
The problem had so many facets; he brought up one in this
conversation.

Aldous: IF SHE WANTS US, DARLING WE CAN GO BACK THERE. IS SHE
ALONE? SHE PROBABLY DOESN'T WANT TO BE ALONE. MAYBE WE
SHOULD GO. (Silence.) SHE SAID SHE WANTED TO WRITE A STORY SO I
GAVE HER A PEN. (Another silence.) WHEN I THINK OF THE ADMIR-
ABLE THING WHICH WAS IN MY LITTLE BOYS' SCHOOL.
Laura: YES? A ROUTINE?
Aldous: WELL, I MEAN WE HAD THIS CARPENTER'S SHOP, WE COULD
ALWAYS SPEND OUR SPARE TIME THERE WHEN WE WANTED TO, AND
THIS WAS COMPULSORY TWO OR THREE HOURS A WEEK. THERE WAS

[5] Paul Reps: *Zen Flesh Zen Bones.*

THIS CARPENTER WHO WAS THE SCHOOL HANDY MAN, BUT HE WAS A TRAINED CARPENTER. WE WENT THROUGH ALL THE EXERCISES WHICH THE APPRENTICE HAD TO LEARN—ALMOST UP TO THE MASTER WORK. THIS IS WHAT "MASTERPIECE" MEANS: THE APPRENTICE LEARNS ALL THE THINGS, AND FINALLY HE PRODUCES HIS FINAL EXAMINATION AS PH.D.

Laura: REALLY?

Aldous: IN THE CASE OF A CARPENTER THERE WOULD BE ALL THE DIFFERENT KINDS OF MORTICES, DOVETAIL, AND SO ON—VARIOUS THINGS JOINED TOGETHER.

Laura: WHICH IS VERY DIFFICULT.

Aldous: VERY DIFFICULT. YOU SEE, ALL THE SURFACES WOULD BE ABSOLUTELY PLANED—YOU WILL HAVE LEARNED TO PLANE ABSOLUTELY EVEN.

Laura: DID YOU DO THAT?

Aldous: YES. YES, WE WENT RIGHT THROUGH THE DIFFERENT KINDS OF MORTICES, DOVETAIL, AND SO ON—JUST AS A MEDIEVAL APPRENTICE WOULD HAVE DONE.

Laura: WELL, BUT . . .

Aldous: THEN WHEN WE HAD DONE ALL THIS SORT OF EXERCISE, THEN WE WERE ALLOWED TO DO WHAT WE WANTED—TO MAKE A SLEDGE OR A BOX OR A BOOKCASE—AND WE DID IT—BUT ALWAYS UP TO THE VERY HIGHEST STANDARDS. I MEAN, THERE WAS ABSOLUTELY NO NONSENSE OF THESE THINGS BEING NAILED TOGETHER; THESE THINGS WERE ALWAYS DONE DOVETAILED.

Laura: BUT HERE THEY DON'T DO THAT—EVEN PROFESSIONAL CARPENTERS.

Aldous: GOOD CABINET WORK IS STILL DONE IN THIS WAY, BUT OF COURSE NOWADAYS IT ISN'T REALLY—I MEAN, IT'S QUITE DIFFERENT.

Laura: BUT IN THIS SCHOOL THEY DON'T DO ANYTHING: THEY JUST STAY THERE ALL AFTERNOON JUST RUNNING AROUND.

Aldous: WELL, ONE OF THE PROBLEMS IS WAGES. I MEAN, THERE WAS THIS EXCELLENT MAN WHO DID ALL THE ODD JOBS AROUND THE SCHOOL, BUT WHO WAS AN OLD-TIME ARTISAN WHO GOT THROUGH ALL THIS HIMSELF. BUT HE WAS A VERY SHREWD MAN: IT WAS A PLEASURE TO BE WITH HIM. AND HE COULD TALK; AND HE HAD DELIGHTFUL PHRASES—LIKE WHEN HE SHARPENED A TOOL HE SAID, "NOW IT IS SHARP ENOUGH TO CUT OFF A DEAD MOUSE'S WHISKERS WITHOUT ITS WAKING UP." BUT ALL THAT IS GONE NOW. BUT WHAT SHOULDN'T HAVE GONE IS THE PREFECTLY SENSIBLE THING OF PROVIDING BOYS WITH SOMETHING TO DO.

Laura: SHALL I MAKE US SOUP? WOULD YOU LIKE SOME SOUP?

Aldous: YES, THAT WOULD BE NICE.

Aldous lecturing at M.I.T., 1960

Glimpses

From February through April 1962, Aldous was a research professor at the University of California at Berkeley. We had driven there in the beginning of February and found a pleasant apartment not far from the campus. It promised to be an interesting period for Aldous. He had enjoyed lecturing and giving seminars in other universities—Santa Barbara, MIT, the Menninger Foundation. But the period at Berkeley did not turn out to be as stimulating as we expected. Later I felt that it was partly my fault: I should have stayed there longer and somehow made more people aware that Aldous was available and accessible to all kinds of persons, except possibly those who insisted on treating him as a curious "historical monument." Anyone who had a sincere concern or interest, anyone who had a real question or made an honest attempt to answer, would always find in Aldous an unhurried, sympathetic listener, ready to offer active, effective participation. Except for the few who were close to him, most people did not realize that Aldous, as a man, a novelist, and a philosopher, was as much interested in bankers as in educators, in acrobats as in scientists, in charming women more than in eminent literati. This variety of interests was one of his distinguishing characteristics.

There are only a few letters of that period, from February to April 1962, for we spoke on the phone almost every other day, took trips together, and Aldous often came home to Los Angeles.

In his letters to me Aldous hardly ever quoted other authors, but in the following one he does. I was then working on *You Are Not the Target*. His attitude as he helped me through that book was enchanting; he made me feel he had such fun in doing it. He was so delighted when he found a quotation that crystallized my thought that he would literally come running with it, like a child with a new gadget.

2533 Hillegass
Berkeley 4
Cal.
5.II.62

My Darling, everything duly arrived . . . assorted mail and your letter about Pismo—which I loved. And in spite of this stupid little flu, I love you—though it was difficult, when you were here to manifest anything except a cough and a wheeze. That's one of the worst things about not being well: one's ailments eclipse one's feelings and shut out other people, even those one loves the most.

I am sending herewith some passages from Chateaubriand's *Génie du Christianisme* and Musset's *Confession d'un Enfant du Siècle.* How similar the experience of that post-war, post-revolution generation was to ours! And how close its diagnoses of the *maladie du siècle* are to your diagnoses of the sickness of *our* century. You might like to use these quotes somewhere in your book—particularly Chateaubriand's remark about "the vagueness of the passions" becoming more widespread as civilization advances and the primitive drives find no natural outlets.

I have just been listening to a broadcast by an American historian on the life of the troops during the Civil War—a record of inconceivable incompetence and inefficiency, resulting in tens of thousands of unnecessary deaths and incalculable amounts of avoidable suffering. So this too is an old story!

Goodbye, my darling. Ti voglio bene.

. . . .

Chateaubriand speaks of a psychological state common already in his day (beginning of the nineteenth century). It is a state in which "the faculties, intensely active but at the same time restricted, are exercised only upon themselves, with neither aim or goal. The more a society advances towards civilization, the more widespread becomes this condition—the condition which we may call the vagueness of the passions." Another product of advancing civilization is a great increase in theoretical knowledge about man and his behaviour. This theoretical knowledge, imparted in books and articles, "makes the individual clever without having experienced life. One becomes undeceived without having been deceived; one is left with desires but with no illusions as to the objects of desire. One's fantasy is rich and abundant; one's existence is poor, arid and disenchanted. The mind is full; but the world one inhabits is empty; without having made use of anything one is dissatisfied with everything. This state of soul embitters life to an incredible degree. In the attempt to employ those powers which it nevertheless feels to be useless, the heart twists and turns in a hundred ways. The ancients knew little or nothing of this secret anxiety, this poison of bottled-up passions fermenting inwardly. An active political existence, the games in the gymnasium, all the activities going on in the forum and city square—these filled up their time, gave scope to their energies and left no room in the heart for ennui and causeless anguish."

. . . .

Alfred de Musset, writing of the generation that had grown up after the revolutionary and Napoleonic wars and became men after the Battle of Waterloo, says:

"A feeling of extreme uneasiness began to ferment in all young hearts. Condemned to inaction by the powers which governed the world, handed over to vulgar pedants of every kind, delivered to idleness and boredom . . . the young felt in the depth of their souls an insupportable wretchedness. The richest became libertines; those of moderate fortune followed some profession and resigned themselves to the law or the army; the poorest, if they were intelligent, gave themselves to philosophy and plunged into the hideous sea of aimless effort . . . Young men found employment for their idle powers in a display of despair. To scoff at glory, at religion, at love, at all the world, is a great consolation for those who do not know what to do. They mock at themselves and in doing so prove the correctness of their attitude to life. And then it is pleasant to believe oneself unhappy when in fact one is merely idle and bored."

These are thought-provoking considerations, though, at least in our time, young students are not as morbidly gloomy as they were at the beginning of the nineteenth century. Whatever the cause, those few months that Aldous spent at Berkeley seemed to him excessively quiet, in spite of the fact that his public lectures[1] were enthusiastically attended by capacity audiences.

The following notes, made while Aldous had the flu, were for a project which did not materialize and to which Aldous referred as "a reflected travel book about California." Aldous was constantly amazed

[1] Information about the recorded lectures of Aldous Huxley is available from "Recipes for Living & Loving" by Laura Huxley
1540 Washburn Road, Pasadena, California 91105

at the fabulous development in California of such diversified fields as electronics, mysticism, vine culture, space exploration—"rich mixed feeding," he called it.

I was in bed with a touch of flu. A portable radio was among the furnishings of my apartment and, reaching out from under the bed-clothes, I kept twiddling its dials in search of something fit to listen to. Twiddling and twiddling—twiddling from toothpaste lyrics to the leitmotivs of beer and cigarettes, twiddling from hit tunes and the cater-wauling of contraltos in simulated orgasm to blood-of-the-lamb revival-ists, sportscasters and the Altruistic Finance Company offering, in dulcet tones, to lend me whatever sum I might ask for, on no security, and the first of the thirty-six easy, easy payments would be postponed (what generosity) for two whole months. After half an hour of this I had come to feel, a bit paranoiacally, that I was the victim of a huge con-spiracy of Anti-Egghead discrimination. But help was at hand. A Good Samaritan appeared carrying a tiny FM radio. She plugged it in and adjusted the dial.

Suddenly, blessedly, I found myself in the middle of the first move-ment of Mozart's C minor piano concerto. My sickbed was in Berkeley, and Berkeley has a non-commercial broadcasting station, precariously supported by the subscriptions of the eccentric minority that likes to listen only to what is worth hearing. For the duration of my influenza, I was able to while away the uncomfortable hours by tuning in to good music of every kind, time, and place, to lively discussions about art and politics and philosophy, to lectures and impromptu talks on every con-ceivable subject from Oriental religion and strontium 90, space explor-ation, race riots, and why Johnny can't read. Rich mixed feeding.

The enormous affluence of our Western world is cultural as well as economic. Behind the barrage of irrelevances laid down by the commercially sponsored mass media, an incalculable treasure of facts, ideas, and imaginings lies waiting for anyone who cares to help himself. All science is now popularized, all history is in paperbacks, all music recorded. From Lascaux to the Guggenheim Museum, from Ur to Moore, from the great Pyramid to Brasilia, every notable piece of painting, sculpture, and architecture has been photographed, repro-duced, and copiously—sometimes, one feels, a little too copiously—written about. Hundreds of critics report on all the world's literatures, hundreds of historians of ideas are hard at work digesting all its philosophies and summarizing, for the benefit of non-believers, all its religious beliefs. What a profusion, what a fantastic variety, of intellec-tual possessions are ours for the asking.

Lying there in bed, with just enough of a temperature to keep my mind hoppingly alive, but a little too much for any kind of serious work, I listened and reflected; took in the random profusion of cultural treasure and reacted to what I heard with random thoughts of my own —thoughts that assented, thoughts that disagreed and objected, thoughts at a tangent, miles away from their point of departure in what was coming over the ether—vast synthetic random bits and pieces. Piano music, the Tantra, radioactive fallout, the psycho-social bases of apartheid—there they were, all coming out of my tiny radio set.

How could things so disparate, so obviously incommensurable, be reconciled? In what great unifying principle were all rooted? In my overactive brain the questions kept popping up again and again. And because my body temperature had risen a couple of degrees above normal, I seemed to myself to be on the brink of an answer—of *the* answer. My temperature as I write these words is back to 98.4°. Today I can only pose the questions.

Here then, looked at in colder blood, are the problems that fever made me imagine I had all but solved. Listening for a few hours to a succession of aesthetically satisfying and intellectually stimulating broadcasts, one is impressed, first of all, by the fantastic richness and diversity of modern culture. And this fantastically rich and diversified culture, one goes on to reflect, is merely a little cave scooped out of a psycho-physical universe incomparably richer, subtler, more intricate and pregnant with an infinitude of potentialities. The human mind is an instrument, among other things, for censoring and simplifying reality. It is a symbol-making machine whose function it is to impose some kind of conceptual order upon the bewildering succession of unique events, upon the huge brute fact of one damned thing after another—or, to be more exact, of ten to the nth damned things after ten to the nth other damned things, ad infinitum.

In the world-views of earlier civilizations more than ninety per cent of what we now know to be the facts were, either unavoidably or through voluntary ignorance, left out of account, and the vacuum created by their absence was filled by objectified metaphysical notions and theological fantasies. The result was a picture of the cosmos, bearing little resemblances to the original, but delightfully clear in outline, understandable at a glance and satisfyingly coherent. Thanks to advances in the natural sciences, in medicine and anthropology, in historical research, in the analysis of language and the processes of thinking, feeling, and perceiving, the percentage of unavoidably omitted facts has fallen from somewhere in the nineties to (let us hopefully say) somewhere in the high seventies, and with this vast increase in our knowledge about things and the languages in which things are described has gone a corresponding decline in the relevance of the notions, in terms of which our word-worshipping fathers imposed an all too rational order upon such few facts as they were able to recognize or chose not to ignore. Today we are confronted by an enormous agglomeration of diversified facts, and as yet we have found no generally acceptable principles of explanation to take the place of those once convincingly plausible symbol-systems which have now lost their power to give any kind of utilizable order to reality. Each class of facts is ordered in terms of its own appropriate symbol-system; but there is no comprehensive symbol-system capable of giving order to the subsidiary systems. Our home-made world of explanatory concepts threatens to become almost as bewildering as the given world of unique events.

Consider, for example, that mystical experience, about which so much was said in the talk on Oriental religion which followed that Mozart Concerto. The experience of a Light which is also and self-evidently Love; the realized self-transcendence into solidarity with a universe which, in spite of death, in spite of inescapable pain and all our gratuitous cruelties, is revealed by the Light as being fundamentally All Right. We talk about this experience, we set out to "explain" it, in a variety of different languages. There is the language, for example, of the depth psychologist, who assures us that mystical experiences are simply the revivals of some obscure memory of infantile bliss at the mother's breast, or, better still, of foetal bliss within the womb. (What utter bosh! But let that pass.) Passing now from the couch to the laboratory, we can discuss the matter in the non-subjective languages of biochemistry and neuro-physiology. Mystical experiences, in terms of these languages, are odd states induced either by anoxia, or by some temporary upset in the normal balance of the enzymes within the brain. These upsets may occur spontaneously (in other words, for reasons we do not yet understand); or else they may be brought on by intensive meditation, by the approach of death, by breathing exercises, by ascetic practices of the kind that alter blood chemistry, or by the deliberate ingestion of psychedelic drugs. Leaving the laboratory, we enter the church and start to explain things in the language of theology. Mystical experience is now spoken of as a grace which is infused from the Outside. Mortifications, spiritual exercises, and enzyme-upsetting drugs are not the causes of this grace; they merely open mental doors and lower physiological barriers. Alternatively, there is no infusion from Outside; there is only discovery, if we choose to talk the language of Buddhism, of an Inside which is identical with the Nature of Things; there is only the realization that "mind from Mind is not divided."

We see, then, that the unique events, to which we give the name of "mystical experience," can be given a measure of conceptual order, can be "explained" and made to "make sense" within the more or less completely incommensurable frames of reference, to which these various languages refer. But within what larger frame of reference can these divergently sense-making explanations be combined so as to make a deeper, more comprehensive sense? Into what totally expressive lingua franca can the various dialects of chemistry, psychiatry, theology, and transcendental operationalism be translated? At 100.4° I could almost believe that I knew this lingua franca. At 98.4° I know very well that I do not.

Some day, I suppose, the enormous confusion of given reality and the bewildering multiplicity of scientific and philosophical frames of reference will be reduced to something like unity in a single monistic system of concepts. When that happens our hypothetical lingua franca will actually be spoken, or at least set down in the symbols of some new and more expressive dialect of mathematics. Could there be a spoken equivalent of this new dialect? At 98.4° I doubt it. But at 100.4° I seem to catch a glimpse of . . .

Glimpses . . . glimpses . . . Sick or well, Aldous was always catching glimpses. That ability of glimpsing, and expressing in part what he saw, made living fascinating. Aldous could experience immediate facts, moment by moment. Then—outside and inside the present facts—he could simultaneously perceive innumerable other, actual or potential, facts. Always present in his mind was the wonderful place our world could be if we would stop what he used to call our "gratuitous suffering." We often spoke of the creative use of our emotion, which was the field of psychotherapy about which I was writing. This letter is a continuation of our conversation.

2533 Hillegass
Berkeley 4
Cal.
10.IV.62

My darling, I have just read a reference to something that William James said in one of his essays—that we ought not to be content with passively experiencing the emotions aroused by music, or drama, or literature, but should always try to give some active expression to the feelings aroused by art as soon as we can find an opportunity to do so. Here, I feel, is the raw material for an excellent recipe. You feel pity for the suffering of Desdemona or King Lear—then go out and express your compassion for some unfortunate person in real life. You are made joyful by the beauty of a Mozart sonata or an impressionist painting—then try to communicate some joy to other people, or at least use it for your own improvement by some conversion of energy technique. (I don't know what one should do when some nauseating piece of Musak in a restaurant fills one with disgust! Perhaps rush out and vomit.)

Love

A

Aldous gave many lectures[2] that winter. I was always amazed at the ease with which he made public appearances. My experience had been mainly with musicians, or with actors or other performers—including myself—whose preparation before a performance was almost a ritual, and who were nervous and demanding. Aldous told me he had not always been so calm about lecturing.

"What changed you?"

He laughed. "I only had to realize that I wasn't as important as all that!"

Anyone who ever heard Aldous lecture would testify, I am sure, that this realization was evident: it was obvious, in his attitude and in his words, that what was important was not *who*, but *what* was right. If he was speaking of the necessity of treating nature well, he would not elaborate on his own ever present love and wonder of nature, but by vividly describing actual situations with which his listener could identify himself, he would give a clear view of the damage and suffering inflicted on ourselves and our children by the greedy or ignorant offenders of nature.

His manner of speaking in his own living room or in front of two thousand people was almost identical—he spoke to a large group with person-to-person intimacy. There were no "angles" in Aldous voice: it was so soothing and flowing that I was often tempted during his lectures to give in to sleep—and sometimes I did. It was a private joke.

"Did you sleep well tonight?" he might ask me after a lecture.

"I would have loved to, your voice was so beautiful . . . But one of your adoring ladies was staring at me!"

"My poor darling, What you have to put up with!"

This had been a troubled and confusing year. Aldous had lost all his books, notes, diaries in the fire, lost the home where we had lived for the best period of our life together; he had had a debilitating flu and the future state of his health was uncertain; *Island* had been little publicized and grossly minunderstood; when we would have the home I was designing was problematical. None of this stopped Aldous

---

[2] Please see page 141.

from keeping his commitments, as evidenced by the following traveling schedule—and, of course, each trip meant lectures, seminars, interviews, conferences.

MARCH 14-16 Santa Barbara; 17-19 Los Angeles; 19 Berkeley; 27 Los Angeles; 28, 29 Alabama; 31 Philadelphia

APRIL 1 New York; 2 Boston; 4, 5, 6, Syracuse; 7 New York; 8 Berkeley; 14 Los Angeles; 18 Oregon; 22 Berkeley

MAY 2 Los Alamos; 6 Anaheim; 7 Berkeley; 17 Los Angeles; 21 New York, Am. Academy of Arts and Sciences; 25 Philadelphia; 26 San Francisco, etc.

This is the man referred to, by some of the world press when he died a year and a half later, as almost blind and bitter, separated from humanity, escaping reality in his ivory tower of protected seclusion—dissolving, no doubt, in a solution of LSD.

"Think how many beautiful trees they had to cut down to print that muck!" Aldous would wistfully remark about sensational tabloids.

"In Los Alamos," Aldous told me, "two out of three people are scientists, Ph.D.'s at least, with an I.Q. of 160 or over." I wonder if it was because of these facts that Aldous chose to give in Los Alamos his lecture on Visionary Experience? This lecture, which generally began with the question: "Why are precious stones precious?" bypasses the Intelligence Quotient and explores that other world of the mind—unmeasurable and unfathomable, familiar to mystics and artists, to children and poets—that world of which we all may have, even if only once in a lifetime, a luminous glimpse.

The hall was filled with the cream of the scientific community. As Aldous spoke, smoothly building bridges from poetry to chemistry to mysticism, the atmosphere of the hall became almost religious—as though, by merely speaking of the visionary world, Aldous had all but a vision-inducing magic.

Aldous made a few short notes of that trip:

Visited the animal laboratory. Twenty-three generations of mice, one strain irradiated, the other not. The life span of the irradiated mice down by 25% of the weight, of offspring by 50%. The line will die out in time. Accumulated recessive mutations, lower resistance, decreased viability. In the sub-basement a "whole body counter" in which human and animal can have their radiation measured. All muscle is radioactive since one per mil of potassium gives out gamma rays. Little boys become more radio-active at puberty as they put on more muscle in relation to total weight. Little girls put on fat and become less radio-active.

Another note:

What brilliant light! and in the afternoons high clouds, which finally diminish in tiny balls and fishes of vapour in the blue.

The letter that follows was from Oregon, where Aldous had gone to meet his brother Julian, who was lecturing there. What a delight it was to see the two brothers together! Completely different in character, yet that same enormous capital of intelligence and knowledge and discipline, that same active commitment to the preservation and evolvement of the nobility of man. Their common interest was Evolutionary Humanism.

"The central belief of Evolutionary Humanism," wrote Sir Julian Huxley, "is that existence can be improved, that vast untapped possibilities can be increasingly realized, that greater fulfilment can replace frustration. This belief is now firmly grounded in knowledge: it could become in turn the firm ground for action."[3]

On this immense ground Aldous and Julian met, listened, and communicated their ideas as though discovering each other for the first time, delighting and stimulating each other's brilliance, originality, and humor. There was always action when the two brothers met. Once Julian and his wife Juliette, a Humanist at every moment of her life, came to see us for Christmas. Between scientific meetings and laboratory visits, social gatherings and walks in the hills, we also "did" Disneyland; I had been there before and have been since, but never have I had so much fun, never have I had such appreciative, amused, and lively guests.

Sheriton-Portland Hotel
Portland, Oregon
18.IV.62

My darling, I got here without incident and was installed in a ground-floor room looking out on a swimming pool in this enormous hideous hotel. Julian seems well though a bit tired. We drove out yesterday in beautiful weather to the Bonneville Dam. Magnificent country—and the fish making their way up the "fish ladders" at the side of the dam were fascinating. They have made experiments with salmon on "endless fish ladders"—they climb twenty feet from pool to pool against the stream of falling water, then are lowered to the bottom and start again. One fish climbed 6,646 feet in 5 days, and its muscles, when it was

[3] *The Humanist Frame* (New York: Harper & Row, 1961).

killed, exhibited no signs of fatigue (measured by accumulations of lactic acid). All the fish climbed rather faster after going up 1,000 feet. And they do all this on an empty stomach. None of them have eaten for weeks, nor will eat for the rest of the summer.

In the evening I talked with the professor of psychiatry at the Medical Center here—he is working on the problem of recognizing the children who will be specially vulnerable to schizophrenia and devising ways in which they can be supported, at school and within the family, so that they may avoid the disease in spite of their inborn tendency towards it. It was most heartening to find that anything so sensible is being thought of and worked at.

This morning we visited the zoo where a female elephant has just given birth to a 220 pound baby—a most unusual event for elephants in captivity, and one which has excited the city of Portland in a quite extraordinary way. The baby, I must say, is very touching—and it is fascinating to see the other female elephants, as well as the mother, clustering around, like Aunts and Grannies, with an intense solicitude for the little creature (who anyhow weighs twice as much as you do!).

Tonight Julian speaks and I suppose there will be a discussion afterwards. Now I must get ready for dinner. Goodbye, my darling, keep well and don't get too tired.

Your

A.

On the back of a postcard:

Tuesday night

Here we are at the end of a most beautiful drive through pastures, wheat fields, rice paddies, olive and orange groves, forests and mountains—to the foot of this huge extinct volcano. Tomorrow we are to be taken round by a forester. Let's hope it won't be rainy.

Love

A.

Between lectures and seminars Aldous flew often to Los Angeles, where I would meet him at the airport. This particular time I left home earlier than usual because I knew that the airport had been remodeled and that there were new locations for the different airlines. But the remodeling was not only in the airport. When I arrived in the vicinity I found everything changed; whether the directions were poorly placed or I misread them, I found myself on a one-way freeway on which I was free only to go faster and faster away from where I wanted to go. When I finally found a way to turn around, it was already too late to meet the plane, but there was still time to meet Aldous at the luggage depot. On the way back I lost my way again, and when I finally arrived the parking lot was full. I left the car in the street and ran frantically toward the luggage depot. I could see Aldous in the distance, his tall figure exuding, even from far away, an aura of dejection. He was standing near a taxi. I ran toward him, calling, but I was too far for him to see me and my frantic call was covered by the traffic noise. Aldous had in his hand the white box containing the gardenia he brought me almost every time we met—he would always find a gardenia in Hollywood Boulevard or at the San Francisco Airport. In those few seconds, as I was running toward him, something in the attitude of his body, in the way he was looking around without really seeing very far, in the manner in which he held the flower box, made me realize the eagerness with which he had looked forward to our meeting, and his disappointment in not finding me there. Somehow this enormously successful, wise, sophisticated man looked like a hurt lonely child, astonished by a sudden injustice. Those thoughts pierced me as I was trying to shout: "Aldous! Aldous . . ."

He was speaking to the driver and about to enter the car, when finally he heard me and suddenly a light turned on—I shall never forget his lightning change from dejection to delight—and my own pounding heart.

Oh, What Am I? Tell Me, What Am I?

IT WAS DIFFICULT, in those last six months of his life, to know whether Aldous was preoccupied with his health or with the new novel he was writing. At times I thought he was feeling physically weak and in pain; but to my question he would say that it was his novel that was keeping him preoccupied. Then, if on the next day I would bring up the subject of his novel, he would say that he was wondering about the increased weakness, or about his muscular discomfort. I did not know to what extent he *felt* sick. I knew how sick he looked—and wondered if he ever looked at himself in the mirror.

In the first years of our marriage I had often noticed that at times, although Aldous might look pale and tired, he still felt well. I also had noticed that he did not realize he looked tired and that it was better not to tell him. But in the summer of 1963 there was something far worse in his looks than tiredness. It was a ghost-like face that looked at me. My heart would sink, and I wondered, does he ever look at himself in the mirror? I knew that, partly because of his lack of vanity, partly because of his eyesight, he rarely used the mirror. He shaved without looking in the glass—but what if once he did? I found the answer to my question in this passage from an unfinished manuscript.

In 1900 I looked in the glass and saw the pale child who, less than three months before, had been shipped home from India, skeleton-thin after a bout of dysentery. Was that really me? Or was it really the all-important being whose existence I experienced in here, where Edward Darley was the center of the universe? Sixty years later, as I rasp the gray stubble off my chin and cheeks, I find myself asking the same question. Am I that alien presence in the glass, that hardly recognizable caricature of the man who used to climb mountains and go to bed with beautiful women? Or am I this still active mind, this hardly impaired capacity to perceive and feel and think, this God-like awareness that has created all the worlds in which, successively or simultaneously, I have lived?

He thought about the worlds we create and in which we live until he died. He knew, and at times said, that he was living on borrowed time. But "borrowed time" was not, for a man of Aldous's temperament, "waiting time." Once in a while he wondered about the length of his loan—most of the time he used it to its limit. To the last he thought about new ways of writing about man—the multiple amphibian—and his worlds. Since he was too weak to write, he welcomed recording instead of taking notes. The following dialogue is quoted verbatim and took place three days before he died.

Laura: WHEN YOU WOKE UP THIS LAST TIME, WHAT TIME DID YOU WAKE UP?

Aldous: SEVEN, I SUPPOSE.

Laura: OH, YOU HAVE BEEN AWAKE FOR A WHILE. . . .

Aldous: YES, I THINK SO.

Laura: HAVE YOU A NEW IDEA FOR WORK? A NEW KIND OF LITERATURE? (I was referring to something he had said earlier in the night when he had awakened.)

Aldous (slowly, deeply, longingly): WELL, I CAN SEE THAT ONE CAN WRITE THE GREATEST BOOK EVER WRITTEN, IF ONE KNEW HOW . . . I MEAN I KNOW HOW, THEORETICALLY, BUT IN PRACTICE, OF COURSE, IT'S SOMETHING RATHER DIFFERENT.

Laura: FROM WHAT YOU HAVE WRITTEN UP TO NOW?

Aldous (very low, hesitatingly): REALLY, FROM WHAT ANYBODY HAS EVER WRITTEN . . . BUT THEN IT'S SUCH   IT'S ENOUGH   ALMOST THE   ALMOST THE WHOLE COURSE OF LIFE.

Laura: HOW DIFFERENT?

Aldous (with a wonderful, happy emphasis, in a voice unexpectedly like his strong, vital self): BY BRINGING IT ALL IN!

Laura: AT ONCE?

Aldous: SOMEHOW.

Laura: LIKE YOU WERE SAYING YESTERDAY—ABOUT ALL THE UNIVERSES?

Aldous: THAT'S IT—AROUND A CENTRAL STORY WITH EPISODES.

Laura: YOU MEAN, YOU WANT TO DO IT LIKE BACH, IN ALL THESE DIFFERENT WAYS . . .

Aldous: WELL, I MEAN BACH IS MUSIC AND THIS IS SOMETHING ELSE.

Laura: CAN YOU DO YOUR NEW NOVEL LIKE THAT?

Aldous (such longing in his voice): WELL, IT WOULD BE MARVELOUS IF I COULD.

Laura: CAN YOU APPLY IT TO ANY LITTLE THING, EVEN A LITTLE SHORT STORY?

Aldous: NO, I WOULDN'T WANT TO.

Laura: DID YOU JUST WAKE UP WITH THE IDEA?

Aldous: YES. (Long silence.) WOKE UP WITH THE IDEA . . . THERE WAS A IDEA BEGAN COMING IN . . . CORRELATING . . .

Laura: THE IDEA CORRELATED QUITE CLEARLY THEN . . .

Aldous: QUITE CLEARLY—YES.   POSSIBLY . . . I MUST DRINK SOME MORE OF MY ORANGE JUICE. . . .

Laura: SHALL WE DO SOME LETTERS AFTER BREAKFAST?

Aldous: WE MIGHT, I THINK . . .

Laura: OR MAYBE YOU CAN DO SOME OF YOUR WORK—THE ARTICLE,[1] I MEAN—IT'S MORE IMPORTANT THAN THE LETTERS.

Aldous: YES.

Laura: IF YOU CAN DO SOME MORE ON THIS BUSINESS OF ALL THE UNIVERSES AT ONCE. . . . IS THAT WHAT YOU MEANT, ALL AT ONCE?

Aldous: YES.

Laura: AND YET IT'S DIFFERENT FROM A POLYPHONIC THING, IS IT?

Aldous: WELL, IT HAS TO BE VIRTUALLY ANALOGOUS TO POLYPHONY ...

Laura: BUT YOU CANNOT SPEAK ALL AT ONCE . . .

Aldous: WELL, NO, ONE CAN'T, AFTER ALL. IT'S NOT LIKE BACH WHERE YOU CAN HAVE FIVE PARTS GOING ON. WHEN YOU HAVE WORDS, YOU INTERRUPT THE THING. . . . EACH PART BLURS THE OTHER.

Laura: THAT'S PROBABLY WHY PEOPLE WRITE OPERA—SO THEY CAN HAVE A POLYPHONY OF WORDS AND MUSIC AND PAINTING AND DANCING?

Aldous: I MEAN, THIS IS WHAT WAGNER HOPED TO DO AND DIDN'T. UNFORTUNATELY, HE WAS AN UNSPEAKABLY VULGAR MAN. . . .

Aldous often said about his writing that he was never certain what was to develop until he had worked it out. Generally he concentrated on one chapter at a time and liked to finish it before starting on the next.

"I am fooling about with notes for a novel. I will have to wait and see what is going to be," he had said to a friend in the spring of 1963. He did not work at full speed on this novel for several reasons; mainly, I believe, because he felt weak—and bewildered about his weakness. However, he kept up his many activities. In March he went to Rome to

---

[1] "Shakespeare and Religion" in *Aldous Huxley, 1894-1965*. A memorial volume (Harper & Row, 1965).

participate in the FAO assembly on "Man's Right to Freedom from Hunger." On this occasion he met Pope John, who was already very ill. Also during those last months Aldous wrote several essays, gave a few lectures, and in the summer we went to Stockholm, where Aldous contributed much to the impetus of the Congress of the World Academy. Then it seemed best for each of us to visit our families: Aldous in London and I in Italy, where he joined me after three long, and for me anxious weeks. We wrote to each other almost every day. Here are excerpts from his letters.

[August 1963]
I keep asking myself what I ought to do in the immediate future—in the probably not very long future that is left me. How to be more loving, more aware, more useful or (if that isn't possible) more content and accepting. So far the answer hasn't come but perhaps it will— especially if you help me find it. . . .

. . . I am feeling reasonably well—though not very energetic—well enough to do what I have to do, but without the extra power to do what one would like to do in the way of creating something or initiating some new course of action. But one mustn't complain. And anyhow, unexpected things may happen—unforeseen changes occur. . . .

. . . you must forgive me, my sweetheart, for being so gloomy and burdensome. I haven't yet learned to accept the fact of not feeling very well, of being mentally and physically diminished—to accept and to make the best of it. But I hope to learn. Meanwhile please be patient with me and remember that underneath the gloom and the sense of being lost, I love you very much. . . .

. . . here it is unseasonably chilly and rainy—but the country is beautiful and there are wonderful clouds when the sun comes out between the showers—like Constables and Turners. And maybe I have some good ideas for my hypothetical novel!

"Hypothetical" was Aldous's way of describing his uncertainty in his strength and in the length of his borrowed time. The novel was to be autobiographical in outline but not in details. For instance, Aldous was six, not eleven years old, in 1900; he and his family never lived in India; he was not a professional historian; and so on. In this yet untitled work, where fiction and facts mingled, Aldous wanted to describe the many different human beings that a man could be, particularly one living during the phenomenal sixty years of this century. In this sense such a novel could not have been written before, because never, in such a short space of time, have there been such profound and startling changes— "explosion" is a better word. Aldous wanted to show how the universes we perceive and feel—one on each side of our skin—interweave, and how they affect each other in an unending, interchanging circle. He also wanted to show how our potentials are sometimes developed and sometimes stunted by the technology that is part of our culture. As an example of the first, he would sometimes open his lecture[2] on Human Potentials with a reminiscence:

May I begin with a small piece of childhood recollection? I remember as a very small boy seeing Queen Victoria going for her afternoon outing in Windsor Park. She was drawn along in a bath chair by a very fat Shetland pony and accompanied by her faithful servant Brown, perhaps at the speed of two and a half miles an hour. She was a very remarkable spectacle. She was then over eighty, with a circumference considerably greater than her height, and at that time it seemed to be the absolutely natural speed and natural means of locomotion for an old lady of this dignity and age. But since then, only fifty or sixty years later, I have seen old ladies of comparable age and comparable dignity stepping on the gas on the flat Pennsylvania turnpike or cornering at enormous speeds in their Maseratis on the Grande Corniche or the passes of the Alps.

One reason this reminiscence is significant is that it shows very clearly that certain potentialities in human beings which were never suspected at all are in fact constantly being actualized by advances in technology. Nobody seeing Queen Victoria at the beginning of this century could conceivably have imagined that old ladies could have this kind of rapid reaction time and pleasure in going at the enormous speeds which in fact many of them do at present.

In this case Aldous was looking at man-made changes; in another mood he looked at changes in nature that had taken place during his lifetime. In June 1961, Aldous was in London with Julian and made an excursion to the place of his childhood. He wrote: ". . . trees I saw planted are now 60 feet high with trunks five feet in girth. How posthumous one feels! One could wallow in the feeling, and that would be literature. But I have no inclination to bring literature into life. React to now in terms of now, not in terms of then."

In the opening chapter of his novel, he brings life into literature and plays with the interaction of here and now and then and there. For a

[2] See footnote p. 141.

time I was in doubt whether these pages should be published: from a literary point of view it may be argued that they are not as polished as other of Aldous's writing; on the other hand, wouldn't it be possessive and egoistic of me to keep this first (and last) chapter of his work in progress in a safe? For what? For whom? Aldous's thoughts and feelings at the end of his life are more important for us, here and now, than as a historical piece for posthumous evaluation. I know that many will find these pages very meaningful, will find in them a reflection of some of our own doubts and questions—and perhaps some answers. "What am I?"—first asked by the eleven-year-old Edward Darley— was to be the leading wand by which, through space and time, Aldous would *"bring it all in!"*

The year was 1900, and on that bright May morning I was precisely eleven years old. How vividly, across the enormous gulf of time, I remember that day! Vividly—but in patches—discontinuously. The spotlight is turned on and then turned off again at the whim of an inexplicably capricious nervous system. Between memory and illumi- nated memory I find myself groping in a blank of darkness. Recall has to be supplemented by imagination, history by historical fiction. Retro- spectively we are all the heroes and heroines, the fascinatingly bad girls or triumphant villains of a Waverley novel—often several Waverley novels. When there are no available facts (which there generally aren't, for we record very little and forget practically everything), we invent a set of pseudo-facts more plausible than the unlikely and pointless happenings of real life, more creditably (or, if we prefer it that way, more discreditably) "in character" than the successive irrelevances of minute-to-minute thinking, feeling and willing. How easy it would be to construct a linear narrative, a straightforward tale that would read like the simple truth! But the truth is never simple. If the straightforward tale carries conviction it is precisely because it is not the truth, but an elegantly streamlined novelette. At the risk of seeming confused and digressive, I shall stick as closely as I can to the complex realities of the autobiographical process—a process that supplements facts with pseudo-facts, inference and rationalization, because it is not the truth, but an elegantly streamlined falsehood. There are no true confessions; there are only autobiographical Waverleys of various degrees of merit. The bad Waverleys are straightforwardly plausible, the good ones are not. Inevitably so; for to be good, an autobiographical Waverley must necessarily be complicated, digressive and full of inconsistencies. Every life is a set of relationships between incompatibles. To get to know oneself, one must get to know all the disparate fields of which, at any moment, one is the center. There are visceral fields, psychological fields, cultural and historical fields. And every sentient, acculturated pattern of cells that calls itself "I" depends for its very existence on this, on that and the other. I am a function of you and it. And all these I-you-it fields extend through time as well as in space, reach back into the past and forward into the future. Moreover, everything that calls itself "I" exists simultaneously in the universe of experience and the universe of notions; in the world of one damned thing after another and the world of orderly thinking; in the privacy of smell and colour, pleasure and pain, and in the public domain of words; among brute happenings and within the home-made cosmos of intelligible symbols. "Let me have a two-page synopsis of your story line," says the movie producer. The story line of a good autobiographical Waverley looks like the crisscrossing of half a dozen broken switchbacks, each of them bristling with innumerable tangents to infinity.

Well, as I was saying, the year was 1900 and that morning I was eleven years old. I had slept later than usual, and it was after seven when I awoke (and this is one of that day's brightly illuminated memories) from a dream in which I was back in India and had come rushing in, after lessons, shouting, "Mother! Mother, where are you?" And of course she was in her little study at the back of the bungalow, sitting at her desk. "Mother!" I threw my arms around her and kissed her, again and again. "That's enough," she said. But I went on kissing her. "That's enough," she repeated and dipped her pen in the ink. "Run along and play. I'm writing." "But, Mother . . ." I heard myself protesting as I woke up. Behind the drawn red curtains the room was suffused with a rosy twilight. Where was I? Outside, somewhere beyond the curtains, a cuckoo was calling, "Cuckoo"—and suddenly I remembered. This wasn't our bungalow, this was Aunt Frances' house in Surrey. "Cuckoo"—and today was my birthday. My birthday! The mood of sadness in which I had awoken from my dream gave place to a gloating exultation.

For the past two or three days a growing heap of packages had accumulated, tempting but inviolable, on the table of what was still traditionally called the nursery. I jumped out of bed, tiptoed into the next room and eyed my treasure. There were square parcels, oblong parcels, squashy parcels without corners, flat parcels that obviously contained books. The grand opening, I knew, was to be a public event, after breakfast. At this early hour my birthday rights were strictly limited. A single, minor virginity—that was all I was now entitled to take. The battalions of lead soldiers, the clockwork train, the chemistry set, coveted airgun—these would come later. For the moment I must be content with a mere book. I picked up one of the flat parcels, crept back to my room, drew back the curtains and, climbing into bed, undid the string. "To Edward Darley, for his birthday, with sincere good wishes from Colonel and Mrs. Craik."

Well, that was pretty decent of them. But then I looked at the title page.

HIPPOPOTAMIA

A Book of Pachydermatous Nonsense

A book for babies! Hot and tingling, the blood rushed up into my cheeks. Just because I had cried at their bloody Christmas party—cried because Willy Craik and the other boys had been so beastly to me about having let the side down at Up Jenkins. "Edward," my mother had whispered in her most upsetting tone of shocked disapproval, "how old are you?" And my father had told me to pull myself together. A moment later I overheard what he said to the Colonel. ". . . such a cry-baby. We don't know what to do about it." The Craiks, it was obvious, hadn't forgotten. Their present, I felt sure, was a deliberately insulting reminder of what had happened last Christmas. Pachydermatous nonsense, indeed! And I'd been reading Shakespeare and Dickens and Thackeray for years. Not to mention books about astronomy, X rays and evolution. *And* Cicero, of course, *and* Xenophon, Sallust, Ovid.... Whereas their precious Willy, that great lout who was eighteen months older than I, couldn't spell and was still struggling with gender rhymes and the third declension. Why not give *him* this kindergarten stuff? I was on the point of throwing the Craiks' insulting gift across the room. Then curiosity got the better of me and, still furious, I opened the volume at random. Printed in bold black type on the right-hand page was a single couplet.

> **Year follows year, and still the Hippopotami**
> **Keep asking, "Oh, what *am* I? Tell me, *what* am I?"**

I read it again—this time aloud.

> **Year follows year, and still the Hippopotami**
> **Keep asking, "Oh, what *am* I? Tell me, *what* am I?"**

On the opposite page was a picture in full color of a young hippo in the act of self-interrogation. Standing on his hind legs and dressed all in black, like the Prince of Denmark, he was gazing intently at his own image in a cheval glass. Behind the glass stretched an expanse of William Morris wallpaper and to the left, with an elaborately carved frame, was a Pre-Raphaelite painting of an auburn girl-Hippo in the pose and costume of the Blessed Damozel. On the right, obviously (as I now remember it) by Sir Joshua, was a portrait group—aristocratic father Hippo, mother Hippo in muslin, and three small Hippo children —with a ducal park and a statue of Hippo-Diana in the background.

Looking over Hamlet-Hippo's shoulder, I studied the reflection of a huge bulging face that, for all its grotesqueness, wore an expression of the most painful uncertainty, of what, fifty years later, the Existentialists would be calling *angoisse*. The rubbery lips were parted and seemed, as I looked at them, to move. I could actually *hear* the murmured soliloquy. "What *am* I? Tell me, *what* am I?" In the seemingly solid floor of Animal Faith this question from the nonsense universe of Hippopotami had suddenly opened trap doors into plunging abysses. Up to this moment it had all been so obvious, so completely self-evident. What am I? My answer to that question had been the same as God's: I am that I am. Hamlet-Hippo had now reformulated the equation. (What-am-I?) am that (What-am-I?) am. I scanned once more the signs of agonized uncertainty on that huge bulbous face in the cheval glass. Then I got out of bed and, crossing the room, sat down at the dressing table in front of the white-framed mirror.

Under an uncontrollable explosion of red-brown hair, a pair of greenish eyes stared back at me. Outside, in the garden, the birds were going about their morning business—the thrushes making thrush noises, the blackbirds blackbird noises, the rooks cawing, the sparrows identifying themselves by the shrill chatter of sparrows. *They* knew precisely what they were. But what about *me?* I stuck out my tongue, and the child in the mirror did the same. I made the kind of faces that one makes when one is angry, when one is hurt, when crying, when laughing at somebody. Rage, pain, grief and derision bounced back at me. I whispered, "*What* am I?" and, this time, the lips in the looking glass really moved. "What *am* I?" Answer: Edward Darley. "Edward Darley," I said aloud. "Edward Darley, Edward Darley, Edward Darley, Edward Darley . . ." Reiterated, the names lost all meaning, broke down into a succession of nonsense syllables: Edward Darley—Abracadabra. Edward Darley—Doodle-doddle Chiffchaff. So what am I, what *am* I?

Hamlet-Hippo had introduced me to psychology and metaphysics, had set me asking the questions which, in different forms and in changing contexts, I would go on asking through all the rest of a long life.

In 1900 I looked in the glass and saw the pale child who, less than three months before, had been shipped home from India, skeleton-thin after a bout of dysentery. Was that really me? Or was I really the all-important being whose existence I experienced in here, where Edward Darley was the center of the universe? Sixty years later, as I rasp the gray stubble off my chin and cheeks, I find myself asking fundamentally the same question. Am I that alien presence in the glass, that hardly recognizable caricature of the man who used to climb mountains and go to bed with beautiful women? Or am I this still active mind, this hardly impaired capacity to perceive and feel and think, this God-like awareness that has created all the worlds in which, successively or simultaneously, I have lived?

Today I know that one can answer these questions in terms of one or another of the various brands of philosophical jargon—can answer them in a way that the top of one's head will find convincing. To the rest of the organism, conviction will never come from any kind of talk. It comes only from the lived experience, moment by moment, of what happens when one fully and consciously accepts the fact of being this creator of worlds and at the same time that parody, that unkind and surely unrealistic caricature of oneself.

In 1900, needless to say, I knew neither the theoretical nor the practical answers to Hamlet-Hippo's self-questioning before the mirror. And as I sat there, looking at myself, the original What-am-I? ramified out into all kinds of subsidiary questions. What was I really? The brilliant boy, two years ahead of his contemporaries in book learning? Or the cry-baby, two years behind them in self-control and the art of behaving like an English gentleman? The model child who won all the prizes was also the feeble outsider, bullied, made fun of, at the best contemptuously tolerated by the louts he envied and despised. Which was the genuine me?

And anyhow, I went on to reflect, these were the public Edward Darleys, the ones that other people knew about. But there were also the Edward Darleys about whom only *I* knew anything—the *sotto voce* whisperer of dirty words, the Peeping Tom forever on the lookout for what my sister Maud, with a giggle, called "sights." And there was another, a still more clandestine Edward Darley—the "I" who descended every night into the shamefully delicious Other World, where the still childish rudiments of self-inflicted pleasure were associated with my mother's perfume and the softness of her skin when I kissed her good night; were associated at the same time with that hot afternoon in the stables behind our bungalow, when little Ali, the *sais's* son, had discovered to his delighted amazement that I, too, was circumcised and would respond to his playfully innocent advances with as much enthusiasm as any Muslim. And there were other voluptuous incitements and accompaniments—memories of the administration of suppositories; the limerick about the Young Lady of Ealing; the reproduction of Boucher's painting of La Petite Morphil with no clothes on, opposite page 87 of Mrs. Craik's big book on French art. This most clandestine of Edward Darleys had never been taken in the act; but his existence had evidently been suspected. My mother had taken me on her knee and, in a grave, alarming tone, had spoken of bad habits and the danger, if one succumbed to certain temptations, of going blind or even insane. And, dropping his ordinarily jocular manner, my father had taken me for walks and, with obvious embarrassment, had talked about self-control and manliness, about duty and the Empire and Lord Roberts. I would have liked to be a hero; and meanwhile my mother's cautionary anecdotes had scared me into detecting in myself the preliminary symptoms of amblyopia and imbecility. Never again, I vowed. But after a week the clandestine Edward always reasserted his rights. Well, just this once, just for a minute or two. And there I was—back again with good-night kisses and suppositories, with Ali in the stables and La Petite Morphil bottom upwards on her rumpled bed. The net result of all that preaching was that the secret and delicious Other World became a world of guilty pleasure. And now there was this war in South Africa and my father had gone with his regiment to fight the Boers. My nocturnal memories of good-night kisses and those afternoons in the stables were mingled now with memories of another kind, memories of the strange Dutch names of battles, memories of Bluebell and Dolly Gray. Haunted by patriotism, the more public members of my unhappy family of Edward Darleys felt guiltier than ever. Never, never again—except this once. What *am* I? Tell me, *what* am I?

What they told me here in Surrey was flattering. Aunt Frances and my grandfather approved of me. They loved books; so did I. They had both been precocious scholars; so was I. For them I was really the model child—a bit too sensitive perhaps, but that would pass; a bit too self-centered and introspective, but then I had been ill, I was a victim of the Indian climate. As for the smut-mutterer, the Peeping Tom, the ultimately clandestine Edward Darley of my nightly Other World— they were too innocently high-minded, I felt sure, even to imagine that such creatures existed. But what about Fräulein Lili? Fraulein Lili had been imported from Munich to look after Maud (more as an elder sister, Aunt Frances liked to say, than as a governess) and was the grownup with whom I had the closest and most continuous dealings. Did *she* know as little as Aunt Frances and my grandfather? Was *she* as pure, idealistic and ingenuous?

"Meuchler!" she had said the other morning when, having blundered by-accident-on-purpose into the unlocked bathroom while she was in the tub, I was elaborately overacting the part of someone looking for his bedroom slippers, someone to whom it has never even occurred that there were such things as nipples and pubic hair. "Meuchler!" And she had given vent to one of her rare, her perturb-

And all day long the Hippopotami
Kept murmuring, "What am I? Oh, tell me what am I?"

The accompanying woodcut showed a young Hippo in ~~/~~ the agonizing

act of self-interrogation. Standing on his hind legs and

~~drx~~ clothed all in black, like the Prince of Denmark ~~every~~

culture is a wardrobe ~~of well worn costumes~~

~~finishing school for performing animals~~ he was gazing

intently at his own distraught image in a cheval glass. ~~"What~~

~~am I?"~~ It was a funny picture and the rhyme was richly

comic. But, even as a child, I knew obscurely that

~~xxxxxxxxxxxxxxxxxxxxx~~ beneath the nonsense lay plunging gulfs

of metaphysical darkness. ~~Cxxxxxxxxxxxxxxxxxxxxxxt-~~

~~xxxxxxxxxxxxxxxxxxxxxxxxxxxmmm~~ "What am I?" asked the

~~soliloquy~~ soliloquizing Hippo~~potamus~~." And what am I? ~~that the~~

little boy I once was used to wonder, as he lay on his
stomach
~~couch~~ in the blue bedroom, poring over ~~that old book of~~

~~Sibylline nonsense. Inside my skull~~ the question has

~~gone on reverberating~~ ever since. It ~~asked~~ ~~echoed there~~ when

~~I was seven, it~~ ~~still echoing now that I am~~ seventy-three.

What am I? Yes, what am I? And what, while we're on the subject

of identities, are you? You, my mother. You, my wife and

children and grandchildren? You, my transient bedfellows? You,

my ~~German~~ enemies doing your dutiful best to kill me?

And you, my bosses, ~~and my~~ subordinates -- what are you? And

what are you, my culture-heroes and exemplars -- my Dostoevskis

and Clerk Maxwells, my Gautamas and Wordsworths. And what are

~~you~~ the strangers? ~~You~~ my fellow passengers in buses, fellow

listeners at concerts, fellow shoppers at Woolworth's and the

~~and the~~ supermarket? ~~xx What are~~ you, the fascinating, inac-

cessible women glimpsed out of the windows of ~~coach~~ That you,

Reproduction of a draft manuscript page of Aldous's unfinished novel ingly loud and derisive laughs. "You're a promising hypocrite," she added in that almost too perfect English of hers. "In a few years you should be almost as good at it as I am." And that evening, when she came into my room to say good night, "What do you mean to think about before you go to sleep?" she had asked. I said I really didn't know. "German grammar?" she gravely suggested. In my anxiety to cut short a conversation on so ticklish a theme, I failed to detect the irony in her words and answered with all the seriousness expected of a model child that, yes, I would think of German grammar. "What about German girls?" she asked. "For example, the German girl in the bathtub this morning?" I started to protest: she mustn't imagine that I had seen anything, I really *was* looking for my slippers. Fräulein Lili laid a hand on my mouth. "Silence is golden," she said. "Good night, Edward. Have fun with your German grammar." And with that she was gone, leaving me with a disturbing sense that she knew too much, too accurately, too intimately. I would have liked, I even made a resolution, to prove her wrong. But, needless to say, within five minutes of her departure I had conjured up the phantom of Fräulein Lili's naked- ness—knees, thighs, a submerged navel, dark hairs in the hollow under a raised arm, a soapy hand lathering round white breasts. And now here was little Ali in the stable, here were the suppositories . . .

But here too, breaking through those memories of the night, was that cuckoo, calling me back from my unavowable Other World to the above-board universe of model children and their birthdays.

And then suddenly I remembered last year's birthday in India. My presents had been opened immediately after breakfast. Father had given me four companies of lead soldiers and a magnificent knife with three blades, a gimlet, a screwdriver, and a hook for taking stones out of horses' hoofs. Mother's presents were an Oxford Book of English Verse, a microscope and a framed reproduction of Watts's *Sir Galahad*. "Where shall we hang it?" There was a lively discussion, a fetching of nails and picture wire and hammer. What fun! But as soon as *Sir Galahad* had been installed above my bed, my mother looked at her watch. "Time to go to work," she announced. My happiness collapsed like a pricked balloon. "But I thought you were going to show me how to use the microscope," I protested. "We'll have two hours for that this evening." But this was no ordinary day, this was an extraor- dinary day—and on this extraordinary day those two hours allotted to me every evening were not enough. "But, mother . . ." My voice broke and I started to cry. "Edward, why can't you be reasonable?" "Why can't *you* be unreasonable?" my father asked. "What do you mean?" "Can't the distinguished lady novelist *ever* take a morning off?" "My mornings are sacred," she said. He shrugged his shoulders. "Scribble,

scribble, scribble. It's an addiction—like chewing betel." I forget what my mother answered. All I remember is that her face, ordinarily so expressively mobile and animated, went stony with repressed anger. She turned and walked away to her study, leaving me to my misery and resentment. My father sat down on the floor. "Let's look at your soldiers," he said. I sat down beside him; but my mind was with my mother in the study. Even on my birthday I was thinking, her work meant more to her than I did. Those bloody novels of hers—how I hated them! Hated them even though in public, and, with part of my mind quite genuinely, I was inordinately proud of them. "My mother writes books," I used to boast whenever I got into conversation with a stranger, and I would quote the reviewers. "Thoughtful and distinguished. . . ." But with the other half of my mind I felt that the memorable achievement was at my expense. The time and attention she gave to her writing were time and attention that ought to have been given to me. I loved her with the intensity that springs from hopelessness. Mine was the exacerbated passion of one who knows that he has a successful rival. "Scribble, scribble, scribble. . . ." My father could smile with indulgent irony and shrug his shoulders. He had been married for the best part of fifteen years. Besides, he had other resources—friends, a profession, polo, sexual alternatives. I had no resources, and my passion was still new and had never been assuaged. For me, that scribbling was not a joke; it was a tragedy.

Punctually at one o'clock my mother emerged from her study. "Come along, birthday boy," she gaily called. I forgot all my grievances and ran to her. Together we walked into the dining room. It was an Anglo-Indian feast—curry and tinned peas, tinned pineapple and a cake with pink icing. Then, pop! my father uncorked the champagne. They drank my health and, making a face (for to me the stuff tasted like medicine), I returned the compliment. "And now," said my father with mock solemnity, "let us drink to the Great Work and its celebrated authoress, George Eliot Junior." Bravo!" said my mother sarcastically. "I didn't think you'd ever heard of George Eliot." "I have," I eagerly volunteered. "I've read *Silas Marner.*" "What we need now," said my father as we rose at last from the table, "is a long siesta." My mother shook her head. "I'm going to finish my chapter," she said. "No, you're not." He caught her by the wrist as she started to move toward the study. "Let me go!" For an answer he picked her up and carried her bodily, protesting all the way, to their bedroom. "Sleep well, Edward," he called from the threshold. The door slammed. Still hiccuping from my half glass of champagne, I lingered sadly in the dark corridor, then turned and went reluctantly to my room. There was Sir Galahad. His strength was as the strength of ten, because he had no bad habits. I lay down under the mosquito net, closed my eyes and thought of La Petite Morphil.

And now the siesta was over. It was late afternoon, and we had moved out onto the verandah. Father was sitting in one of the wicker chairs, smoking his pipe. Mother was lying in the hammock. I stood there, looking at her, just looking and looking. How beautiful! As though the face were lighted up from the inside. And she kept smiling to herself (after all these years I can remember myself remembering that look of quiet rapture)—smiling to herself about some secret that was at once too precious to be divulged and to enormous to be hidden. And that secret, I knew, had nothing to do with me. It was their secret. I *didn't* count.

"Stop mooning about," my father said. "Why don't you play with your soldiers?" Obediently, but full of hatred, I sat down on the floor and started to arrange my Highlanders and Grenadier Guards in a hollow square. For a long time nobody spoke. Then I heard my mother's voice saying, "Darling." Hopefully, I looked up at her. But she wasn't talking to me. That shining face of hers was turned toward my father. He smiled back at her, reached out an enormous hand and with an outstretched forefinger touched the tip of her nose. "My little Cesario," he said. "Your little Cesario," she echoed. "Why do you call her Cesario?" I asked suspiciously. "Cesario was a boy," my father explained. "A boy?" "A boy who was really a girl called Viola. It's in a play by Shakespeare. White tights and a red velvet doublet. Your mother was acting that part the first time I ever set eyes on her." "At Lahore, in eighty-seven," she elaborated. Then she turned again to my father, "What would have happened if you hadn't come to that performance of *Twelfth Night?* Or even if I'd been playing Olivia instead of Viola? I'd have gone back to England after the cold weather. I'd have married a Sanskrit scholar like my uncle. Or a political economist like my brother-in-law. Or perhaps even one of my father's curates—God forbid. Instead of which . . ." "Instead of which," he said, "you suddenly found yourself in the army, married to a mindless cavalry officer." "Who isn't really mindless," she said. "He only pretends to be." "Just to annoy George Eliot Junior?" my father questioned. "Why do you want to annoy her?" He shrugged his shoulders. "I hadn't bargained for George Eliot. All I bargained for was little Cesario." The smile of quiet rapture gave place to a frown. "Cesario—and in the intervals, what? The perfect *mem-sahib?* The standard army wife? No, thanks!" She sat up, dropped her feet over the side of the hammock and, suddenly brisk and business-like, stood up. "Come, Edward," she said. "Time for us to try the new microscope." I jumped up and followed her into the study.

Looking back, I can see myself as I sat in front of the dressing-table mirror, I can remember myself remembering the enigmatic conversation of the previous year. If I remembered it so vividly, it was because I didn't really know what it was all about, because, in my incomprehension, I felt so bitterly aggrieved at being left out, so deeply hurt by the realization that there were contexts in which I was of no importance, in which, so far as my mother was concerned, I didn't even exist. It was not until much later that I fully understood what they had been talking about—and by that time, needless to say, the knowledge was irrelevant. It had come too late to . . .

A hand was laid on my shoulder. Startled almost to the pitch of terror, I uttered a little cry and opened my eyes.

"*Guten Morgen, lieber* Edward."

Nun-like in a long white dressing gown, her dark hair still in plaits, Fräulein Lili was standing behind my chair.

"It's only me," she went on in her almost unaccented, her positively *too* correct English.

Only Fräulein Lili . . . it was a relief, of course, to discover that the hand on my shoulder had not been a ghost's or a burglar's. But relief was tinged with a certain apprehension. For all her youth and her dazzling good looks, I never felt at ease in Fräulein Lili's presence. There was something enigmatic about her, something even obscurely menacing.

"Didn't you hear me come in?" she asked.

I shook my head. Fräulein Lili had an almost feline gift of noiselessness.

My gesture evoked a tiny smile of satisfaction that gleamed for a moment and was gone again, leaving the marble-smooth face as impassive as ever. That impassiveness was one of the things in Fräulein Lili that I found most disquieting. She knew everything about me— knew it, so to say, from the inside, by some kind of direct participation that was yet compatible with an amused and slightly contemptuous detachment, sometimes with the most devastating of ironies. To her, my secrets were an open (and obviously rather boring) book. But what did I know about her secrets? Looking into that statue's face of hers, it was impossible to find any clue to what was going on in her mind. And other people evidently shared my feelings. I remembered the conversation I had overheard, two or three days earlier, between Aunt Frances and Mrs. Bloxam. In her loud, almost military voice, Mrs. Bloxam had started to talk about "that German girl of yours, there's something unnatural about her. Does she *never* smile?"

"She doesn't have much to smile about," Aunt Frances had explained.

It was hard for me to follow the story in all its details; but the gist of it, as I now reconstruct it from my memories of the fragments I understood, is plain enough. Her mother had died when Fräulein Lili was still in the nursery, and she had been brought up by a doting father. Brought up like a little princess, with everything money could buy—servants, borzois, high society, ermine muffs, holidays in grand hotels on the Riviera. Then, when she was eighteen, crash! Her father, the financial wizard, had overreached himself. There were ugly rumors, then a judicial investigation and the uncovering of enormous swindles, then a warrant for the wizard's arrest. But the warrant was never served; as the police came up the stairs to get him, he put a pistol to his head and blew his brains out. The now penniless orphan had gone to live with her half sister, the wizard's child by an earlier, less distinguished marriage. It had been the prelude to yet another tragedy. Lili was young and beautiful; her half sister had five children and was running to fat.

"So you can imagine what happened. She had to leave in a hurry. Her brother-in-law . . ."

"You mean, he tried to . . .?"

"You know what men are," Aunt Frances had said.

But what *are* they? The remembered words had raised the insistent Hippopotamian question. What was anybody?

Fräulein Lili broke a long silence. "When I came in," she said, "you were talking to yourself." I shook my head emphatically. "Yes, you were," she quietly insisted. "Something about thousands of miles. What was it?"

I tried to answer; but the words stuck in my throat, and a moment later I was uncontrollably sobbing.

"Thousands of miles away from your mother—was that it? *Armes Kind.*" She ran her fingers through my hair. "But it won't be long now. Three or four months, that's all." She went on stroking my hair. I pulled out a handkerchief and blew my nose. "My mother never came back," she resumed. "What would have happened to me if she hadn't died. I'd be somebody different. Different—perhaps better—whatever *that* means."

Suddenly there was a noise of water being run into a bathtub. Then a door banged, slippered feet thudded on linoleum and, from half way along the corridor, Maud began calling, "Edward," and again more insistently, *"Edward!"* The voice was still squeaky, still childishly modulated, but its tone was peremptory. From the moment of my return from India, Maud had appointed herself to be my governess—a governess of the old school, nosy, bossy, chronically censorious. "Time for your bath." She came hurrying into the room. "And wash your ears,

for a change. They were just filthy. . . . Oh!" Taken aback by the sight
of Fräulein Lili, she broke off and, suddenly abject, began to apologize.
"I'm sorry. I didn't know. I mean . . ."

Fräulein Lili turned an expressionless face in her direction and said
nothing.

"I mean, I wouldn't have shouted," Maud went on, more abjectly
than ever.

"Shouting is seldom necessary," said Fräulein Lili.

Maud hastened to agree with her.

"And now go and see if that bath is overflowing."

"Sisters," said Fräulein Lili, as the sound of footsteps receded along
the passage. "Elder sisters." She wrinkled up her classically blank face
into an expression of disgust, and slowly shook her head. Had Maud in
some way reminded her, I wondered, of her own elder sister—the elder
sister who got so upset because her husband had tried to do what
anyone who knew what men are would naturally have expected him to
do? "And now," she added, "you'd better go and have your bath."

I marched off reluctantly toward yet another of those agonizing
ordeals by cold water which, in those days, were supposed to be good
for the health and morals of little boys.

Maud, when I got there, was still in the bathroom.

"Did you run any hot water?" I asked.

"Not a drop," she assured me. "You're supposed to have a *cold*
bath."

"Not on my birthday."

"Every day." She was already gloating over my imminent
martyrdom. "In you get!"

"Not so long as you're here," I answered. "Get out."

"I'm staying here to see that you don't cheat. You'll *say* you had
your bath—but how does anyone *know?*"

"Get out!"

"Won't."

"You will," said a familiar voice. Fräulein Lili had made another of
her noiseless entrances and was standing there, behind us, in the door-
way. "You will go and get dressed. And don't forget to wash *your*
ears."

"But Fräulein Lili . . ."

"At once."

Maud stood there for a few seconds, poised on the brink of rebellion;
then, quailing, averted her eyes.

"All right," she grumbled. "But see that he doesn't cheat."

She left the room. Fräulein Lili closed the door after her and locked
it. Taking a bath towel from the rack, she unfolded it and sat down on

the cork-topped stool that stood between the tub and the washbasin.

"Hurry up," she commanded.

I took off my pajamas. "Do I *have* to?"

"Hurry up," she repeated.

I braced my spirit for crucifixion; then, gritting my teeth, stepped into the tub, sat down and immersed myself three times (that was the ritual) in the icy water and scrambled out. Fräulein Lili enveloped me in the towel and started to rub me down.

"There," she said when I was dry.

She handed me the towel. I took it, walked over to the rack and draped it carefully over the top rail. From behind me, suddenly, startlingly, came a sound of laughter, muffled, at first, then full-throated, uninhibited. It was though some long-imprisoned creature of the wilds had suddenly broken out of its cage.

Was she laughing at *me?* I turned on her aggressively. "What's the joke?"

"*So hold und schon und rein,*" she gasped. Then, recovering her breath, "It's a line of poetry," she explained. "Somebody I knew once quoted it to me. I was suddenly reminded."

Mystified, I asked her what it was that had reminded her.

"Your little *Erziehungstuck.*"

"*Erziehungstuck?* What's that?"

Fräulein Lili was silent for a few seconds. Then, beckoning, "Come here," she called.

I looked at her. The face which, only a few moments before, had been as expressionless as that of a marble Artemis, was glowing now with a wild hilarious mischief. "What do you want?" I asked suspiciously.

Cautiously I approached.

"Nearer." I took another step. "Nearer." Yet another, and I was standing beside her. Fräulein Lili slipped an arm around my waist, effortlessly lifted me off my feet and laid me, struggling vainly (for she was far stronger than I) across her knees. "It's *this,*" she said, and a cool cupped palm rested first on one buttock, then on the other. "The *Erziehungstuck.* The upbringing Morsel. The Organ of Education."

With as much dignity as my present posture would permit me to assume, I told her that my people didn't believe in that sort of thing. Maud and I had never been spanked—emphatically *never*.

"Yes, I know," said Fräulein Lili. "No corporeal punishment. It was the first thing your aunt told me when I came here to look after Maud. And she said the same thing when *you* arrived. Well, I'm just a Fräulein now, and Fräuleins have to do as they're told. But what a pity, what a *pity!*" She patted the Organ of Education. "And how ungrateful to the Herr Gott," she added, "seeing that it was He.who created the *Erziehungstuck*—created it for this express purpose." The gentle pats modulted, *crescendo,* into a succession of harder and harder slaps.

"Ow! Ow!"

And then (what *am* I! tell me *what* am I?) I found myself remembering Hamlet-Hippo. I, the protesting victim of an outrage, I, who was nevertheless discovering this new kind of excitement, this obscure pleasure in being outraged—what *was* I?

"*So hold und schon und . . .*" Smack!

"Stop it!"

"Just one more," Fräulein Lili pleaded.

"No."

"Please."

"All right then." (Tell me, what am I?)

For what seemed a very long time nothing happened. Then, resoundingly and with stinging force, the final hardest slap was administered.

"You beast!"

"*Du armes Kind, was hat man dir gethan?*"

"I hate you!"

"No, you don't," Fräulein Lili assured me. "On the contrary . . . Shall I kiss it to make it better? *So hold,*" a kiss, "*und schon,*" another kiss, "*und rein, rein, rein*"—a whole shower of kisses. Then, briskly, she set me on my feet, arose and pushed back the stool on which she had been sitting. "And now we must hurry, or we'll be late for breakfast."

Twenty minutes later, buttoned up in my Norfolk jacket and with brilliantine on my hair, I was once more the model child. Maud had gone ahead to say good morning to her white rabbits in their hutch in the stable yard. The model child was alone with a model governess. And what a model! Starched Eton collar, white blouse, more than ankle-length navy-blue skirt Fräulein Lili's disguise was impenetrable. She examined me, gave a last perfectionist's touch to my tie, and we were ready.

"*Vorwärts.*"

At the foot of the stairs that led down from the nursery floor to the wide landing at the head of the main staircase, we were intercepted by Aunt Frances' maid. Mrs. Dibdin would like us to come to her room before we went down to breakfast. We knocked and were told to come in. Gently propelled from behind by Fräulein Lili, I entered. propped up against pillows and with a board across her knees, Aunt Frances was busily writing. A pile of books were piled up on the night table and a couple of volumes lay open on the broad expanse of the bed beside her.

Aunt Frances and Mother—two sisters, but how unlike one another! And their difference was not merely chronological; they were separated by much more than the eighteen years of Aunt Frances' seniority. Mother was impulsively quick, Aunt Frances deliberate. Aunt Frances was always predictably her serious, concentrated and deeply conscientious self; Mother was changeable like spring weather—hilariously gay, then sad almost to the point of despair, then suddenly happy again, happy to the point of recklessness or rapture. Mother was beautiful and fascinating; I loved her, not as a Higher Being, but horizontally, so to speak, as a kind of fairy creature inhabiting a world that was on the level of my own, but alien, of another, a magically different order. Aunt Frances wasn't beautiful—had doubtless never been beautiful; she was majestic, she inspired a kind of awe. I loved her, loved her profoundly, but loved her always from below upwards. That she looked, sitting up in the huge fourposter, like an enthroned queen was appropriately symbolic. Symbolic, too, was her appearance. Splendidly aquiline, her rather prominent nose might have been one of those characteristically regal features handed down, generation after generation, through a long ramifying line of kings, empresses, princes of the blood, assorted bastards. Less typically regal were the broad high forehead, the observantly kindly eyes, the mouth at once resolute and almost tremulously sensitive, the general air, indescribable and yet unmistakable, of high intelligence and a concerned goodness. The throned queen, it was obvious, was also something of an intellectual and an artist.

Aunt Frances had been reading; but as I entered the room, she put down her book and, holding out her arms, called, "Many happy returns of the day!" I approached; she laid her hands on my shoulders and kissed me. "Dear Edward—dear, *dear* Edward." Her voice was rich, beautifully modulated, vibrant with feeling, intrinsically convincing. It was a voice that made everything she said seem truer than the truth, sincerer than sincerity, better than goodness. "Better," Fräulein Lili had said, "better—whatever *that* means." But what it meant was obvious. Being better meant being more like what this thrilling voice said that one ought to be.

Aunt Frances turned to Fräulein Lili. "And you, my dear—thank you, thank you. Edward has been very fortunate to have you as his guide, his big sister."

Fräulein Lili gravely inclined her head. "One does one's best."

"With the happy result," said Aunt Frances, "that *he's* been doing his best. I've seen it, Edward," she went on, "and I'm proud of you."

Borne on that intrinsically truthful, that more than sincere voice, her pride was contagious; I felt it as an expansion of the heart, a tingling up and down the spine. What was I? Aunt Frances was telling me. I was the heir of two noble traditions—the Darley tradition of public service, the scholarly tradition of the Garths. A worthy heir, an heir who, already, was demonstrating his ability and (more important) his declared willingness to live up to those traditions.

The charismatic voice was still. It was my turn to say something; but I was too deeply moved, too close to tears, to be able to speak. Aunt Frances kissed me again.

"And now you must go and have your breakfast."

I nodded speechlessly and, followed by Fräulein Lili, walked out of the room. At the head of the staircase she laid a hand on my shoulder.

"Take three deep breaths. It'll make you feel better. More like a credit to your family," she added with an earnestness whose ironic intention did not become apparent to me until long after the event.

I halted and took three long breaths. Then three more. Fräulein Lili patted me on the back.

"Now you're ready for anything." And she led the way into the dining room.

Silver-haired, aquiline and ascetic, my grandfather Garth was already in his place at the head of the table.

"Many happy again-comings of the day," he flutily called as I made my entrance. (The re- in "returns" was inadmissibly Latin. In my grandfather's view, Cicero and the Norman conquest had utterly corrupted our fair Saxon tongue.) "Many happy again-comings." And, addressing me as though I were a contemporary of Earl Godwine and the Confessor, "May God bless you, my dear Eadweard," he added in a graver, more professionally clerical tone.

"Amen," I felt constrained to mumble, and blushed with embarrassment. Outside of church and on weekdays, references to God were as bad as dropped aitches or Cockney diphthongs. But after all, I charitably reflected, Grandfather was a clergyman and so presumably couldn't help it. Not to mention the fact, of course, that he was dodderingly old and quite obviously completely cracked.

"Come, Eadweard, and sit by me."

I obeyed, but with ill-disguised reluctance. Sitting next to Grandfather was a privilege which I always did my best to leave to Maud, who didn't mind. Maud was lucky; she had been born with the gift of bilocation and could be in two places at once. An adult would talk to her and, looking brightly intelligent, Maud would seem to be listening, would even make appropriate noises whenever a pause in the discourse seemed to require them. "I see." "Isn't that interesting." "Yes, of course." And all the time she had been wandering at large in the private world of her daydreams. Lacking this talent, I had to suffer the consequences of always being in the same place as my body. To sit next to Grandfather was to be constrained, so far as I was concerned, to pay attention to Grandfather. He would talk embarrassingly about God, or Jesus, or not-I-but-Christ-in-me, and I had no choice but to squirm and listen. And then there was all that drivel about our fair Saxon tongue. No alien adjectives, only home-grown mark-words of suchness. And don't say "omnibus"; say "all-men's wagon." Don't talk about bicycles and perambulators; call them tway-wheels and childer-wainlets. Having to pay attention to Grandfather's nonsense was bad enough. What was still worse was having to pay attention to Grandfather himself—to the acrid smell of him, to his trembling hands and messy feeding, to the strange noises proceeding from somewhere beneath his soup-stained clerical waistcoat—long-drawn-out bubblings and sometimes for . . .

How vividly, even after more than sixty years, I remember these things! I can actually see those food stains on the clerical waistcoat, can hear that fluty voice and the obbligato of visceral noises, can feel again little Eadweard's emotions of boredom, exasperation and resentful embarrassment. But as well às living memories of a child's eye view of the tail-end of life, I have my present experience of the tail-end of life. I know at first hand the nature of that old man's world from which, across impassable gulfs, my poor grandfather believed himself to be communicating with the nine-year-old inhabitant of an incommensurably alien universe. To the uncomprehending and therefore pitiless child who once answered to my name, the tremblings and the borborygmi seemed disgusting to the point, positively, of obscenity. As for the talk about childer-wainlets and Christ-in-me, it was just foolishness and bad taste, just a symptom of senile imbecility. In fact, of course, all that my grandfather was doing then was what I—the caricature of the man whose second cousin once removed was little Eadweard—am doing today: getting ready for death and, on the side, finding diversion in an innocent intellectual hobby. My hobby and the frame of reference within which I try to practice the *ars moriendi* are not the same as his. But the differences are accidental. Essentially the Andrew Garth of 1900 and the Edward Darley of 1963 belong to the same species.

"Come, Eadweard, and sit by me."

As soon as I was seated, my grandfather started to talk about the two kinds of birthdays. Anniversaries of one's first nativity or of the second. Of being born into the world or of being born anew unto God. A man might be eighty years old by one calendar, and only three by the other.

He advanced a trembling hand, picked up his cup and very cautiously raised it to his lips. The cup wobbled, coffee slopped over the rim and rained down on the tablecloth.

I thought of that story in Grimm's Fairy Tales about the little boy who had had the bright idea of making a small wooden trough for his grandfather to feed from. My grandfather, meanwhile, was tremulously wiping his mouth.

"By that other time-lore," he said ("chronology," of course, was out of the question). "By that other time-lore I am hardly older than you are." He shook his head. "To think that one waited sixty years before allowing oneself to be born! Will *you* choose to wait so long for your true birthday? I hope not, dear boy. Oh, I hope not!"

There was a silence, broken only by the muffled trills and rumblings of a complaining stomach. In a dimension of time that was neither God's nor man's the burgeoning neoplasm was celebrating yet another of its accelerated birthdays. Christ-in-me or cancer-in-me? In the battleground of the old man's tortured body the opposing forces would soon be fighting it out. Meanwhile, uncomprehending and pitiless, little Edward heard only the rude noises and was sardonically disgusted.

There was a sound of voices and approaching footsteps. Smelling of hay and rabbits, Maud came trotting into the room. Enormous in brown tweeds, and smelling of yesterday's cigars, Cousin Hugh came striding after her.

"Many happy returns, young man."

Cousin Hugh had the voice of a drill sergeant with adenoids—loud and yet indistinct, harsh but somehow furry, a voice that always made me think of doormats, clothes brushes, hedgehogs. I forced a smile and thanked him for his good wishes. Under the black bristles of a closely clipped mustache, those very red and horribly juicy lips of his were like sea anemones.

"Nine years old today," he rasped, as he took his place at my grandfather's left. "So how many *days* old? One, two, three." He snapped his thick fingers and, when no answer was forthcoming: "Can't you even *multiply?*" he asked. "Nine times three hundred and sixty-five. Quick! One, two, three!" Another snap of the fingers. Boiling with hatred and on the brink of tears, I shook my head.

Cousin Hugh shrugged his shoulders. "Aren't children taught *anything* nowadays?" He unfolded his napkin. "It may interest you to know, Edward, that you're exactly three thousand two hundred and eight-five days old. Plus two for leap years. Which means—let me see . . . ." He took a sip of coffee. "Seventy-seven thousand eight hundred and eighty-eight hours." Then he picked up *The Times,* opened it out and disappeared into the morning's news.

Under the table, Fräulein Lili, who was sitting next to me on my right, comfortingly patted my knee. But all she said aloud was, "Eat your porridge now."

"Hours!" my grandfather was saying. "Hours." He shook his head in mournful disapproval. "Such a shame that we gave up *stound* for an outlandish word like 'hour.'" And being barred by the rules of his odd game from regretting the fact, he sadly rued that it had so fallen out. Then, addressing himself to Fräulein Lili, "Our good old Saxon *stound*," he explained, "is the self-same word, root-wise, as your own German *stund*."

Fräulein Lili raised her long-lashed eyelids, gave the old man an almost imperceptible smile and said, "How interesting." Then, turning to me, "Don't you think so, Edward?" she asked.

"Very interesting," I dutifully echoed.

My grandfather smiled with pleasure, then addressed himself to the difficult task of buttering a piece of toast.

From Fräulein Lili's side I caught an almost imperceptible whisper. "Bravo, *Heuchler!*" Could it be that *that* was what she was saying. I glanced at her; but all I saw was, averted and classically blank, the marble profile of Artemis.

"What's the news from South Africa?" my grandfather now inquired.

"Better from *our* point of view," Cousin Hugh replied "Decidedly worse from the point of view of our young pro-Boer here." Over the top of his paper he shot a challenging glance at Fräulein Lili.

Pro-Boer . . . How I hated him for pronouncing that dreadful word. And yet it was perfectly true. Fräulein Lili made no secret of her sympathy for our enemies, those incarnations of evil against which we were now crusading.

"You'll be sorry to hear," Cousin Hugh went on, "that your precious Mr. Kruger isn't doing so well."

"Isn't that what everyone expected?" Fräulein Lili mildly inquired. "After all, if little David has no sling, it's pretty obvious that Goliath will end by winning the battle."

Chivalrously, my grandfather came to her support. Fräulein Lili, he insisted, was not to be blamed for following the lead of her Kaiser.

"Not to mention the most extenuating circumstance of all," said Cousin Hugh. "Our little pro-Boer is only twenty years old and outrageously pretty. *Schon hübsch.*" Under his hogged mustache the sea anemones had contorted themselves into a leer that was at once lustful and teasing.

Fräulein Lili looked at him for a few seconds in silence, then turned to the window and began to talk about the weather.

An hour later, after the Grand Opening, I was out in the garden with my new airgun—out in a world of fantasy where I was stalking tigers, Boers, rhinoceroses, Redskins. Bang—and the charging rhino had fallen at my feet. Bang, Bang—I had killed De Wet, I had bagged my thirteenth man-eater. Tiptoeing out from behind the Wellingtonia, I saw a cock sparrow foraging among the bushes in the rose garden. "If you *must* kill something," Aunt Frances had said, when I thanked her for the airgun, "kill the pests—as many rats as you can. And sparrows. Nothing else. Do you understand?" I understood—and here was my chance, the third since I had sallied forth with my weapon. I raised the gun to my shoulder, and carefully took aim. The charging rhino was doomed. I pressed the trigger. There was a mild pop. With an agitated chirp, the sparrow flew away. "Damn!" From the heroic world of fantasy I had been precipitated, yet once more, into humiliating fact. "Hands up, De Wet!" Bang! But in fact, I gloomily reflected as I reloaded, in fact I'd been incapable even of killing a sparrow.

"Cuckoo," the wandering voice began to call—derisively, it seemed, "cuckoo, cuckoo . . ." I walked into the kitchen garden. At the sound of my feet on the gravel, a fat pigeon, strutting along the path in front of me, noisily flapped its wings and headed for the woods. I looked about me for sparrows; but the only bird I could see was a cock chaffinch among the radishes. "Get out!" I shouted—and under his breath one of the more secret Edward Darleys added a swear-word and a four-letter obscenity. The chaffinch darted off, circled the garden and settled finally on the lowest branch of an apple tree some twenty yards from where I was standing. "Cheeky little devil!" I decided to give him a good fright, raised my gun, pointed it vaguely in the direction of the apple tree and, pop! let fly. The chaffinch fluttered wildly, then closed its wings and fell like a stone.

Horror! And yet what a marvelously good shot. But I had given Aunt Frances my word of honor. . . .

My first impulse was to run away, to pretend it wasn't me, that nothing of the kind had occurred. And anyhow all I had intended was to give him a fright. What had happened was just an accident. It wasn't my fault. Nobody could say that it was I who had killed him. But in fact, in fact. . . .

I turned back and slowly walked over to the apple tree. The chaffinch was lying there on the bare ground. There was no blood, no sign of a wound; the little body was unstained, undefaced. Those tiny claws pathetically reaching reaching up toward the sky, that polished beak and the round black eye, that smooth feathery coat of many colors, wings barred with white, the gray-green cap above brown cheek and neck, the russet of the breast modulating at the throat into rose color—how strange and beautiful, how unimaginably elegant, how perfect! and mysteriously perfect! A minute ago this tiny embodiment of perfection had been a living creature. Now it was dead. I raised my hand and looked at it because it belonged to a living creature. But one day that creature would die. This moving, feeling hand would be no more than an appendage to a corpse. What *was* I? I was someone who was going to die.

Duchardy

A Wars Huxley
August 2nd
1962

One Doesn't Know

SEPTEMBER, OCTOBER, NOVEMBER. . . . From August 29, 1963, the day we arrived from Europe, to November 22, the day Aldous died, it was a slow but unrelenting diminuendo.

It is in periods of illness that it is a burden to be well known, for there is the added stress of secrecy, of trying to preserve one's privacy. To all appearances our life was the same. Aldous was writing and preparing to go on a lecture tour in the East. He always kept engagements —was loath to inconvenience people by cancelling commitments that had required so much preliminary organization. As usual, local friends and others passing through California would call up, to make plans to meet. Invitations to events of interest or requests for interviews—all the usual occurrences of our life—continued as though Aldous were well. My own life had never been so involved with the public as at this time. My book was at its peak of popularity. I had been scheduled for lectures and appearances; I received calls and letters from people in urgent need, who hoped and believed that one or two meetings with the author of a book which had already helped them were essential for the solution of an urgent problem. Since spring I had put off seeing people who had been working with me previously. I could not bring myself to cancel their appointments unless I could give them a very solid reason.

Unfortunately, there was a solid reason: Aldous was dying. Disclosing that fact might have relieved me of many obligations, but it would also have put an enormous weight on my shoulders. Friends and admirers would have pressed around us with their love and encouragement—but also, unwittingly, with their grief and hopelessness. I was afraid their feelings would affect me and rob me of that strength I was jealously keeping for Aldous.

The rumors that Aldous was dying might be picked up by reporters, and I would have had to deal with them. A famous woman reporter from Europe called only a few days before Aldous died. I had one of the most harassing telephone conversations with her I can remember. I had been avoiding her like the plague, but somehow she got me on the phone. I said that Aldous and I were leaving for the country; the doctor had ordered silence and rest for his voice because of a prolonged laryngitis, and we were leaving town this very moment. If I had recorded the conversation, it would be interesting to publish it, although no one would believe it. The woman said that she had come six thousand miles to see Huxley (of course she had come to see as many celebrities as possible, not just Aldous) and that she was not going back without interviewing him.

"But he must not speak; the doctor has ordered absolute silence," I told her.

"I will just give him a look! It will not tire him to be looked at!"

How lucky she would have felt if I had told her that Aldous was in the next room, dying! That would have been a scoop! Through her voice and her words one could, even on the telephone, feel the voraciousness of this woman—ready to use anything for a headline. Fortunately this type of journalist is rare, in either sex and in any nationality.

Of course, it was not this kind of difficulty I was trying to avoid with my silence. I did not expect, nor have I ever had, many experiences of this sort. What I wanted to avoid was other people's reactions. Many people naturally wanted to visit Aldous. If they did, they would have known it was for the last time. In spite of themselves, their emotions would have spilled over onto Aldous and me.

It is very difficult for me to receive consolation—not because of a false sense of pride, not because I want to hide my pain—but because almost involuntarily I feel, in the consoler, the projection of his own pain onto me. When we lost everything in the fire, I had strongly experienced the consoler's interpretation of my loss. Now I needed all my concentration; I did not want to be distracted by anyone's sadness, even if it were in sympathy with Aldous. I did not want to be distracted. Fortunately, there were a few friends who could help. They were told. They believed also, as I do, in the power of thought-emotion even when not expressed. The though-emotions aroused by Aldous's condition would have been of affection on one side, but, overpoweringly, on the other, of hopelessness. This hopelessness, even unspoken, would have spilled over onto Aldous and me—feelings are as solid as tangible objects. I did not want tons of hopelessness converging on us.

There was another preoccupation: how and when should I tell

Matthew, Aldous's son, about his father's condition? I wrote to him, then kept the letter for days, hoping that a change might warrant a delay. At the same time Aldous had to cancel his lecture tour in the East, where he had planned to visit his son. Aldous then decided to tell Matthew himself, and also Julian and Juliette, the reason for the cancellation.

Following are the two letters, one by Aldous and one by me, in chronological order, describing the situation:

September 14, 1963

Dear Matthew:

This is the letter I have been hoping I would not have to write—for it is to tell you that Aldous is very sick. This started in June, 1960, but it had not been considered grave until last April.

In June, 1960, Aldous had a little bump on the tongue, which, from biopsy, was found malignant. After visiting several doctors we decided that Doctor Max Cutler was the best, and still think he is. In June Aldous went to the hospital and Dr. Cutler put eight radium needles in the tongue for five days. Aldous was very weak and low for the rest of the summer, but by autumn he had completely recovered and his tongue was, and still is, in perfect condition. . . .

. . . Cutler's optimism left him completely early this April when he found in Aldous's mouth, in the jawbone, a new cancer. Not a metastasis of the original cancer—a new cancer. Again there were decisions to make; on April 23rd we came to New York to the hospital to see Dr. B. I wanted at this time to tell you the situation, but that very day, on the plane coming to New York, we read our mail. There was a letter of yours which I will never forget; it was the first one I had read where you were bubbling with confidence and happiness, the first one in which you loved the present and believed in the future. It was all too rare and beautiful to destroy. You were speaking about Judy and the children and about the new excellent job offered to you. Had your letter arrived a few minutes later, we could not have taken it in the plane with us, and probably I would have called you. We stayed in New York only a few hours, and did not call.

Again there was the choice between a vast radical deforming operation with no hope of full recovery and palliative cobalt therapy. Dr. Cutler presented this to Aldous in such a way that he remained very hopeful, and agreed to cobalt therapy for three weeks. But Dr. Cutler was no longer hopeful because of the multiple cancer. However, he suggested not to change any of our plans yet, and if it were possible at all, to take Aldous to Europe.

Aldous was very weakened this time by the cobalt therapy, in spite of all the other therapies we did to counteract this debilitation. His voice began to get low and this, he was told, was a normal reaction to radiation. Dr. Cutler is a very gentle man, and has kept Aldous' morale high. It is not difficult so far to keep from him the gravity of the situation. It seems strange that this man, who has such a clarity of mind and such knowledge, does not seem, in this case, to know or want to know.

I was not sure he could make it to Europe until the last moment. We went to Stockholm on July 28, and then Aldous went for three weeks to England. In spite of his weakness this stay in England was very pleasant for him; he went away every weekend to beautiful places with Julian and Juliette; they gave him the intellectual climate which he needed. But he looked so bad, and his voice was so low that Juliette (or Julian, I don't know which) asked a doctor friend to come to the house. Aldous took the doctor aside, explained to him the situation, and asked him not to speak about it to his relatives. He also went to a specialist in London—the first time he went to a new doctor without me—so for the first time he was bluntly told that even in case of full recovery his vocal cords would be permanently affected and his voice remain very low. I think this shocked him at the time, but a few days after he came to Italy and the two doctors we saw there reassured him in general, and told him that probably his voice would be normal again. . . .

But what is obvious is that Aldous has been getting worse since we arrived here two weeks ago. The cancer is now in the glands of the neck, growing visibly. It does not bother his swallowing or breathing, but he is very weak—although he gets up every morning, eats four meals a day, takes a walk sometimes and does a little work. Yesterday he cancelled his lecture tour in the East scheduled for October. . . .

He does not—or does not want to—realize how sick he is; never mentions death. Cutler and I go along at his speed and play it by ear. At times Aldous feels very sick—but always gives himself a different and plausible reason: the trip, the heat, now this low grade infection. He looks and sounds very sick. Throughout this Aldous has never had pain that aspirin could not control—the maximum aspirin he took has been three a day. But now, worse than any specific pain, is the general muscular discomfort and ache in the bones, which he feels specially in the morning. He has taken a sleeping pill, Amytal, these last few nights. He eats well but obviously does not assimilate. In these last two weeks he has had every day a new discomfort or pain, like shortness of breath, backache, neck ache, and general exhaustion and depression. Last night—it was the first since I have known Aldous—he said he would prefer *not* to go to a good English movie. I proposed that, because he was so dejected that I thought it might distract him for an hour or so. He may or may not write you and J. and J. I would prefer that he did tell you in his own way and time. But now I feel that you must know. *Nobody knows.* Cutler, Ginny Pfeiffer (who has helped us in every way) and the other doctors have collaborated so that no one ever heard of x-rays or operations. We have been going in and out of hospitals under an assumed name. I beg of you to keep this status quo. The publicity, as well as the sympathy and concern of friends would be more exhausting and unbearable items for us both.

Please write or phone me here in my studio. Here I can speak freely; we are, more than anything else, taking care of Aldous' morale, and we don't want to upset in any way the protection that somehow Aldous himself has built. Cutler has been a remarkable psychologist with Aldous, for, without ever lying to him, he has managed never to say anything brutal. Maybe he can do this because he also loves Aldous.

> Love to you and Judy
> Affectionately
> Laura

California 29.ix.63

Dearest Julian and Juliette,

You must be back from Africa, I imagine, by now—but meanwhile Africa has come to us, with a vengeance, in a frightful heat wave with temperatures day after day of 105 and 80 degree nights. In my own case meteorology has been compounded by a spell of ill health, due to the after effects of a long course of radiation which I had to take this spring. I hadn't told you of this trouble before, since it hadn't seriously interfered with my activities and there seemed to be no point in spreading unnecessary apprehensions. It started in 1960, with a malignant tumour on the tongue. The first surgeon I was sent to wanted to cut out half the tongue and leave me more or less speechless. I went from him to my old friend, Max Cutler. . . . Cutler recommended treatment with radium needles and so did the Professors of Radiology and Surgery at the U of Cal Medical Centre at San Francisco, whom I consulted. I took the treatment in the early summer of sixty, and it was remarkably successful. The tumour on the tongue was knocked out and has shown no signs of returning. However, as generally happens in these cases, the lymph glands of the neck became involved. I had one taken out in sixty-two, and this spring another mass appeared. This was subjected to twenty-five exposures to radioactive cobalt, an extremely exhausting treatment from which I was just recovering when at last I was able to make the trip to Stockholm and London. Since my return there has been a flare-up of secondary inflammation, to which tissues weakened by radiation are peculiarly liable, often after considerable intervals. Result: I have had to cancel my lecture tour, much to Mr. ————'s distress. (Incidentally, he hoped that you, Julian, might take over some of my cancelled engagements; but I told him I thought this wouldn't be feasible for you at this time. However he still may ask you.) Another handicap is my persistent hoarseness, due to the nerve that supplies the right-hand vocal cord having been knocked out either by an infiltration of the malignancy, or by the radiation. I hope this hoarseness may be only temporary, but rather fear that I may carry it to the grave.

What the future holds, one doesn't know. In general these malignancies in the neck and head don't do much metastasizing. Meanwhile I am trying to build up resistance with the combination of a treatment which has proved rather successful at the University of Montreal and the U of Manila—the only institutions where it has been tried out over a period of years—and which has been elaborated upon by Professor Guidetti, of the University of Turin, who has read papers on his work at the two last International Cancer Congresses, at Buenos Aires and Moscow. I saw Guidetti while in Turin and was impressed by some of his case histories, and with Cutler's approval we are carrying out his treatment here. When this damned inflammation dies down, which it may be expected to do in a few weeks, I hope to get back to regular work. For the present I am functioning at only a fraction of normal capacity.

Much love to you both from both of us.

Ever your affectionate,
Aldous.

The Polish Rider

In a simple whitewashed bedroom overlooking a large expanse of still wild Hollywood hills, Aldous worked from the autumn of 1961—and there two years later he died.

There were two pictures on the walls. Over his bed a refreshingly naked, lovely girl of about fifteen bending down to dry her feet (Dégas's "After the Bath"). The other, also a reproduction, was Rembrandt's "The Polish Rider," one of Aldous's favorite pictures.

In those last painful days there was very little that gave Aldous any pleasure. He could not listen much to music, but he was still interested in books and in news reports and Ginny read to him every day. It was his marvelous capacity to *listen* that, more than anything else, made those last weeks bearable—for, even when in great discomfort, he was able to direct his attention to what was read to him and away from his pain. Also one of the techniques of *The Art of Seeing* helped him especially at this time. It is one of the simplest and most effective of the imagination techniques: with the mind's eye one looks at a white dot on a deep black background—the dot swings with a small pendulum movement. This simple technique, which Aldous had used for years to improve his eyes, now helped him to go to sleep.

Aldous still enjoyed looking at things, if they were near and in strong light. One morning I thought he might enjoy looking at "The Polish Rider." I also hoped that by means of this picture I would have an opportunity to tell him how much he had given to me during our nine years together, the many new, beautiful, and significant experiences I had lived through and with him. One of these was a new and deeper way of seeing paintings. By reminding him casually of this, one of his many gifts to me, I might find a way of telling him what was in my mind: "I want you to be sure to know, before you go, that this piece of life we had together has been a blessing."

Such a simple thing—but how to say it? Not with words, of course, but with feelings and acts. The reason I wanted a verbal reinforcement just then was that a few days before he had said dejectedly, "This illness, darling—this is the very last thing I wanted you to have to put up with."

During the last weeks of his life, Aldous's mind was extraordinarily active, and since he was too weak to make notes he was relieved to have a small tape recorder near his bed. The following conversation, which took place while we were looking at "The Polish Rider," as well as the dialogue in the following chapters, are all verbatim transcriptions. The few words spoken are interrupted by long silences, dreadful spells of coughing, the noise of removing the picture from the wall, propping up the bed.

Laura:. . . JUST THAT MOMENT OF SUNSET—IT IS SUNSET, ISN'T IT?
Aldous (very slowly): I SUPPOSE SUNSET OR SUNRISE.

Even in this small detail one can see how our minds were working. Aldous, who was dying, was not choosing to see a sunset in that painting—indeed, it might be a sunset or a sunrise—while I, instead, was superimposing my own crepuscular feeling on the painting.

Laura: I LIKE THE RELATIONSHIP BETWEEN THE HORSE AND THE MAN;
   IT SEEMS TO ME THE PERFECT RELATIONSHIP BETWEEN TWO PEOPLE
   OF A DIFFERENT SPECIES.
Aldous: THE GREAT CONFIDENCE OF THE MAN IS SO WONDERFUL, ISN'T
   IT?

What revealing, nostalgic feeling there was in that remark! Weak and ill, Aldous acutely felt deprived of confidence. It was not only the art of Rembrandt that he was admiring today in this particular painting; it was also the character of the subject. "The Polish Rider" represents a young, confident cavalier, daring and romantic. How far this was from Aldous's present state! Aldous always was deeply romantic at heart, although he would not often manifest this aspect of himself publicly. He had a kind of longing admiration for those who could lead a life of adventure and risk. Besides, "The Polish Rider" was associated with a romantic meeting we had in New York in the summer of 1955. I don't know whether Aldous was consciously thinking of that. I was. Aldous had been passing the summer vacation in Connecticut with his son and his family. He wrote me almost every day. I wish I had the letter asking me to go to New York for a week's vacation with him; only he could have written it so tactfully and yet so straightforwardly as far as details were concerned, so inviting and yet so self-effacing.

New York was exhaustingly torrid and humid—but our own inner meteorology, as Aldous liked to say, was good. It was then that I saw paintings in a way I never had before. Aldous took me to the Frick collection. He knew each painting in it, and its location. This was true not only of this small museum; it was also true of most of the great galleries in Europe and America. I remember an autumn day in the Louvre. We had been seeing paintings for quite a while. Exhausted, I felt like a vignette in *The New Yorker:* sitting in the middle of the vast cold hall, no longer capable of enjoying the overpowering abundance of masterpieces, looking instead only at my shoes, which I was hopelessly trying to stretch with my bare hands. All the while Aldous, fresh as though we had just started out, his open raincoat fluttering about, was running, actually running, from one painting to another, as if he were greeting old friends and he did not want to miss any of them—occasionally checking a detail with his enlarging lens. Then he suddenly stopped, surprised, "This painting used to be on the west wall; I wonder why they moved it."

That summer day in New York he had taken me leisurely from one painting to another, saying so little—almost nothing—but what he said illuminated the pictures. As Kenneth Clark wrote, "Aldous had an astonishing faculty for seeing what an artist really meant."[1]

Before I had gone to New York, Aldous had sent me a postcard reproduction of "The Polish Rider." Now at the Frick Museum we were looking at the original. Leisurely and casually he would show me a line here, a certain stroke there, a point of light and shadow. Looking at Bellini's "St. Francis in Ecstasy," he commented on the many ways to achieve ecstasy—through abstinence, fast, and solitary confinement; through plants, herbs, or their chemical equivalent; through disciplines of concentration, hypnosis, meditation; through the complete expression of love. When we looked at "The Polish Rider" he called my attention to small points of light which he said gave a magic quality to Rembrandt's paintings. Sometimes he would tell me a funny story about a painting: "Do you know why the Gioconda has that mysterious smile? Leonardo had engaged a young man to tell her dirty stories during the sittings . . . she really wanted to laugh but had to contain herself and only smile. . . ."

Now, nine years later, these memories engulfed me as we looked at

---

[1] *Aldous Huxley, 1894-1963.* A memorial volume (Harper & Row, 1965).

"The Polish Rider"—for the last time.

Laura: THAT WAS THE FIRST TIME I REALLY SAW PICTURES—WHEN WE
WENT TO THE FRICK MUSEUM: I REALLY NEVER HAD BEFORE, I
REALIZE . . .

And there is some mumbling on the tape—good heavens! was that
all I could say? I wanted to tell him so much more—for instance, about
his beautiful gesture that first evening in New York. I had arrived in the
afternoon and we had gone to an early dinner at a restaurant on the
West Side. It was still closed, and we walked up and down the sidewalk, talking. I was complaining about myself—how little I achieved in
spite of hard work. I was elaborating on this, trying to prove to him that
I really had achieved very little in comparison to the amount of work I
put into my varied careers. He listened intently, then abruptly he
stopped walking. "But what do you mean?" he exclaimed. "What you
have accomplished is this," and made a vague gesture toward me.
"This . . . what?" I did not understand.
Aldous was silent for a moment; he was trying to convey something
to me that was not easy to convey. I was standing in front of him,
completely attentive.
Then Aldous made a beautiful gesture, a creative circular gesture
that included my whole person and whatever emanates from it. As his
long arms returned to their normal position, he said, with enormous
conviction and definition: "This—*what you are.*"
I understood, to a point, what he meant then; I understood increasingly in the following years. Aldous was expressing the importance of
being—of what you are. He did not depreciate material accomplish-
ment and success, but, as I realized more and more, he meant that the
most important achievement in life is to be "the best of what we are."
"What is man for?" He often started out with that question in his
lecture[2] on human potentialities. Then he would answer his own
question: "As an act of faith, and I think it is an act of faith which is
shared by most people who are concerned with human decency and
liberty, I believe that man is here for the purpose of realizing as much
as possible of his desirable potentialities within a stable and yet elastic
society."
He was not giving me a lecture that evening—or any other evening.
Nothing could have been more unlike a lecture than that vast, princely
gesture and those simple words: "This—*what you are.*"

[2] See footnote, p. 141.

Another day, during the same week, we went to the Metropolitan Museum and had lunch there. I remember it because it was one of the few times Aldous spoke about Maria. Lunch was served in a gallery with a glass roof. Aldous looked pale in the cold and greenish light. The large potted plants gave to the place the feeling of a winter garden, deserted and quiet. Something moved Aldous to speak about the previous summer when he had been traveling with Maria: "I thought she was so well then—you remember when we went to Tarquinia. She looked and felt well." I said nothing, but remembered how my heart sank when I saw her. She did not look well to me, but perhaps, in comparison, she looked well to Aldous. After that week in Rome they had gone to Paris, where Maria began to have pain and the doctor advised them to return home immediately. Even after Maria was given another course of X rays and felt wretchedly sick with nausea and discomfort, Aldous had not realized that the end was near. When the doctor told him, only a very few days before the end, that there was nothing more to be done, the news had come as a shock to him. "You see, I did not realize Maria was dying . . ."

And now, does he know that *he* is dying? He had realized late that she was dying—but in time to prepare himself and her for that last experience together. How late will be time enough for him to know, to realize, to experience? Should I tell him now, while looking at "The Polish Rider"? We hardly ever spoke about the past. He would understand immediately what I meant if now I spoke about that distant summer in New York, if I spoke of the feeling of adventure and romanticism and mystery with which our lives had been colored—if I could tell him that in many ways he *was* that adventurous Polish Rider he so admired—if I could tell him. . .

"Aldous, I want to tell you. . . ."

Suddenly he was seized by violent coughing.

I gave him oxygen.

The moment, the only moment, was gone.

Defeated, I put "The Polish Rider" back on the wall.

The Almost Boundless Nature
of Ego-Ambition

ALDOUS AND I would often tell each other our dreams at breakfast. We would not interpret much, but rather speak about the feeling of the dream. Sometimes Aldous would joke about the different interpretations that might be made by the well-known "oracles," or schools of psychology. Aldous's view was that not *all* dreams are of great significance—he would say that since the brain has some thirteen billion cells, and since the number of intercellular connections made every second is staggering, the number of possible combinations is infinite. In an immense telephone circuit the wires sometimes get crossed, resulting in an accidental combination; the same can happen to the dreamer, due to circumstances independent of himself. However, Aldous did not underestimate the dreaming faculty. We recounted our dreams because one of the best ways to induce dreams is to give attention to dreams. Now that we were living with Ginny and her children, we spoke even more freely about dreams to encourage the children to do so, too. We let them tell us their dreams at breakfast, not interrupting or commenting much, but showing approval when they remembered what they dreamed.

I have only one letter of Aldous's telling me about a dream. At the end of May 1962, Aldous and I went to New York. He was to give a talk and receive a medal from the American Academy of Arts and Letters, and I was to meet my publisher and discuss my book with him.

After a week in New York we went to the airport together but flew in opposite directions: Aldous went to Berkeley, and I flew to Italy for rest and inspiration before starting the ardous and, for me, new job of finishing *You Are Not the Target* and getting it ready for publication.

We both would return to Los Angeles at the same time twelve days later.

In Italy I went to Siena, a magic place, for three days, and then returned to my family in Turin. There I found Aldous's letter.

31.V.62

How are you, my darling?

At this end of the world another problem has arisen. I noted, just after getting back from New York, that a gland on the right side of my neck was swollen and tender. Cutler went over my neck very carefully and concluded that the swelling might be due to some kind of local infection. If so, it should go down by June 12th, when he wants to see me again. If it hasn't gone down by then, he suggests taking the gland out and, if a biopsy shows that the swelling is due to a metastasis, perhaps take out two or three other smaller glands near by. This would involve relatively minor surgery. Fortunately this kind of metastasis involves only the local glands and has almost no tendency, unless it is left to develop for a long time, to spread to other areas.

I had a very unpleasant dream during the night when I first noticed the swollen gland—a dream about some nameless and faceless person who was going to kill me, and who kept explaining that it really wouldn't hurt, provided it was done in the right way and in the right place—and he kept making preparations and leading me from one room to another. So the unconscious evidently got a shock! It is a relief to know that, even at the worst, it is not, so Cutler says—really serious. And meanwhile—perhaps just *because* death seems to have taken a step nearer—everything seems more and more beautiful, the leaves on the trees, the flowers, the sky, the green unwrinkled sea as we flew over it this afternoon, and my memories of you and all the people I have loved or felt concerned about.

I went yesterday to see an extraordinary exhibition of Chinese paintings at the De Young Museum in San Francisco—200 pictures from 900 AD to 1700, lent by Chiang Kai Shek, who took the treasures with him when he retreated to Formosa. Such marvels—but unfortunately very hard to see, as they were under glass and the glass was full of reflections. Good-by my love. Be well and happy and don't feel too concerned about this business of mine. It is more of a nuisance than a threat. Give my love to everyone.

Yours,

A.

The gland was taken out on July 4, 1962. Aldous was in the hospital only two days. He did not suffer. The gland was malignant, but Dr. Cutler reassured me that he was confident Aldous would get well.

In the period just preceding his death, I felt that Aldous's dreams were more meaningful than ever before. In those days more and more urgent were the questions. Did Aldous know that the end was near? Why did he not speak of it? Should I say something about it?

I had given him so many openings. One was to read to him the draft for *The Psychedelic Experience*[1] by Doctors Leary, Metzner, and Alpert. This book is an instructional manual, based on the Tibetan Book of the Dead, on how to guide a person through a psychedelic session. The instructions given to the aspirant to a higher life are the same as those given to the dying person: the aspirant is seeking freedom from compulsive and ego-centered passions and desires; the dying one is losing the body through which passions and desires are expressed. Both are urged and helped to experience a state of egoless freedom and to accept love as "the primary and fundamental cosmic fact." As we read it, it would have been natural for Aldous to make some remark about death. Instead he ignored any personal application and spoke only about how these techniques could be used for people who were not dying *bodily,* but dying only to their *ego.* He discussed what would be the best way to end the session, to help people bring back and apply to their daily life the "gratuitous grace" they had just been given.

There are two diametrically opposite views about dying. One is the the best way is to go without knowing it, to slip away—hopefully when sleeping. The other view—less prevalent but more spiritually enlightened—is that one should die as aware and clear-minded as possible; that death is one of the great adventures of life, and one should not miss it or block it by unconsciousness. In this view, it is thought that the future life of the "soul" or "consciousness" or "mind" (whatever word one uses for that which pervades the body and gives it life) is influenced to a great extent by the thoughts and feelings at the moment of death.

Aldous believed in the latter. I was the natural one to help him—but how could I do it if we did not speak about it now, when death seemed around the corner? The few people acquainted with the situation had different reactions.

"It's wonderful that he is not speaking about death; that's the best thing that could happen; he does not realize how sick he is," some of them said. But others, who knew Aldous well, were as worried as I was. One of them was Ginny.

"He trusts you so completely," she reminded me, "he certainly would not expect you to let him go without knowing—he relies on you for that."

[1] University Books, 1964.

Aldous was not trying to spare me by pretending not to know the seriousness of his condition, for he could have discussed it with Ginny or some other person. There were two possible explanations of the fact that seemingly he did not expect death so soon: one was the organic protection that is present in many people when they near death; the other was his ingrained philosophy: "Sufficient unto the day is the evil thereof." This was a principle he had cultivated by constant practice. It had sustained him when Maria was dying; it sustained him when he was dying. But during those last weeks I did not fully realize that he was, once again, practicing what he preached: to live here and now, whether you were to die tomorrow or in a hundred years! In my trepidation that is might indeed be tomorrow, I was constantly alert to any opening from him on the subject of death—feelings, ideas, anything.

The essence of Aldous's life, probably of the life of any creative human being, is the dual capacity to be receptive, to be open to *im*-pression, and at the same time to be capable, through talent, emotions, intelligence, work, and discipline, of *ex*-pression. When these two activities are in balance, there is usually also a balance in the individual. I believe that this was the source of Aldous's basic strength: He was wholly open to impressions, and these impressions were transformed into artistic ex-pressions. During the summer preceding his death, the major reason for his depression was the feeling of not being able to create, to express. Of the *im*-pression/*ex*-pression activity, Aldous was well aware; he often spoke about his good luck in being able to make a living with his favorite occupation. How often he would help people, financially or otherwise, simply because he felt sorry for someone obliged to make his living at something he disliked or even hated!

But now this man, for whom expression at a high level had been as natural as breathing, was physically unable to write and at times barely able to speak—yet his mind was active and there was little doubt that it was painful for him to keep this effervescence within, and muted.

For me there were two major problems. One was that discussing his dreams, ideas, feelings should not be made momentous, should arise smoothly and naturally. The other was that the slightest pressure discouraged Aldous by making him realize even more how "feeble" (that is the word he often used) he was.

In the week preceding his death his mind was more than usually active. He was taking a small amount of one of the drugs which doctors prescribe in cases of discomfort and pain, called Dilaudid. As usual, Aldous took the minimum dosage. This drug, not one of the psychedelic group, put him to sleep, but it also stimulated areas of consciousness not usually brought to the surface.

Reporting one's own dreams is difficult enough; in reporting another's dreams, it is almost certain that we distort them. Even with the utmost honesty and good will, I could not recount Aldous's dreams relying only on my memory. But because he intended to take notes for future writing, the tape recorder was near his bed and these dreams are in his own words. His ability to express himself even when he had barely the strength to breathe was again remarkable and a great help. Yet only a fraction of the atmosphere of these dialogues comes through the printed word. For on the tape one hears and feels the effort of speaking, the breathing, as loud as the words themselves, the long pauses, the hissing of the oxygen. Hearing the tape re-creates the whole situation—the room, by now like a hospital room; the smell of disinfectant and medicaments, the bandage on the right side of his chin, the wasted body in the orthopedic bed.

I tried to find questions that would stimulate the expression of what he was experiencing—questions to lead him on, but not to press him. The questions had to be phrased in such a way as not to reveal *my* anxiety but to bring forth *his* thinking. They were asked between his sipping of a spoonful of orange juice, having the slant of the bed changed, taking a pill, and sinking into exhaustion.

On this tape there is some talk about reading the second part of his essay "Shakespeare and Religion." Then:

Laura: I THOUGHT YOU MIGHT REPEAT WHAT YOU SAID IN THE MORNING WHEN YOU WOKE UP—SO THAT YOU WOULD BE SURE TO HAVE IT.
Aldous (astonished): REPEAT WHAT, DARLING?
Laura: ABOUT THE DREAM . . .

It was now eleven o'clock in the morning of November 19. About six o'clock that morning Aldous had told me his dreams, and now I was trying to bring them back to his consciousness.

Laura (speaking in a vague uncertain manner): IS IT ENOUGH—WHAT YOU HAVE . . .?

I was vague on purpose; I wanted Aldous to help *me* remember.

Aldous (mumbling): I DON'T KNOW . . . IS ENOUGH . . . BUT YOU CAN'T . . . IT IS THE EXACT QUALITY OF THE THING . . . (Almost suddenly, the words become more alive and defined.) I REMEMBER FEELING SO EXTRAORDINARILY EXCITED.

A few days away from death, yet in those last days this remark is repeated several times, alternately with his saying how completely exhausted he was. The voice is low but the words are definite.

Aldous: . . . FEELING SO EXTRAORDINARILY EXCITED BECAUSE IN SOME
  SENSE, I WAS LIVING THE THING OVER, BUT PRACTICALLY SIMUL-
  TANEOUSLY . . . THAT I WAS LIVING WHAT I HAD BEEN THROUGH IN
  SLEEP, AND IT WAS STILL GOING ON . . . THIS WAS THE MARVEL OF
  THE THING. BUT EXACTLY WHAT I WAS DREAMING OF I DON'T KNOW
  BECAUSE I WAS QUITE INCOHERENT.
Laura: YOU WERE NOT INCOHERENT WHEN I SPOKE TO YOU.
Aldous: NO, BUT I NEVER WENT INTO DETAILS ABOUT WHAT IT IS . . . I
  DON'T THINK I EVEN KNEW THEN.
Laura: WELL, WHEN I CAME AT TWO O'CLOCK YOU WERE SPEAKING
  ABOUT. . .

There was great hesitation in my words; first, because I wasn't sure of what to say and, secondly, because I hoped Aldous would fill in my hesitation.

Laura: WHEN I CAME IN THE NIGHT YOU SEEMED TO HAVE SOME FUNNY
  DISCOVERY, BUT I COULDN'T GET WHAT YOU WERE TALKING ABOUT.
Aldous: WELL, THERE ARE TWO DISCOVERIES. (Aldous is speaking
  slowly and low, but with a determined tone.) ONE IS THAT PART OF
  MY ENTHUSIASM FOR DELAUDID CONSISTS IN THE FACT THAT FOR
  SOME EXTRAORDINARY REASON I WAS LIVING UNDER THE ILLUSION
  THAT THE SECOND HALF OF EACH NIGHT, WHEN I GOT MY DELAUDID,
  I WAS SOMEHOW BEING CARRIED AROUND IN A JET PLANE, AND
  AND THAT I CAME IN, IN THE MORNING, FEELING THIS STRANGE AND
  WONDERFUL FEELING OF ELATION. . . .

"Feeling this strange and wonderful feeling of elation." No one could have imagined, seeing Aldous then, that he could feel elation.

Aldous: NOW WHY SHOULD I HAVE THOUGHT THAT?

As a child would ask: "Why are the stars in heaven?" so would Aldous ask unanswerable questions in an astonished enchanting way, his whole tone an innocent, gigantic question mark.

Aldous: SUDDENLY I REALIZE THAT I HAD BEEN LYING IN BED ALL THE
  TIME.
Laura: OH, BUT YOU TOOK IT FOR GRANTED THAT YOU WERE BEING

CARRIED AROUND IN A JET PLANE . . . BECAUSE YOU NEVER MEN-
TIONED IT. IT WAS SO NATURAL TO YOU, PROBABLY, THAT YOU
NEVER MENTIONED . . .
Aldous: YES—SOMEHOW I ASSUMED THAT THE TWO FORMS OF EXIS-
TENCE WERE DIFFERENT . . . (Heavy coughing registered on the
tape. Long pause.)
Laura: YOU KNOW, YOU DIDN'T HAVE ANY DILAUDID LAST NIGHT—
YOU DIDN'T SEEM TO NEED IT. IS IT THEN YOU DISCOVERED THAT
THE TWO SIDES OF THE NIGHT WERE OCCUPIED IN A DIFFERENT
WAY? (Pause. Heavy breathing.) AND WHAT ABOUT THE OTHER DIS-
COVERY?
Aldous: WELL, THE OTHER DISCOVERY WAS VERY ODD INDEED.

Here Aldous's voice took that special tone characteristic of him
when he was fascinated and amazed. "Very odd indeed" is said in a
smiling whisper, a bit awed and a bit amused, a delight to hear.

Aldous: IT SUDDENLY DAWNED UPON ME THAT THAT'S WHAT I HAD
BEEN THINKING.
Laura: THAT YOU HAD ONE EXISTENCE HERE AND ONE EXISTENCE
SOMEWHERE ELSE?
Aldous (in a low voice and with a sense of wonder): IT SHOWS THE
ALMOST BOUNDLESS NATURE . . .
Laura: THE WHICH NATURE?
Aldous: THE ALMOST BOUNDLESS NATURE OF THE EGO-AMBITION. I
DREAMED, IT MUST HAVE BEEN TWO NIGHTS AGO . . .

Here there is a violent attack of coughing. Long silence—but the
thought is in the air; there was no need of questioning. I knew that as
soon as he had enough breath he would continue. He did, in a tone full
of wonder.

Aldous: . . . THAT IN SOME WAY I WAS IN A POSITION TO MAKE AN ABSO-
LUTE . . . COSMIC GIFT TO THE WORLD. I DON'T EXACTLY KNOW
HOW—BUT ANYHOW IN DOING THIS I HAD BEEN SORT OF FLYING
AROUND IN IMMENSE SPACES—AND I HAD BEEN LOOKING IN AT
WINDOWS AND HELPING PEOPLE, AND THAT SOME [long pause, and
then great emphasis on the next four words] VAST ACT OF
BENEVOLENCE WAS GOING TO BE DONE, IN WHICH I SHOULD HAVE
THE SORT OF STAR ROLE. . . .
Laura: BUT HOW BEAUTIFUL! THAT MUST HAVE GIVEN YOU A BEAUTI-
FUL FEELING. . . .

Aldous: . . . AND THEN PEOPLE WERE SAYING, WELL, THIS MUST BE A DRESS REHEARSAL REALLY, AND WE'LL GET DOWN TO THE REAL THING ANOTHER TIME.

Laura: THE PEOPLE YOU WERE SEEING THROUGH THE WINDOWS?

Aldous: WELL, I WASN'T SEEING ANYBODY—THIS WAS JUST GOING ON IN SOME STRANGE WAY . . . (Another dark attack of coughing, sounding as though it could be the last. Long silence. Hissing of oxygen tank.)

Laura: DID IT LAST A LONG TIME?

Aldous: NO. AND THEN THE NEXT NIGHT—AT LEAST I THINK IT WAS— IT IS VERY DIFFICULT FOR ME TO KEEP THE CURRENT OF THESE THINGS—I KEPT SAYING "WHEN DO WE START?" AND PEOPLE JUST LAUGHED.

Laura: WAS IT WHEN YOU SAID, "WHEN ARE WE GOING TO START THIS ASCENSION IN A BALLOON?"

Aldous: NO—WHEN ARE WE GOING TO START THIS ENORMOUS COSMIC WORK. . . .

Laura: TO WHOM DID YOU SAY IT?

Aldous: I DON'T KNOW TO WHOM IT WAS. BUT IT WAS A SORT OF GENERAL QUESTION, THE ANSWER TO WHICH WAS ALWAYS SHRUGGING THE SHOULDER AND A LAUGH. AND . . . THIS WHOLE THING HAS BEEN VERY STRANGE BECAUSE IN A WAY IT WAS VERY GOOD—BUT IN A WAY IT WAS ABSOLUTELY TERRIFYING, SHOWING THAT WHEN ONE THINKS ONE'S GOT BEYOND ONESELF, ONE HASN'T.

Laura: YES.

Aldous: AND I WAS ALWAYS SORT OF BUMPING MY HEAD AGAINST WALLS—IN AN ATTEMPT TO GET OUT AND DO THESE THINGS.

Laura: WOULD THE THING GO ON IN A TIMELESS WAY? OR DID YOU KNOW IT WAS ALL NIGHT? OR WHAT?

Aldous: WELL, IN THE NATURE OF DREAMS, NATURALLY, THESE THINGS . . .

Laura: WHAT KIND OF FEELING WOULD YOU WAKE UP WITH?

Aldous: WELL, I BEGAN WITH THIS MARVELOUS SENSE OF THIS COSMIC GIFT, AND THEN ENDED UP WITH A RUEFUL SENSE THAT ONE CAN BE DECEIVED—BUT NEVERTHELESS ONE MUST GO ON. (The voice is even lower now.) BUT IT WAS VERY IMPORTANT TO FIND THE TRUTH OF THE MATTER. (Pause. Almost inaudibly.) I'D LIKE SOME MORE OXYGEN, DARLING. (Long pause.)

Laura: IT SOUNDS AS THOUGH IT WERE SIMILAR TO AN LSD INSIGHT.

Aldous: IT WAS AN INSIGHT, BUT AT THE SAME TIME THE MOST DANGEROUS OF ERRORS.

Laura: THE MOST DANGEROUS OF ERRORS?

Aldous: YES.

Laura: IN WHICH WAY?

Aldous: INASMUCH AS ONE WAS WORSHIPPING ONESELF. (Long pause.)

Laura: HOW DID THIS COME TO YOUR MIND NOW? WE DIDN'T SPEAK ABOUT IT.

Aldous: NO, WE DIDN'T. THESE THINGS HAVE COME AS A SORT OF SERIES OF ENLIGHTENMENTS INTO WHAT I HAVE BEEN TALKING ABOUT AND FEELING IN THESE LAST DAYS.

Laura: LAST NIGHT, WHEN I CAME, I THINK YOU MUST HAVE HAD A DREAM ABOUT—YOU SPOKE ABOUT THE "BALLOON ASCENSION."

Aldous: YES. WELL, THIS WAS PART OF IT—THAT WE WERE INSIDE THIS SPACE AND WANTED TO GET OUT, AND THAT THIS HAD ALL BEEN PREPARED FOR IN SOME WAY.

Laura: IT WAS VERY REAL TO YOU BECAUSE WHEN I DID NOT—YOU KNOW—REACT—YOU SAID, "WELL, ONE OF US MUST BE MAD." REMEMBER?

Aldous: I DON'T REMEMBER.

Laura: YOU SAID, "WHEN DO WE START THIS BALLOON ASCENSION?" DO YOU REMEMBER?

Aldous: I VAGUELY REMEMBER THAT.

Laura: WAS THERE A FEELING OF DIFFERENT SPACES INTO WHICH WE WOULD GO?

Aldous: NO. NO, THE SENSE WAS THAT I HAD SORT OF PROPHESIED TO MYSELF OF GOING OUT INTO UNIVERSAL SPACE, BUT IN FACT WAS STILL INSIDE AN ENORMOUS SORT OF AVIARY—AN ENCLOSED THING.

Laura: INSIDE WHAT?

Aldous: AN AVIARY.

Laura: AN AVIARY! OH, I SEE—THAT'S VERY INTERESTING! THAT'S PROBABLY WHAT WE ARE IN, NO?

Aldous: YES, I KNOW. BUT THE POINT IS—IT'S VERY INTERESTING TO SEE HOW EASY IT WOULD BE TO SUCCUMB TO A COMPLETELY FALSE REVELATION.

Laura: OH, I SEE. YOU MEAN THE DANGER OF REVELATION: YOU MEAN YOU COULD TAKE THIS TOO SERIOUSLY?

Aldous: YOU CERTAINLY COULD.

Laura: WELL, CAN YOU TAKE IT, IN PART, SERIOUSLY?

Aldous: OH, YES! ONE CAN SEE WHAT IS GOOD IN IT, AND WHAT IS BAD.

Laura: DO YOU WANT SOME MORE OXYGEN?

Aldous: NOT FOR THE MOMENT. (Cough. Pause.)

Laura: WELL, THEN WHEN YOU ARE NOT UNCOMFORTABLE, IT'S RATHER INTERESTING WHAT YOU ARE GOING THROUGH, ISN'T IT?

Aldous (with low voice, but with extreme definition): YES . . . VERY.

Aldous giving a commencement address

Our Business Is to Wake Up

ALDOUS WAS AS completely detached from his past books as he was dedicated to his current writing.

He usually had to correct his work several times. I don't remember his ever being much worried about essays or preparing for lectures, but when he was writing *Island* he was "stuck" a few times. Once or twice he left that novel and wrote something else—for instance, *Brave New World Revisited*. This type of writing he did with ease and enjoyment. *Island* was difficult: its message could have been conveyed in a form other than a novel, but Aldous felt that by fusing the message with a story, he would reach a larger and more varied audience.

When Aldous would occasionally have a peculiarly gloomy and pensive look for no obvious reason, I learned that often that expression indicated a writing problem. As far as I know, Aldous did not often discuss his writing with friends. I remember one time, when speaking with a small group of friends about frustration in writing, Aldous said, "A man is alone with his problem." Making a general statement which really represents a personal problem is something most of us do often—but this was one of the very rare instances when Aldous did so. He was speaking about himself.

How well I understand, now, this being alone with a writing problem! Evidently this can happen to an experienced writer as well as to one, like me, for whom reading and writing are unusual activities; it was only in 1960 that I began taking notes and then wrote a book. Neither did I have the habit of reading. For a major part of my life I was a concert violinist and I had to concentrate my energy on practicing or on activities related to violin playing. Reading was a kind of luxury that I could allow myself only rarely, like going to a masked ball. My first thought when I would see Aldous reading in the morning was to wonder why he wasn't doing something more useful with that best time of the day. How amused Aldous had been once when I asked him that!

Aldous would sometimes joke about my disinclination to read. On one of my first visits to him after Maria's death, I told him about my nonreading habits and asked him which one of his books he would recommend that I read; I had read only three or four. Now I wished to know, from him, which was his most important novel. He liked *Time Must Have a Stop;* however, *Point Counter Point,* he added with absolute detachment and a slightly amused tone, "was thought to be somewhat important as a picture of the English society of that time." He went in the other room and brought a copy of *Point Counter Point.*

"Oh, how long!" I said, without thinking.

Aldous laughed. "But you don't *have* to read it."

"Yes, yes, I must," I said with the determination of a martyr.

And I did. I found it very depressing and told Aldous that it was now his responsibility to cheer me up.

In any case, it was pleasant to have Aldous take care, so lovingly, of my ignorance. He would tell me about anything he had read in the scientific field which was new or of special interest for my work. Sometimes he would read to me a beautiful passage or give me a quotation which would enhance what I was writing.

His system of reading was extremely helpful, not only for him but for me also. Aldous always read with a pen—he would mark passages which were of special importance, sometimes comment on them with a few words on the page itself, then at the end of the book note the subject and the page. For instance, on the two back pages of *The Way of Zen* by Alan Watts, Aldous has about thirty entries. Picking one at random: "29, humanness better than righteousness."

On page 29 of the text, the following paragraph is marked:

It was a basic Confucian principle that "it is man who makes truth great, not truth which makes man great." For this reason "humanness" or "human heartedness" was always felt to be superior to "righteousness," since man himself is greater than any idea which he may invent. There are times when men's passions are much more trustworthy than their principle. Since opposed principles, or ideologies, are irreconcilable, wars fought over principle will be wars of mutual annihilation.

Unfortunately, I have now very few books marked in this way. The fire destroyed his 4,000 volumes, most of which contained these private reference annotations.

On a melancholy Sunday of that last November of his life, a lifelong friend brought Aldous a copy of his latest book, which he had inscribed to Aldous. After his friend left, I was looking at the new volume. Books are to me a never ending source of wonder and pleasure—miraculous capsules in which almost everything can be found. I love them as objects. The feel of the paper and the type of print, the weight of a book and its smell, the design and color and quality of jacket are to me intriguing and fascinating. A wall filled with books is a wall of magic.

On this autumnal afternoon, I was standing near Aldous's bed with the new book in my hand, praising it—it was beautifully proportioned, a pleasure to touch and admire. I was talking about it, trying, I think, to prevent Aldous from knowing what I was seeing in his deadly pale face, in his destroyed body. I thought he might like to speak about this book. It was a very learned one, which would have been difficult for me to read. I wanted to cheer up Aldous—or at least try.

"This is a very beautiful book, Aldous," I said. "It probably is very good."

"Don't be so sure"—almost cavernously, without a trace of his usual humor, he answered.

"Well, I think I am going to read it." I was speaking very lightly; I wanted to introduce a facetious note, and the subject of my reading had been one. "Aldous, I think I am going to take the decision to start reading a book from cover to cover. Don't you think it is a good idea?"

With a dark, tired voice, Aldous said, "I don't think so; you seem to be getting things in some other way."

I repeated, "But I thought it was about time I started reading."

Aldous was silent for a moment. Then, in an unusually grave tone, he said slowly, "Don't botch [or bitch?] yourself up by reading."

He said it with great seriousness and unequivocal definition. I was surprised, not so much by the thought, but by the way he expressed it. It was unusual for him. I thought: "I will bring up the subject another time." He was now obviously tired and wanted to rest.

The chance to discuss it did not come again. We were keeping his little strength to finish the article he had promised *Show* magazine for the fourth centennial of Shakespeare's birth. Aldous was worried about its not being finished by the promised date. He was always ahead of deadlines; this one was November 15. But I had called New York at the beginning of November, and Aldous was relieved to hear that the deadline was extended to November 30.

The article, "Shakespeare and Religion," was two-thirds written, most of it typed by Aldous; one and a half pages handwritten, in large letters, with a marking pencil. This was now to be corrected and the last third written.

It was during this last part of the work that, for the first time, I was right there during Aldous's creative process—for he needed, for the first time, physical help in writing. Aldous had never had a secretary or dictated. He worked alone, first by making handwritten notes, then typing his work several times. In the case of a book, the finished work would be retyped before it was sent to the publisher; in the case of articles, he often sent his own copy. Even for his voluminous correspondence he did not want help. Whenever I suggested a secretary, he said that answering letters himself was faster than dictating, reading and signing them. I envied the speedy way in which, between breakfast and lunch, usually on a Sunday morning, he would answer dozens of letters. He would read a letter, "scribble" (to use his expression) an answer, address it, stamp it, seal it, and put it in the stack of outgoing mail— all, so to say, in one breath. When Aldous decided to write a letter—or when he decided anything—he would generally do it at once.

But in these last weeks most of the correspondence remained un- answered. I took care of the urgent letters. Aldous dictated a few, but what was worrying him was the unfinished article. Since actual writing was physically impossible for him now, and dictating was extremely difficult because speaking soon brought on a cough, we planned that I would read aloud what he had already written and that he would stop me and make his corrections—all while we were being recorded. Then the tape would be transcribed by a good friend, C.P., who was also occasionally our secretary and who knew the situation. I could not send these tapes to an outsider, for Aldous's voice would have immediately and shockingly revealed his condition. Then I would read aloud the transcript and Aldous would correct it—always with the recorder going. Finishing this article required of him a superhuman effort. Here he was, almost completely deprived of physical energy and dexterity, yet, more than ever, he knew that it was necessary to say *now* what he felt must be said.

He was not used to dictating, nor did he like it. He often said that he had to work a great deal to make his talks ready for printing—and tedious work it was, he commented. In 1961, when we were in India for the commemoration of Tagore, many speeches were made. One of them was by the then vice president Radhakrishnan; I hardly ever heard Aldous express such wholehearted admiration. He said that the vice president had spoken in such absolutely perfect English that the speech could be printed exactly as he had spoken it. "Not even a comma would have to be changed," Aldous commented.

"Darling," I said, "you also speak perfect English; can't your speech be printed as you spoke it? It sounded wonderful."

"Oh, no!" he replied with emphasis. "Mine will have to be

corrected; it would not read well at all. But his—it was absolutely perfect." Aldous had publicly expressed his admiration for Radhakrishnan when he became president of India: "More effectively than any man living, Dr. Radhakrishnan has contributed to the building of the bridge of understanding which, now, at long last, connects our two cultures—the Indic and the European. For this we all, here in the West, owe the President a debt of gratitude, a tribute of sincerest admiration."

Again that day, when he started slowly to speak into the microphone the new part of his article, he remembered Radhakrishnan's perfect speech. With the little tape recorder on his bed, and the microphone in his hand or mine, Aldous was now formulating his thoughts slowly, with enormous concentration. One could "see" him thinking. I felt that I was witnessing an extraordinary event: the process of creation made through an organism that was being de-created.

Soon after Aldous's death the article was sent, punctually, to *Show* magazine; the proofs, in two copies, arrived some days later. I immediately sent one to Julian and Juliette. By return I received the following letter from Juliette.

Julian has just read to me the article you sent. Not so much Shakespeare and Religion as Shakespeare and Death. It is the most poignant and beautiful search for the immortal thoughts of man—on his death bed. Only Aldous could have taken that pilgrimage, on his last journey here. I sit here, in the room he used when he stayed with us, his photographs on the wall before me, and my heart full—he is so vibrant in these lines—so strong in courage and acceptance—so piercingly lucid. It is indeed "a human document of great importance—it is a field of immortal corn—the corn was orient and immortal wheat" and I feel an immense unbounded gratitude to Aldous for having left this with us, as a testament. It is also unbelievable that he should have achieved this, with the pain and illness. Thank you for having flown it out so quick, you must have known how it would shine in the darkness, and inspire us.

What would Juliette have said if she had witnessed the way this last work was brought to completion?

It was not only knowing that this was, in all probability, Aldous's last creative contribution that gave me a feeling of awe; it was not only *what* he was expressing. It was the *way* he was speaking, with the low exhausted voice continuously interrupted by coughing, by malaise, by exhaustion. It was the atmosphere of the room, the smell of the

medicinals, the bandages and the oxygen, the feeling of death enveloping us. Aldous was speaking his essay—but, at times, my interfering
ego would make me feel that he was speaking to me. Of course he was
not speaking to me, he was speaking to his readers. But I would
wonder: does he mean this for me? Is he saying this because he knows
he is going to die? How would he write about "Shakespeare and
Religion" if he were not ill? What he was saying in this essay was not
completely new; but what a difference between reading these thoughts
on the printed page and hearing, seeing him slowly and gravely speak
those thoughts. It was a battle between the forces of destruction and the
forces of creation which was taking place in this marvelous being.
Totally deprived of strength, with hardly enough energy to breathe,
Aldous seemed to me, now for the first time, the warrior-prophet
urging once more his fellow men to an acuter perception, to a wider
acceptance of Human and Religious Reality—urging us, for the last
time, to Attention and Love.

I could give no help—except by being mechanically efficient and,
above all, by putting my ego, my thoughts and feelings and fears, out of
his way, out of my way ("If you can get out of your own way, you won't
be in anyone else's."[1]) I had not read the essay before. We started from
the beginning. I was reading slowly enough for Aldous to make corrections, stopping to ask him about words I could not understand in the
typed script. I started to read expecting an interesting article about
Shakespeare but found, with increasing palpitation, that it was largely
about death.

The first mention of death was a general objective one at the
beginning of the article: ". . . in a world of perpetual perishing and
inevitable death." Shortly after followed comments and quotations on
the death of Falstaff. I kept reading objectively. Half a page later there
was a quotation from *Measure for Measure* with Aldous's comments on
the judgment of departed souls. I went on reading, trying to remain
detached, trying to read clearly, to understand what Aldous meant.
Soon followed comments on the death of Shakespeare, with the
conclusion that almost anything is possible, especially on a deathbed. I
continued reading to find, in a few more lines, the speech of the Ghost
to Hamlet about the horrors of purgatory. And immediately after:

Claudio gives utterance to the same fears. Death is terrible not only in
its physical aspects, but also and above all because of the awful menace
of Purgatory.

[1] *Island.*

> Ay, but to die, and go we know not where;
> To lie in cold obstruction, and to rot;
> This sensible warm motion to become
> A kneaded clod; and the delighted spirit
> To bathe in fiery floods, or to reside
> In thrilling region of thick-ribbed ice;
> To be imprison'd in the viewless winds
> And blown with restless violence round about
> The pendent world; or to be worse than worst
> Of those that lawless and incertain thought
> Imagines howling! 'Tis too horrible!
> The weariest and most loathed worldly life
> That age, ache, penury, and imprisonment
> Can lay on nature is a paradise
> To what we fear of death.

These are shocking lines even when read to oneself in ordinary circumstances; they are powerful enough to put chills in one's spine when one hears them spoken by a competent actor—but if you want to know their full power, imagine reading them aloud to your dying husband.

"But this is his work," I kept telling myself; I must concentrate only on speaking clearly, every syllable slowly and clearly. I had the good fortune of studying with the incomparable speech teacher and artist, Geltrude Fögler. As the crescendo of Death closed in on me with mounting intensity, I made the utmost effort to concentrate on her wise counsel: "Love the words."

This death bombardment had taken me completely unaware. If I had read the script before, it would have perhaps been easier, but I had not. I had the feeling that Aldous did not want to discuss it, that if I had taken these deadly references as an opportunity to speak about his death, not only would he not have allowed it, but he would have felt even more depressed to be needing physical help to write. The more death was mentioned, the more I did my best to put myself in that state of dynamic passivity which Aldous had so often practiced. Hearing the tape now confirms my feeling that at that time Aldous wanted, most of all, to finish his work, and preferred not to digress.

This is from that tape:

Laura (reading): "HOW SHAKESPEARE MANAGED HIS PRIVATE LIFE WE DO NOT KNOW; ALL THAT WE KNOW IS THAT IF HE DID INDEED GO THROUGH A DARK NIGHT OF COSMIC DESPAIR, HE WAS POET ENOUGH TO BE ABLE, IN WORDSWORTH'S WORDS, 'TO RECOLLECT THE EMOTION IN CREATIVE TRANQUILLITY' AND TO USE HIS EXPERIENCE

AS THE RAW MATERIAL IN A SUCCESSION OF TRAGIC DRAMAS THAT
WERE FOLLOWED, DURING THE LAST YEARS OF HIS PROFESSIONAL
CAREER, BY A SERIES OF ROMANCES IN WHICH STRANGE AND IM-
PROBABLE ADVENTURES ARE ACTED OUT IN AN ATMOSPHERE OF
ACCEPTANCE, OF FORGIVENESS, OF A CONVICTION THAT, IN SPITE
OF ALL APPEARANCES TO THE CONTRARY, GOD'S IN HIS HEAVEN AND
ALL'S RIGHT WITH THE WORLD."

I felt on safer ground now; how to use creatively pain, frustration,
and illness was one of our themes. I interrupted the reading to say,
"That's what you do? That's what the writer does, he gets all upset and
then he writes it up?"

There is silence on the tape. Aldous probably made some kind of
affirmative, weak noise or gesture. By then he could hardly move his
head. I made another attempt.

Laura: WELL, YOU WILL HAVE A LOT OF WRITING TO DO AFTER THIS EX-
PERIENCE! (No response from Aldous. A silly lonesome laugh from
me. Then immediately I continue reading) ". . . AND ALL'S RIGHT
WITH THE WORLD."

Soon after, I interrupt again.

"THUS THE SOILED FICHU IS THE BESTIAL CARICATURE OF WOMAN-
HOOD, FOR IN WOMAN 'BUT TO THE GIRDLE DO THE GODS INHERIT,'
THE REST IS ALL THE FIEND'S"—WHAT DOES HE MEAN?
Aldous: . . . THIS INSATIABLE SEX LIFE, WHICH IS INTRINSICALLY EVIL.
Laura: BUT IT SAYS THE CONTRARY, UP TO HERE IS GOD'S . . .
Aldous: NO, DOWN TO HERE.
Laura: IS FIEND'S.
Aldous: GOD'S.
Laura: BUT TO THE GIRDLE DO THE GODS INHERIT, THE REST IS ALL
THE FIEND'S . . .

I suppose I was using my ignorance here as a safeguard; but I did
not escape for long. In a few lines the words of a short, massive
statement came upon me crushingly, as falling boulders:

Laura: "SICKNESS, DECREPITUDE, DEATH LIE IN WAIT
                              FOR EVERYONE.
'TO-MORROW, AND TO-MORROW, AND TO-MORROW,
CREEPS IN THIS PETTY PACE FROM DAY TO DAY,
TO THE LAST SYLLABLE OF RECORDED TIME;

AND ALL OUR YESTERDAYS HAVE LIGHTED FOOLS
THE WAY TO DUSTY DEATH. OUT, OUT, BRIEF CANDLE!
LIFE'S BUT A WALKING SHADOW, A POOR PLAYER
THAT STRUTS AND FRETS HIS HOUR UPON THE STAGE
AND THEN IS HEARD NO MORE: IT IS A TALE
TOLD BY AN IDIOT, FULL OF SOUND AND FURY,
SIGNIFYING NOTHING.'"

Later a reference to Shakespeare's last play: "BUT WE CANNOT BE SURE OF THIS, NOR CAN WE BE SURE OF THE FACT THAT HE HIMSELF HAD INTENDED IT TO BE THE LAST."
And Aldous? did he know that his was his last?

Laura: ". . . SHAKESPEARE'S OWN RELIGION CAN BE INFERRED IN MANY CASES FROM THINGS DROPPED ALMOST CASUALLY BY HIS CHARACTERS." WELL, THIS IS WHERE IT FINISHES, AND THE REST IS DONE ON THE TAPE—ON THE OTHER TAPE. . . .

Aldous, almost inaudibly, asks for the tape.

Laura: WELL, THE OTHER TAPE—WE DON'T HAVE IT. I THINK YOU SHOULD BE VERY PLEASED, DON'T YOU? DO YOU WANT ANYTHING ELSE?
Aldous (practically inaudibly): NO. (After a moment) EXCEPT BE PLEASED WITH MYSELF.
Laura: WHAT?
Aldous (clearly and seriously, but with a shadow of humor): EXCEPT BE PLEASED WITH MYSELF.

Between the first two-thirds of the essay (the typewritten part and the last part, which he spoke directly on the tape), Aldous had managed to write by hand a little over a page. This page turned out to be, for Aldous, the most fatiguing part of the article. This may have been due to the day we did it, or to my ineptitude, or to the fact that Aldous realized it was almost impossible for him to work. It is only by hearing the tape on which we read this passage that one can measure the effort Aldous made to accomplish this. Each word is separated from the next by long pauses filled with fatigue, dejection, cavernous breaths. It was only the knowledge that Aldous wanted to finish this essay that sustained me in helping him do it.

Laura (reading slowly, hesitantly): "INTER"   IT SAYS HERE "INTER"
THE   FIRST   WORD—I   ALREADY   DON'T   UNDERSTAND

(Long pauses between words. I am trying so hard, and unsuccessfully.)

Aldous: "INTERPRETATION"?

Laura: IS IT "INTERPRETATION"? (Long silence.) "INTERPRETATION OF . . ."

Aldous: WHAT WAS ALL THIS ABOUT, DARLING?

Laura: WELL, THIS IS THE PAGE YOU WROTE FOR THE . . . THE SHOW MAGAZINE ARTICLE.

Aldous: OH, I SEE   SHAKESPEARE   DIVIDED . . .

Laura: HIS   HIS . . .

Aldous: OH,   WAIT.   WAIT   A   MINUTE   "INTERPRETERS   OF SHAKESPEARE HAVE DIVIDED HIS CAREER INTO FOUR PERIODS: THE WORKSHOP TIME, WHEN HE WAS THE PLAYWRIGHT-TO-BE ARRIVING   LEARNING HIS BUSINESS,   THE TIME IN THE WORLD   WHEN HE MIGHT   BE MATURE ENOUGH TO   WHEN THE POET IS USING HIS SKILL TO MAKE DRAMA OUT OF HISTORY, BIOGRAPHY, AND CHRONICLE FICTION." I THINK IT IS . . .

Laura: "CHRONIC?"

Aldous: ". . . FICTION." I DON'T THINK IT MATTERS, BUT I CAN LOOK IT UP IN A PLACE.   "THE TIME OF THE 'DEPTHS'" INVERTED COMMAS "WHEN . . ."

There is a pause between each word; one hears more breaths, then words; but at this point the pause is so long that one despairs that the next word will ever come. Then, almost inaudibly, my voice:

Laura: ALL RIGHT, ALDOUS, LET GO: I'LL HOLD IT.

Aldous was trying to hold both the page and his magnifying glass; I was holding the microphone. Then again, each word separated by long pauses:

Aldous: ". . . WHICH   IS   THE   SAME   WE   HAVE BEEN   DISCUSSING   IN   THE   EARLIER   PART   OF   THE ESSAY, AND THE TIME IN THE "HEIGHTS". . .

Only Aldous's breathing is heard here, for long minutes. Immobility, except for the tape rolling roundly, hypnotically. Silence, except for the laborious, painful breaths.

Then, in a dejected, heartbreaking murmur:

Aldous: I   DON'T   KNOW   WHAT   IT   IS   . . .

Laura: WELL, WE WILL DO IT . . .

Aldous (more clearly): I KNOW WHAT IT IS ALL ABOUT MYSELF.

Laura: WHAT IS IT ALL ABOUT?

Aldous: IT'S THE LAST PERIOD, THE PLAYS OF THE LAST PERIOD.

Laura: DO YOU WANT TO REST A BIT NOW, THEN WE CAN DO THIS AGAIN.

Aldous (almost inaudibly): I AM EXHAUSTED . . .

The next time we worked, it was a better day for Aldous. He read the handwritten page slowly, but with less effort. After the last phrase, "In our religious context . . ." he asked me to stop the recorder. He was going now to compose directly on the tape. He asked me to show him how to stop and start the recorder. He did not want me to hold the microphone for him; to have control of the machine gave him a greater feeling of comfort and independence. I stood silently by. He would think for a while, then press the button and speak a phrase, then stop the machine and think. Therefore this part of the tape does not have the long silences which occur when the recorder was rolling continuously.

After he had recorded the first two paragraphs Aldous said, almost smiling: "I begin to see how one could develop a technique to write in this way." He was fascinated by the problem and had started to solve it as soon as it presented itself.

Aún aprendo—"I am still learning." This was one of Aldous's favorite mottoes, and his way of life. The motto is the caption for a drawing Goya did in his old age, representing a man, bent by the weight of years and infirmities, haltingly walking with the aid of a staff. *Aún aprendo* was the message Aldous would give to young students who after twenty years of classroom learning were starting out in life; it was the compliment he paid to his great friend Igor Stravinsky on his seventy-eighth birthday. Age is no limit on the process of learning, not only for masters such as Goya and Stravinsky, but for all of us. . . . "The process goes on from the cradle to the grave and, doubtless, beyond" (from a commencement address).

Now, just on this side of the grave, there was a shadow of a smile on Aldous's face. "Yes, I can see how one could do this. . . . It is different . . . . quite different. . . . One has to think the phrase through. . . ." He was doing what he loved to do: he was still learning, while summing up, in those last six hundred words, his views of life and death.

Slowly but steadily, Aldous was speaking about Prospero, the protagonist of Shakespeare's last play, and the necessity of abandoning magic, even white magic, if the aspirant to the spiritual life is to go forward. Then:

"OUR REVELS NOW ARE ENDED. THESE OUR ACTORS,
  AS I FORETOLD YOU, WERE ALL SPIRITS, AND
  ARE MELTED INTO AIR, INTO THIN AIR;
  AND, LIKE THE BASELESS FABRIC OF THIS VISION,
  THE CLOUD-CAPP'D TOWERS, THE GORGEOUS PALACES,
  THE SOLEMN TEMPLES, THE GREAT GLOBE ITSELF,
  YEA, ALL WHICH IT INHERIT, SHALL DISSOLVE;
  AND, LIKE THIS INSUBSTANTIAL PAGEANT FADED,
  LEAVE NOT A RACK BEHIND. WE ARE SUCH STUFF
  AS DREAMS ARE MADE ON, AND OUR LITTLE LIFE
  IS ROUNDED WITH A SLEEP."

PROSPERO IS HERE ENUNCIATING THE DOCTRINE OF MAYA. THE WORLD
IS AN ILLUSION, BUT AN ILLUSION WHICH WE MUST TAKE SERIOUSLY,
BECAUSE IT IS REAL AS FAR AS IT GOES, AND IN THOSE ASPECTS OF THE
REALITY WHICH WE ARE CAPABLE OF COMPREHENDING. OUR BUSINESS
IS TO WAKE UP.

Our business is to wake up! Ironically, at the very moment of the
admonition, my ego again started its painful, presumptuous guess-
work: What should I do now? To what am I asleep? Does he want me
to say, to do something? What is it that I don't understand? Then the
sudden, grateful awakening to the obvious fact: Aldous was not speaking to me in riddles, he was writing his article! And simply expressing,
in six words, what he had said in a myriad of ways, trying to reach
people on all levels, stating a whole life program, not only for his own
last few hours of life—and certainly not just for me!—but for each
awarely conscious being, for each timeless moment.

Aldous: OUR BUSINESS IS TO WAKE UP. WE HAVE TO FIND WAYS IN
  WHICH TO DETECT THE WHOLE OF REALITY IN THE ONE ILLUSORY
  PART WHICH OUR SELF-CENTERED CONSCIOUSNESS PERMITS US TO
  SEE.

To give ways of breaking away from the self-centered consciousness,
ways to realize that our ego is only a movable screen between the small
chamber of our organism and an infinite reality; to show, finally, how
these abstract concepts can be transformed into practical everyday life.
Aldous envisaged and wrote *Island,* his ultimate legacy.

Aldous: WE MUST NOT LIVE THOUGHTLESSLY, TAKING OUR ILLUSION
  FOR THE COMPLETE REALITY, BUT AT THE SAME TIME WE MUST NOT
  LIVE TOO THOUGHTFULLY IN THE SENSE OF TRYING TO ESCAPE FROM

THE DREAM STATE. WE MUST BE CONTINUOUSLY ON OUR WATCH FOR WAYS IN WHICH WE MAY ENLARGE OUR CONSCIOUSNESS.

Did Aldous suspect that the confusion of issues, of ends and means, of use and misuse accompanying the consciousness-expanding movement was going to storm bombastically into a howling hurricane?

Aldous: WE MUST NOT ATTEMPT TO LIVE OUTSIDE THE WORLD, WHICH IS GIVEN US, BUT WE MUST SOMEHOW LEARN HOW TO TRANSFORM IT AND TRANSFIGURE IT. TOO MUCH "WISDOM" IS AS BAD AS TOO LITTLE WISDOM, AND THERE MUST BE NO MAGIC TRICKS. WE MUST LEARN TO COME TO REALITY WITHOUT THE ENCHANTER'S WAND AND HIS BOOK OF THE WORDS. ONE MUST FIND A WAY OF BEING IN THIS WORLD WHILE NOT BEING OF IT. A WAY OF LIVING IN TIME WITHOUT BEING COMPLETELY SWALLOWED UP BY TIME.

HOTSPUR, AS HE IS DYING, SUMS UP THE HUMAN PREDICAMENT WITH A FEW MEMORABLE WORDS:

"BUT THOUGHTS THE SLAVE OF LIFE, AND LIFE TIME'S FOOL, AND TIME, THAT TAKES SURVEY OF ALL THE WORLD, MUST HAVE A STOP."

WE THINK WE KNOW WHO WE ARE AND WHAT WE OUGHT TO DO ABOUT IT, AND YET OUR THOUGHT IS CONDITIONED AND DETERMINED BY THE NATURE OF OUR IMMEDIATE EXPERIENCE AS PSYCHOPHYSICAL ORGANISMS ON THIS PARTICULAR PLANET. THOUGHT, IN OTHER WORDS, IS LIFE'S FOOL. THOUGHT IS THE SLAVE OF LIFE, AND LIFE OBVIOUSLY IS TIME'S FOOL INASMUCH AS IT IS CHANGING FROM INSTANT TO INSTANT, CHANGING THE OUTSIDE AND THE INNER WORLD SO THAT WE NEVER REMAIN THE SAME TWO INSTANTS TOGETHER.

The article was almost finished three days before Aldous died. There was still the last paragraph to be completed. Listening to the tape, one feels that there was a little less darkness; the discussion on his writing reveals Aldous's great patience with my ignorance.

Laura (reading): "THOUGHT IS DETERMINED BY LIFE, AND LIFE IS DETERMINED BY PASSING TIME. BUT THE DOMINION OF TIME IS NOT ABSOLUTE, FOR 'TIME MUST HAVE A STOP' IN TWO SENSES. FROM THE CHRISTIAN POINT OF VIEW IN WHICH SHAKESPEARE WAS WRITING, IT MUST HAVE A STOP IN THE LAST JUDGMENT, AND IN THE WINDING UP OF THE UNIVERSE. BUT ON THE WAY TO THIS GENERAL

CONSUMMATION, IT MUST HAVE A STOP IN THE INDIVIDUAL MIND,
WHICH MUST LEARN THE REGULAR CULTIVATION OF A MOOD OF
TIMELESSNESS, OF A SENSE OF ETERNITY."

Aldous: "WE ARE ON THE WAY TO AN EXISTENTIAL RELIGION OF MYSTI-
CISM . . . WELL ON THE WAY . . ." AND THERE WE STOP, DON'T YOU
THINK? OR WHAT COMES AFTER?

Laura: ". . . THROUGH PROCESSES OF MEDITATION, THROUGH
EXTENDED AWARENESS OF THE MYSTICAL STATE OF MIND, WE ARE
WELL ON THE WAY TO AN EXISTENTIAL RELIGION OF MYSTICISM."

Aldous: HOW DOES IT GO IN THE SCRIPT?

Laura: "SHAKESPEARE WAS NOT, AND DID NOT WISH TO BE A SYSTEM-
ATIC PHILOSOPHER."

Aldous: THAT'S IT.

Laura: YOU MEAN THE FIRST PART?

Aldous: YES.

Laura: WELL, WE DON'T HAVE THE FIRST PART HERE.

Aldous says something.

Laura: THIS ONE? I'LL READ IT THROUGH. WE STOP THERE, WHERE YOU
STOPPED THE OTHER DAY, WITH "MYSTICAL STATE OF MIND?" CAN
YOU STOP WITH THAT PHRASE?

Aldous: "WE ARE ON THE WAY . . ." WELL, I MEAN WE ARE TALKING
ABOUT RELIGION, DARLING.

Laura: BUT YOU HAVE THIS BEAUTIFUL PHRASE SAYING, "THE CULTI-
VATION, THROUGH PROCESSES OF MEDITATION, OF AN EXTENDED
AWARENESS, OF A MYSTICAL STATE OF MIND."

Aldous: NO, I THINK WE MUST END ON OUR SUBJECT MATTER, "SHAKE-
SPEARE AND RELIGION."

Laura: DO YOU THINK WE CAN END THAT PARAGRAPH: "WE ARE WELL
ON THE WAY TO AN EXISTENTIAL RELIGION OF MYSTICISM"?

Aldous: MMM . . . WE CAN JUST END UP: "HOW MANY KINDS OF
RELIGION, AND HOW MANY KINDS OF SHAKESPEARE."

Laura (copies): YOU WANT AN EXCLAMATION?

Aldous: MARK, YES.

Laura: BUT THERE ARE NOT MANY KINDS OF SHAKESPEARE . . .

Aldous: BUT, DARLING, THAT'S EXACTLY WHAT WE'VE BEEN TALKING
ABOUT . . . AND STOP THE DAMN THING NOW.

Laura: DO YOU WANT ME TO READ IT OVER . . . "SHAKESPEARE," IS IT
PLURAL?

Aldous: NO.

Laura: AND RELIGION ALSO IS SINGULAR, THEY ARE BOTH SINGU-
LAR. . . . "HOW MANY KINDS . . ."

Aldous: "KINDS OF RELIGION . . ."

Laura: THE "KINDS" IS PLURAL OF COURSE, AND THE "SHAKESPEARE" IS SINGULAR. "HOW MANY KINDS OF RELIGION! HOW MANY KINDS OF SHAKESPEARE!" THIS IS FUN TO DO—DO YOU WANT TO DO ANOTHER ONE?
Aldous: NO, DARLING, I AM TOO TIRED.
Laura: NO, I MEAN TOMORROW.

The next day Aldous heard this tape, was slightly amused, added a comma.

That was the twenty-first of November.

O Nobly Born!

ALDOUS DIED AS he lived, doing his best to develop fully in himself one of the essentials he recommended to others: *Awareness*.

When he realized that the labor of his body leaving this life might lessen his awareness, Aldous prescribed his own medicine or—expressed in another way—his own sacrament.

"The last rites should make one more conscious rather than less conscious," he had often said. "more human rather than less human." In a letter to Dr. Osmond, who had reminded Aldous that six years had passed since their first mescaline experiment, he answered: "Yes, six years since that first experiment. 'O Death in Life, the years that are no more'—and yet also, O Life in Death . . ." Also to Osmond: ". . . My own experience with Maria convinced me that the living can do a great deal to make the passage easier for the dying, to raise the most purely physiological act of human existence to the level of consciousness and perhaps even of spirituality."

All too often, unconscious or dying people are treated as "things," as though they were not there. But often they are very much there. Although a dying person has fewer and fewer means of expressing what he feels, he still is open to receiving communication. In this sense the very sick or the dying person is much like a child: he cannot tell us how he feels, but he is absorbing our feeling, our voice, and, most of all, our touch. In the infant the greatest channel of communication is the skin. Similarly, for the individual plunged in the immense solitude of sickness and death, the touch of a hand can dispel that solitude, even warmly illuminate that unknown universe. To the "nobly born" as to the "nobly dying," skin and voice communication may make an immeasurable difference.

Modern psychology has discovered how powerful the birth trauma is to the individual's life. What about the "death trauma"? If one believes in the continuity of life, should one not give it equal consideration?

The Tibetan Book of the Dead gives the greatest importance to the state of consciousness at the time of death. The guide always addresses the dying person with the salute "O Nobly Born!" and urges: "Let not thy mind be distracted." The guide keeps reminding the dying person not to become entangled in visions, heavenly or hellish, which are not real, but which are only the illusionary projections of his thoughts and emotions, fears and desires. The dying are exhorted "to go on practicing the art of living even while they are dying. Knowing who in fact one is, being conscious of the universal and impersonal life that lives itself through each of us. That's the art of living, and that's what one can help the dying to go on practicing. To the very end." [1]

"O nobly born!" This mark of respect and recognition is uplifting and seems to me more conducive to better life—here or after—than the image of the sinner beating his breast and desperately begging for forgiveness: "What shall I, frail man, be pleading? Who for me be interceding, when the just are mercy needing?"

November 22, 1963, was to be the last day on earth for two men of good will. Although belonging to different generations, different countries, and different backgrounds, both John F. Kennedy and Aldous Huxley had waged a common fight against ignorance and bad will; both dedicated their lives to helping humanity to understand and love itself. They died on the same day: no imagination could be vivid enough to conceive two ways of dying as antipodal as these. Distorted rumors have circulated about Aldous's death. I reported the actual events of that day in a recording for relatives and a few friends three weeks after Aldous died. These are the facts.

Dear ———

There is so much I want to tell you about the last week of Aldous's life, and particularly the last day. What happened is important because it is a conclusion, better, a continuation, of his own work.

First of all, I must confirm to you with complete subjective certainty that Aldous had not consciously considered the fact that he might die very soon until the day he died. Subconsciously it was all there, and you will be able to see this for yourself, because from November 15th until November 22nd I have many of Aldous's remarks on tape. Aldous was never quite willing to give up his writing by hand for dictating or making notes on a recorder. He used a Dictograph only to record

[1] *Island.*

passages of literature he liked; he would listen to these in his quiet moments in the evening as he was going to sleep. In the beginning of November, when Aldous was in the hospital, Ginny gave us a recorder—a small thing, easily manageable and practically unnoticeable. After having practiced with it myself a few days, I showed it to Aldous, who was very pleased with it, and from the fifteenth on we used it a little every day, recording his dreams and notes for future writing.

The period from November 15 to the twenty-second marked, it seems to me, a period of intense mental activity for Aldous. We had diminished little by little all the drugs as much as possible—only used pain-killers like Percodan, a little Amytal, and something for nausea. He took also a few injections of ½ cc. of Dilaudid, which is a derivative of morphine; the doctor says this is a very small intake of morphine.

Now, to pick up my point again, in his dreams as well as sometimes in his conversation, it seemed obvious and transparent that subconsciously he knew that he was going to die. But not once did he speak of it. This had nothing to do with the idea that some of his friends put forward, that he wanted to spare me. It wasn't this, because Aldous had never been able to play a part, to say a single lie; he was constitutionally unable to lie, and if he wanted to spare me, he could certainly have spoken to Ginny.

During the last two months I gave him almost daily an opportunity, an opening, for speaking about death, but of course this opening was always one that could have been taken in two ways—either toward life or toward death; and he always took it toward life. We read the entire manual of Dr. Leary based on the Tibetan Book of the Dead. [2] He could have, even jokingly, said: "Don't forget to remind me when the time comes." His comment instead was directed only to the problem of "re-entry" after a psychedelic session. It is true he sometimes said things like, "If I get out of this," in connection with his new ideas of writing, and wondered when and if he would have the strength to work. He was mentally very active and it seemed that some new levels of his mind were stirring.

The night before he died (Thursday night), about eight o'clock, suddenly an idea came to him.

"Darling," he said, "it just occurs to me that I am imposing on Ginny—having somebody as sick as this in the house with the two children—this is really an imposition."

Ginny was out of the house at the moment, and so I said, "Good,

_____
[2] *The Psychedelic Experience.*

when she comes back I will tell her this—it will be a nice laugh."

"No," he said with unusual insistence. "We should do something about it."

"Well," I replied, keeping it light, "all right, get up. Let's go on a trip."

"No," he said. "It is serious. We must think about it—all these nurses in the house. What we could do, we could take an apartment for this period, Just for this period."

It was very clear what he meant; it was unmistakably clear. He thought he might remain seriously sick for another three or four weeks, and then he could come back and start his normal life again. This idea of starting his normal life occurred quite often. In the last three or four weeks he was several times appalled by his weakness when he realized how much strength he had lost, and how long it would take to be normal again. A few days before, as he was going to sleep, I had asked him: "What are you thinking about?"

"I was thinking that a way must be found to speed up this recovery; it is true I am better, the back is better, but it is depressing not to have the strength to do something that one wants to do."

Now this Thursday night he had remarked about taking an apartment with an unusual energy, but a few minutes later and all that evening I felt he was going down, he was losing ground quickly. Eating was almost out of the question. He had just taken a few spoonfuls of liquid and puree; every time he took anything, it would start the cough. Thursday night I called the doctor and told him the pulse was very high —140; he had a little bit of fever, and my whole feeling was one of the imminence of death. Both the nurse and the doctor said they didn't think this was the case, but that if I wished the doctor would come up to see him that night. Then I returned to Aldous's room and we decided to give him an injection. It was nine o'clock, and he went to sleep and I told the doctor to come the next morning. Aldous slept until about 2 a.m. and then he had another shot, and I saw him again at six-thirty. Again I felt that life was leaving, that something was more wrong than usual, although I didn't know exactly what, and a little later I sent you and Matthew and Ellen and my sister a wire. Then about 9 a.m. Aldous began to be so agitated, so uncomfortable, so restless. He wanted to be moved all the time. Nothing was right. The doctor came about that time and decided to give him a shot which he had given him once before, something that you give intravenously, very slowly. It takes five minutes to give and it is a drug that dilates the bronchial tubes so that respiration is easier.

This drug made him uncomfortable the time before—it must have been three Fridays before—when he had that crisis I wrote you about.

But then it helped him. This time it made him feel restless. He couldn't express himself but he was feeling dreadful—nothing was right, no position relieved him. I tried to ask him what was happening. He had difficulty in speaking, but he managed to say, "Just trying to tell you makes it worse." He wanted to be moved all the time. "Move me." "Move my legs." "Move my arms." "Move my bed." He had one of those push-button beds which move up and down from both the head and the foot, and incessantly, it seemed, he wanted to be moved up and down, up and down. We did this again and again and somehow it seemed to give him a little relief, but it was very, very little.

All of a sudden—it must have been then ten o'clock—he could hardly speak, and he whispered he wanted "a big, big piece of paper to write on." I did not want to leave the room to find it, so I took a typewriter tablet that was near by, laid it on a large tray and held it. Aldous wrote, "If I go," and gave a direction for his will.

I knew what he meant. He had signed his will, as I told you, about a week before, and in the will there was a transfer of a life-insurance policy from me to ————. I said to him, "Do you mean that you want to make sure that the life insurance has been transferred?"

He said, "Yes."

I said, "The papers for the transfer have just arrived. If you want to sign them you can sign them, but it is not necessary because you already made it legal in your will."

He heaved a sigh of relief at not having to sign. I had asked him the day before to sign some important papers, and he had said, "Let's wait a little while." This, by the way, was his way now to say that he couldn't do something. If he was asked to eat he would say, "Let's wait a little while." And when I asked him the day before to do some signing that was rather important he said, "Let's wait a little while." He wanted to write you a letter. "And especially about Juliette's book, it's lovely," he had said several times. But when I proposed doing it, he would say, "Yes, in just a little while," in such a tired voice, so totally different from his normal way of doing things at once. So, when I told him that the signing was not necessary and that all was in order, he gave a sign of relief.

"If I go." This was the first time that he had said that with reference to *now*. He wrote it. I knew and felt that for the first time he was looking at death—now. About half an hour before, I had called up S.C., a psychiatrist who was one of the leaders in the use of LSD. I asked him if he had ever given LSD to a man in this condition. He said that he had only done it twice, and in one case it had brought a sort of reconciliation with death, and in the other case it did not make any difference. I asked him if he would advise giving it to Aldous in his condition. I told him how I had offered it several times during the last two months, but Aldous always said that he would wait until he was better.

Dr. C. said "I don't know—I don't think so. What do you think?" I said, "I don't know. Shall I offer it to him?"

He said, "I would offer it to him in a very oblique way. Just say, 'What do you think about taking LSD?'"

This vague response had been common to the few researchers in this field whom I has asked, "Do you give LSD *in extremis?*" In *Island* there is the only definite reference I know of. I must have spoken to Dr. C. at about 9:30. Aldous's condition was worsening by the minute—he could not say what he wanted; I could not understand. At a certain point he said something. He said, "Who is eating out of my bowl?" I didn't know what this meant, and I asked him. He managed a faint, whimsical smile and said, "Oh, never mind, it is only a joke." And later on, feeling my need to know a little so I could do something, he said in an agonizing way, "At this point there is so little to share." Then I knew he knew that he was going. However, this inability to express himself was only muscular. His brain was clear and in fact, I feel, at a pitch of activity.

Some time during the morning, a new tank of oxygen was brought in by a young man who had come several times before. He started, rather loudly, to say, "Did you hear that President Kennedy . . ."

I stopped him with a look. Aldous did not notice, maybe because he was preoccupied about the tip.

"Those tanks are heavy; give him a dollar."

Aldous was always in such a hurry to give tips, as though the opportunity to do it were about to vanish. It was the same feeling today. I answered yes, but I was thinking I did not have a dollar in that room, and where was my purse. Aldous must have felt my hesitation because he repeated, "Give him a dollar. There are some bills in my trousers pocket in the closet." He spoke very low, but quite clearly this time.

Then, I don't know exactly what time it was, he asked me for his tablet and wrote, "Try LSD 100 mm intramuscular." Although his writing was not very clear, I knew that this is what he meant. I read it aloud and he confirmed it. Suddenly, something was very clear to me, after this tortuous talking of the last two months. I knew then, I knew what was to be done. I went quickly to fetch the LSD, which was in the medicine chest in the room across the hall. There is a TV set in that room, which was hardly ever used. But I had been aware, in the last hour or so, that it was on. Now, when I entered the room, Ginny, the doctor, the nurse, and the rest of the household were all looking at television. The thought shot through my mind: "This is madness, these people looking at television when Aldous is dying." A second later, while I was opening the box containing the LSD vial, I heard that President Kennedy had been assassinated. Only then did I understand the strange behavior of the people that morning.

I said, "I am going to give him a shot of LSD—he asked for it."

The doctor had a moment of agitation—you know very well the uneasiness in the medical mind about this drug. But no "authority," not even an army of authorities, could have stopped me then. I went into Aldous's room with the vial of LSD and prepared a syringe. The doctor asked me if I wanted him to give the shot—maybe because he saw that my hands were trembling. His asking me that made me conscious of my hands, and I said, "No, I must do this." I quieted myself, and when I gave him the shot my hands were firm.

Then, somehow, a great relief came to us both. It was 11:45 when I gave him his first shot of 100 mm. I sat near his bed and I said, "Darling, maybe in a little while I will take it with you. Would you like me to take it also in a little while?" I said "a little while" because I had no idea of when I could take it. And he indicated yes. We must keep in mind that by now he was speaking very, very little.

Then I said, "Would you like Matthew to take it with you also?"

And he said yes.

"What about Ellen?"

He said yes. Then I mentioned two or three people who had been working with LSD and he said, "No, no, *basta, basta.*"

Then I said, "What about Ginny?"

And he said, "Yes," with emphasis. Then we were quiet. I just sat there without speaking for a while. Aldous was not so agitated physically. He seemed—somehow I felt he knew—we both knew what we were doing, and this had always been a great relief to Aldous. I have seen him at times during his illness upset until he knew what he was going to do, then, the decision taken, however serious, he would make a total change. This enormous feeling of relief would come to him, and he wouldn't be worried at all about it. He would say let's do it, and we would do it, and he was like a liberated man. And now I had the same feeling: a decision had been made. Suddenly he had accepted the fact of death; now, he had taken this *moksha*-medicine in which he believed. Once again he was doing what he had written in *Island,* and I had the feeling that he was interested and relieved and quiet.

After half an hour, the expression on his face began to change a little, and I asked him if he felt the effect of LSD, and he indicated no. Yet I think that something had taken place already. This was one of

Aldous's characteristics. He would always delay acknowledging the effect of any medicine, even when the effect was quite certainly there; unless the effect was very, very strong, he would say no. Now the expression on his face was beginning to look as it did when he had taken the *moksha*-medicine, when this immense expression of complete bliss and love would come over him. This was not the case now, but there was a change in comparison to what his face had been two hours before. I let another half hour pass, and then I decided to give him another 100 mm. I told him I was going to do it, and he acquiesced. I gave him another shot, and then I began to talk to him. He was very quiet now; he was very quiet and his legs were getting colder; higher and higher I could see purple areas of cyanosis. Then I began to talk to him saying, "Light and free." Some of these suggestions I had given him at night, in these last few weeks, before he would go to sleep, and now I spoke them more convincingly, more intensely.

"Light and free and let go, darling; forward and up. You are going forward and up; you are going toward the light. Willingly and consciously you are going, willingly and consciously, and you are doing this beautifully; you are doing this so beautifully—you are going toward the light—you are going toward the light—you are going toward a greater love—you are going forward and up. It is so easy—it is so beautiful. You are doing it so beautifully, so easily. Light and free. Forward and up. You are going toward Maria's love with my love. You are going toward a greater love than you have ever known. You are going toward the best, the greatest love, and it is easy, it is so easy, and you are doing it so beautifully."

I believe I started to talk to him—it must have been about one or two o'clock. It was very difficult for me to keep track of time. I was very, very near his ear, and I hope I spoke clearly and understandably. Once I asked him, "Do you hear me?" He squeezed my hand; he was hearing me. It was 3:15 p.m. according to the nurse's records. I was tempted to ask more questions, but in the morning he had begged me not to ask any more questions, and the entire feeling was that things were right. I didn't dare to inquire, to disturb, and that was the only question that I asked: "Do you hear me?"

Later on I asked the same question, but the hand didn't move any more. Now from two o'clock until the time he died, which was 5:20 p.m., there was complete peace except for once. That must have been about three-thirty or four, when I saw the beginning of struggle in his lower lip. His lower lip began to move as if it were going to struggle for air. Then I gave the direction even more forcefully.

"It is easy, and you are doing this beautifully and consciously, in full awareness, in full awareness, darling, you are going toward the light."

I repeated these or similar words for the last three or four hours. Once in a while my own emotion would overcome me, but if it did I immediately would leave the bed for two or three minutes, and would come back only when I could control my emotion. The twitching of the lower lip lasted only a little bit, and it seemed to respond completely to what I was saying.

"Easy, easy, and you are doing this willingly and consciously and beautifully—going forward and up, light and free, forward and up toward the light, into the light, into complete love."

The twitching stopped, the breathing became slower and slower, and there was absolutely not the slightest indication of contraction, of struggle. It was just that the breathing became slower—and slower—and slower; the ceasing of life was not a drama at all, but like a piece of music just finishing so gently in a sempre più piano, dolcemente . . . and at five-twenty the breathing stopped.

And now, after I have been alone these few days, and less bombarded by other people's feelings, the meaning of this last day becomes clearer and clearer to me and more and more important. Aldous was appalled, I think (and certainly I am), at the fact that what he wrote in *Island* was not taken seriously. It was treated as a work of science fiction, when it was not fiction, because each one of the ways of living he described in *Island* was not a product of his fantasy, but something that had been tried in one place or another, some of them in our own everyday life. If the way Aldous died were known, it might awaken people to the awareness that not only this, but many other facts described in *Island* are possible here and now. Aldous asking for the *moksha*-medicine while dying is not only a confirmation of his openmindedness and courage, but as such a last gesture of continuing importance. Such a gesture might be ignorantly misinterpreted, but it is history that Huxleys stop ignorance, before ignorance stops Huxleys.

Now, is his way of dying to remain for us, and only for us, a relief and consolation, or should others also benefit from it? Aren't we all nobly born and entitled to nobly dying?

Aldous with his aunt, Mrs. Humphry Ward

The World's Fundamental
All-Rightness

. . . Huxley was one of the freest men in the world. And now he is gone: availing himself of a moment of hystorical turmoil, he left a là Huxley, lightly on tiptoe, not to disturb his fellowman, to whom he only wanted to lend a hand.

Indro Montanelli: *Corriere della Sera*
December 15, 1963
Milano

ALDOUS DIED ON Friday, November 22, 1963, at 5:20 p.m. His son Matthew and I were in complete accord about having no funeral. We simply said that Aldous wanted no money spent on this sort of thing, and the flowering salesmanship of the funeral director was cut at the bud. Ceremonies and publicity were thus avoided. Cremation took place with professional witnesses only. The entire cost was $328.50, the minimum. When it was all over, we announced to the press that Aldous Huxley was dead.

As Aldous had often entertained his friends for a walk and tea afterwards, Matthew and I invited a few close friends for the next afternoon, Sunday, the twenty-fourth. We walked for a while on that path in the Hollywood hills that Aldous knew so well—a wistful, nostalgic group. But as the autumnal sunset enveloped us in its softness, we also felt an all-pervading, overflowing sense of gratefulness for the man who had given so much, who had loved so well. His deep, gentle power would continue for a long time to encourage and to inspire.

In the weeks following Aldous's death, I received many messages of love and comfort—but the one which helped me most was one which came from Aldous himself. A few months before he died, he had written to an unknown correspondent, who, with exquisite timing, sent it to me.

". . . I have known that sense of affectionate solidarity with the people around me and the Universe at large—also the sense of the world's fundamental All-Rightness, in spite of pain, death, and bereavement. . . ."

Aldous with his grandson Trev

Epilogue: *Sit Down before Fact Like a Little Child*

ON THE SUBJECT of the art of dying and life after death, Aldous wrote Dr. Osmond (14-xii-1960): "The emphasis, in the last rites, has to be on the present and the post-human future, which one must assume— and I think with justification—to be a reality."

In the following pages an event is reported that occurred fifteen months after Aldous's death, in his post-human future.

I have never undertaken the study of ESP, mediumship, or spiritulism. It was in a casual and roundabout way that, in 1965, I came to have a reading by a medium.

During the year following Aldous's death I was continuously over-burdened with decisions and responsibilities. At that period of low vitality the emotional and intellectual demands were very heavy on me, and I had little help. One day I decided I was not going to worry about the many small items that came up in my mail. For minor decisions I would just try having *yes* days and *no* days.

When the letter that follows arrived, I had been saying *no* all week; so it was time for a *yes* day. It was a long letter form Keith Milton Rhinehart, the head of a foundation in Seattle. It read: ". . . Our members are deeply interested in the parapsychological, the anthropological, philosophical, social and scientific aspects of the societies and cultures of the world, past and present." The letter concluded by asking my participation in a television interview to be filmed at my home.

Since it was a *yes* day, I said *yes*.

We made an appointment to film the interview on November 29. K.M.R. and the cameramen came. K.M.R. was a good interviewer; his questions covered a large range of subjects. Mediumship, ESP, and reincarnation were mentioned, but I dwelt little on them. I feel that in these matters only facts should be communicated, and not our emotions connected with them; it is for this reason that I am attempting to put down the events that follow as an objective report without opinions or emotions—only facts.

We were so involved that afternoon in our work that I did not ask K.M.R. about the foundation whose name was on his letterhead, or about his main line of work. Since he was embarking on a world-wide tour, I took it for granted that his work was mainly lecturing and interviewing. When we finished the filming, K.M.R. said he was very grateful for my interview and wanted to do something for me in return; he would be happy to give me a private reading. I did not know exactly what he meant and reacted to his offer accordingly.

K.M.R. must have realized that I had not understood, for he said, "I don't know whether you know it, but I am a medium." I found out later that he was a very well-known medium. He explained that his foundation was partly based on and sustained by his work as a medium. However, he did not want to limit it to mediumship. For this reason he was going on a world tour to interview educators, scientists, doctors, and healers—some of whom were not at all involved in ESP or mediumship, and some who were openly against it.

He was going to London the next morning; I had an engagement that evening. I asked for a rain check on the reading. We planned he would do it on his return, when he would show me his films before releasing them. I wished him good luck, and somehow I felt he needed it. Some of the famous people he planned to see were busy and difficult to contact: would they find time for an unknown young man who had no introduction and who wanted not only to ask all sorts of questions but also to film the interviewer? I doubted it.

I was surprised when, three months later, he called. His tour had been marvelously successful; he had interviewed and filmed a dozen prominent people in three continents, and had met with wonderful cooperation. He wanted me to see the films.

"Did you see Bertrand Russell?" I asked. I had never met him, but Aldous had spoken so often, admiringly and affectionately, of his old friend.

"I had a wonderful meeting with him," K.M.R. said. "You will see and hear what he has to say; I have a half-hour film of him."

I was amazed. Bertrand Russell, then ninety-four, and frail, and not easily accessible, had found energy and time for an interview with this unknown American.

K.M.R. and I planned to meet the following week to see and discuss his film. I had been a film editor and he thought I might have some useful ideas for the general presentation of this series. But by some mis-understanding he arrived one day sooner than I expected, on an evening of a small dinner party at Ginny's home. I asked K.M.R. to join us for dinner; we would see the films the following evening.

Including K.M.R., we were seven at dinner. J.M., an old friend of Ginny's from San Francisco; a woman illustrator G.E. and her hus-band, a builder; R.M., a close friend of mine; and Ginny and myself. I introduced K.M.R. as a lecturer and interviewer who had just returned from a world tour. I thought he would speak, at dinner, about the prominent people he had visited in Europe and Asia; instead, he was very quiet and rather self-effacing. At the end of dinner he took me aside and said, "I have not forgotten my promise; I owe you a reading. Do you want to have it this evening?"

I had forgotten about the reading. "I would prefer to have it tomor-row when we were alone."

K.M.R. agreed to this. Then, on second thought, he added: "Unless you prefer to have a group reading now with your friends."

I thought it was a wonderful idea. I had never participated in a group reading; neither had my friends. In fact, they did not know what a reading was. This intelligent group was neither in the grips of con-formity nor out on the fringe. The woman painter and Ginny were dedi-cated to bringing up their children in the best way possible in a place, Hollywood, where such a task is particularly difficult; they were also involved in artistic and humanistic activities. The three men were quite different types, and of different degrees of conformity. The most unconventional one, the builder, was the only one who decided not to participate in the reading. I would say that the general feeling about mediumship and life after death was one of varying skepticism and curiosity.

A medium is similar to a telephone; he is a channel of communica-tion between different states of consciousness—possibly the living and the dead. If a few telephones had suddenly appeared in the Middle Ages without their mechanism being explained, people would have con-sidered them the work of the devil—and their users burned at the stake. What? Speak to someone in Florence when you are in Siena? Everyone knows that the two cities are eighty kilometers apart; no one can speak *that* loud—it is *impossible!* And anyone who says he can—or God Forbid, actually does—is decidely suspect. *What?* To be able to communicate between this, our universe, and the invisible universe of the dead—we are not sure it even exists! Exceedingly suspect!

The possession of this mysterious channel of communication does not denote in its owner any specific moral, intellectual, or ethical qualities. But society tends to think so. The opinion society in general has of mediums has, as a matter of course, a superior spiritual nature; while at the other extreme, many people are thoroughly conditioned to react to a medium as to a crook. If a medium cannot perform at the appointed time, our attitude is somewhat intolerant—we certainly do not accept it as we accept a singer's cold. The medium would be immediately discredited by those who are convinced that he is a fraud—and blindly and stubbornly believed by those who think he is omniscient. It is a lamentable situation because it prevents an intelligent and methodical development of valuable talents, whose existence is no longer denied—moreover these talents are more evanescent and vulnerable than those exercised in other arts or professions.

Events related to mediumship and ESP are not the only ones that are difficult to accept and comprehend without some preparation. If the scientific and technical feats of the last ten years had not been widely popularized, how many of us would accept them? Suppose we had not been informed, through press, radio, and television, of the preparations of the last eight years for trips in outer space; suppose we had not seen on the TV screen the launching of space vehicles. How would we react to a man who showed us a blurry photograph of sands and pebbles and announced: *"This is the moon"?* It is easy to predict. We would call him a charlatan or a madman. Now, secure in our knowledge, we all agree that the famous blurry photograph is indeed the moon!

To know is reassuring: not to know generates emotional insecurity. Of corporeal death we are certain—but what comes after? This is, for a vast segment of humanity, one of the important problems of life. Hereafter is a mysterious universe, often feared; its dimensions, immeasurable. We forget that so many of the most important facts of life are immeasurable "How much do you love me?" we ask. "You are so far away tonight," we say to someone who is right near. How can we measure that love, or that distance? Many of us seem to feel better if everything is measured, weighed, catalogued, and put in a neat, tight box, clearly labeled, with no time for contemplation of mystery, no room for expansion. People so inclined hope that science will, some time in the future, give them the security, satisfy the need. It is inspiring that one of the greatest human beings, and one of the greatest scientists of all times, Albert Einstein, did not have that need, for he said: ". . . To know that what is impenetrable to us really exists, manifesting itself as the highest wisdom and the most radiant beauty. . . ."

That evening we had not dwelt on the "impenetrable." It had been a pleasant dinner, the conversation varying from the stock market to traveling, from education to techniques in painting. Mediumship and life after death were not on my mind or on the guests'. K.M.R. had not mentioned mediumship or spiritualism. But when we decided to have a group reading, he explained to us what it was. He spoke very well and with mature authority remarkable in a twenty-eight-year-old man. He explained that he was a medium and that he had a spirit guide who was able to contact other discarnate entities and give us their message. He gave each of us an ordinary three-by-five index card on which was printed in the corner: "Direct your billet to loved ones, guides, friends, or relations in spirit; write full names; place question in center; sign your full name at bottom. Thank you."

We followed instructions. then I placed each card separately in an envelope which I fetched from my own desk upstairs; and I sealed the envelopes. To complete the preparation, K.M.R. asked me to blindfold him with several layers of tape over his eyes, then wrap his head in scarves and towels. This procedure seemed completely superfluous—I had used my own opaque envelopes purposely because I knew that complete blindfolding is almost impossible; the minutest pinhole is large enough to permit a field of vision sufficient for reading. K.M.R. said we could ask for any person we wanted except Aldous; he was so well known that we would feel the medium was using the knowledge he had about Aldous from his writing or other sources. He added that he felt Aldous's presence very strongly.

We were sitting in the living room; the lights were as they normally are, neither very strong nor very dim. Five of us had written one billet each and put it in an envelope—and sealed it. The envelopes had been placed on a table nearby. K.M.R. picked them up one by one, and kept them in his hand for a few seconds. Through this contact he knew the name of the dead person: he knew who the questioner was, and the question. The medium was now in a trance; he spoke very clearly and with definition. In the state of trance, supposedly it is the spirit guide, or control, that is speaking, using the physical body of the medium. The medium took my billet first. I had written it in pencil, very lightly. It was in French, addressed to a Frenchman, a friend of mine who had been murdered about ten years before and whose murderer had never been found. Almost as soon as the medium picked up my billet, he began to give signs of intense suffering. He said that my friend, whose French name he mentioned, had had a horrible death, that his body had been maimed; it was too terrible to speak about. The medium felt my friend did not want to go into the story of the murder, but would like me instead to remember a lovely trip with him to the seashore, the

beauty of nature, the leisurely good time we had. At the moment I
could not remember. The medium insisted—it had been a lovely weekend—he mentioned Ensenada, named other people who were with us.
For a moment, probably overcome by this astonishing presence and the
exactness of what the medium had said about the murder, I could not
remember that trip. At this point the friend from San Francisco, who
also had been a friend of the murdered man, said that we had sent him
photos of that trip. He still had them (mine had been burned in the fire)
—they corresponded exactly to the description the medium was giving,
and which I could then recall.

The medium went on to another billet, Ginny's. She had asked for
her father, who had died twenty years before. Again the medium gave
the name of the man—he said that the date of death and the date of
birth were within a few days from each other, and that the birthday had
occurred only a few weeks ago. All this was correct. The medium
reported that Ginny's father was present; he was thanking his daughter
for what she had done, a few weeks before, in commemoration of his
birthday. "That was the right thing to do," he said. Ginny did not
know at the moment exactly what the medium meant, but the next day
she received a letter of thanks from a friend to whom she had sent a
sum of money on the date of her father's birthday, thinking that that is
what he would have done in similar circumstances, and what he would
prefer as a birthday memorial.

For the next hour and a half the medium spoke to each of the participants, and gave messages from the departed person they had asked
for. We were witnessing a phenomenon totally unexplainable, for
which there are two theories. One is that there is a world of disembodied entities, and that these entities can put themselve in contact
with us through a medium. The other theory is that the medium does
not contact any disembodied entities, but has access to the conscious
and unconscious mind of the person for whom he is reading. However,
at times the latter theory is inapplicable. For instance, that evening
R.M. asked for the deceased mother of a woman friend of his, who was
still grieving for her loss. The medium gave correctly the name of the
mother, who sent her daughter a message that she was serene and was,
at this time, playing their favorite piece on the piano. later R.M. found
that at the *very time the message was given,* the daughter also was
playing the piano—and was playing the same piece! In whose mind
had the medium read this information?

That evening was unforgettable for all the participants; for some of
them it changed their conception of death. I also was impressed, and
wanted now to have a private reading. Throughout the seance the
medium kept saying that Aldous was there.

The next evening the medium and I went to my room, which had been Aldous's room. The reading was a little different now—no bandaged eyes and no writing of billets. The medium and I sat, facing each other, one on each side of a table; it had been Aldous's writing table. The entire reading was tape recorded, except when the medium was speaking about private matters. Throughout the reading there were discussions of the most personal nature.

In the beginning of the reading the medium spoke about the murdered man I had asked about the previous night. He said there were certain facets of the murder which he did not want to reveal in the presence of others. He also said that Aldous knew the murdered man and that now they were both present. They had actually met only once on earth. The personal messages and discussion of matters known only to Aldous and me were interrupted several times by communications such as, "Aldous says that you are going to receive what eventually is going to be considered *classical evidence of survival* of the personality and consciousness—not something that can be explained by telepathy or other theories. I feel you are going to have what is called in technical language 'classical evidence.'" It seemed, according to the medium, that Aldous was very keen on giving proof of survival, and that this proof was not going to be just an incident, or somthing which could be attributed to intuition or imagination or probability, but something which could not be explained away.

The reading was over. It had made a deep impression on me. However, in listening to the tape, one could argue that what the medium said was something he could have perceived in my mind, even in the deep unconscious. This explanation would eliminate the hypothesis of survival of consciousness after bodily death and attribute the communication to ESP. But what happened after the medium was no longer in trance indicates a knowledge outside the conscious or unconscious of any one living person, including Aldous when he was alive.

K.M.R. and I went downstairs. Ginny and her children had started preparations to show the filmed interviews K.M.R. had brought from his world tour. A few minutes before, Gina Cerminara, the well-known writer on parapsychology, had arrived to spend the evening with us and see the films. I realized later than it was fortuitous that she was present for the following occurrence. Now everybody was busy with the projector, screen, and films. K.M.R. was trying to solve the threading of the film when without diverting his attention he said to me, "Please give me a pencil and a paper; Aldous is saying I must write this down." I gave him a piece of paper and Gina Cerminara gave him a pencil. He wrote:

17th page

6th book from left
3rd shelf
or
6th shelf
3rd book from left

23 line

He then handed me the paper, turned back to the projector, and said nonchalantly, "Aldous wants you to look up those books."

I was left with that piece of paper in my hands, wondering. I had not, then, heard of what is known in parapsychology as a "book test." I kept looking at the words and numbers. Then slowly and thoughtfully I went upstairs to Aldous's room, where the reading had taken place. Two walls of the room are covered with bookshelves. I went to the small wall, next to the door, which has six shelves about four feet in length. I counted to the third shelf from the floor, counted to the sixth book from the left, and took it out. It was a book six and a quarter by nine and a quarter inches and had 257 pages. It was a soft-cover book inside a cardboard container, in Spanish. It looked and felt as if it had never been opened before. The title *Coloquio de Buenos Aires,* 1962, published by the P.E.N. Club of Argentina, in Buenos Aires; the printing was finished August 20, 1963. I opened the book to page 17. Before I even counted to line 23, the name Aldous Huxley, from the paragraph in the center of the page, leaped to my eyes. This is the paragraph containing line 23:

> Marcos Victoria: Aldous Huxley no nos sorprende en esta admirable comunicación, donde la paradoja y la erudición en el sentido poético y el sentido del "humor" se entrelazan
> Line 23 en forma tan eficaz. Quizás la mayoría de los oyentes de este coloquio no tengan una idea completa de la riqueza espiritual de esta comunicación a través del resumen que acaba de leernos la fiel traductora y también erudita en disciplinas científicas que es Alicia Jurado. Pero no es culpa de ella, sino de la complejidad extrema del pensamiento del escritor inglés que exige la lectura repetida del texto completo de cuarenta páginas.

I do not know Spanish, but it is a language similar enough to Italian, my mother language, for me to understand quite a bit of it. I looked at those lines, not understanding completely, but fully knowing *la riqueza espiritual de esta comunicación:* "the spiritual richness of this communication." After a few moments the thought came strongly to my mind that this event should have witnesses; and that I should be checked by other people. I marked the place from which I had taken the book—the sixth from the left—by pulling out about an inch the fifth and seventh books on the shelf; the space where the sixth book had been was empty. I put the book back as it was before I touched it. I went downstairs and asked the others to come up. When everyone was in the room, I asked K.M.R. to do what Aldous had dictated. K.M.R. went through the same procedure I had gone through, pulled out the same book, went to the same paragraph. Standing near the bookcase, the four of us stared at that paragraph while Gina Cerminara translated it aloud into English:

> Aldous Huxley does not surprise us in this admirable communication in which paradox and erudition in the poetic sense and the sense of humor are interlaced in such an efficacious form. Perhaps the majority of the listeners to this conversation will not have a complete idea of the spiritual richness of this communication through the summary which the faithful translator, and learned scholar in scientific disciplines who is Alicia Jurado, has just made for us.

Line 23

We were speechless. Then, immediately, the question arose whether Aldous knew of that book and its location. He did not know. Many books had accumulated during the last months of Aldous's life, first during the summer of 1963 when we were in Europe, then during the last three months, when he was too sick to read. This book had arrived either shortly before Aldous's death or after. My sister, who had come from Italy for a visit a few weeks after Aldous's death, had reorganized the library; the location of the shelves in the room had been changed, as well as the arrangement of the books in the shelves. Since she had put the books in order, no one had touched those in that group of shelves near the door.

I had never seen the book before. It is the report of a literary meeting held in Buenos Aires in October 1962. Aldous and I were to go to it, and he was to give an address on "Literature and Science." But we did not go. The paragraph quoted refers to Aldous's last book, *Literature and Science.*

We read the paragraph several times and wrote out the English translation. Having recovered partially from the shock, we began to think that there might be another book. We were looking at the shelves reproduced on page 238.

If various people were asked which was the first shelf, some would start counting from the floor up; others from the ceiling down. On the bottom shelf there were three stacks of books, as in the illustration. We took out the third book from the left. It was a small, black, hardcover book, eight by five and a half, 86 pages, copyrighted in 1961 by the Parapsychological Foundation, Inc. and titled *Proceedings of the Two Conferences on Parapsychology and Pharmacology.* On page 17 the paragraph containing line 23 read as follows:

> Parapsychology is still struggling in the first stage. These
> Line 23 phenomena are not generally accepted by science although
> many workers are firmly convinced of their existence. For
> this reason the major effort of parapsychological research
> has been to demonstrate and to prove that they are working
> with real phenomena.

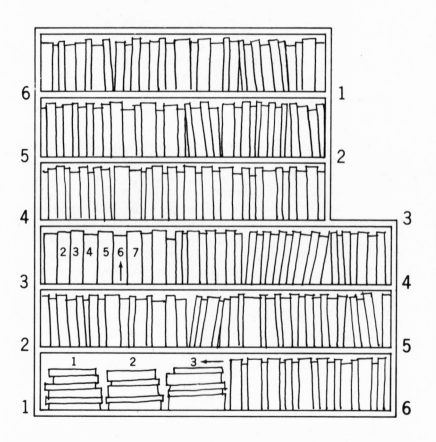

How pointed can one be?

One more book was found that met the requirements of location and page. It was *My Live in Court* by Louis Nizer. If compared to the startling significance of the two preceding messages, this one might seem relatively unimportant. The paragraph containing line 23 describes a man bearing no resemblance to Aldous, *except* for his exceptional height of six feet five. Aldous was six feet four. If one were asked to give a physical description of Aldous, his height would almost certainly be first mentioned. It is as though the intelligence that motivated the two previous events wanted now to give also a physical proof.

We were stunned.

Ginny was the first to recover. She suggested that maybe in any book in that library, on page 17, line 23, one could find something that could relate to Aldous. We gave this possibility a full trial; none of the books we picked at random had, on page 17, line 23, meanings which could be specifically or even remotely related to Aldous or to what was happening that evening.

When I told a few people of this strange occurrence, some suggested the possibility that the medium had browsed among the shelves before the reading. But the medium had never been alone in that room. He was there, the previous night, with six other people, including me, for about fifteen minutes; there was a program on television which we wanted to see. For that program we had brought the television set from another room. Seven of us were present, looked at the program for about fifteen minutes, and left the room again. During the private reading, K.M.R. and I were both in the room for over an hour, sitting at the table. K.M.R. was not in the room alone at any time. Christopher Isherwood made the remark that even if he had been, it would have taken some thousand hours of reading to find three books which, at the specified location, would have had three paragraphs so directly related to Aldous and to the experiment of that evening.

To conclude:

1. I did not know those books or that they were in the library.

2. Neither did Ginny or the medium, or Gina Cerminara, who had never been in the house before.

3. The printers of those two books, one in South America and one in North America, and possibly some other persons, might know the location of those paragraphs in those two books.

4. But those persons did not know the location, or even that the books *were* in my library.

5. My sister in Italy, who organized the library, might vaguely know the location of those three books, but not their content, because she never read them.

6. It must be added that Aldous would not have been able to point out these books in this way when he was alive. Aldous had a marvelous memory, but it was not a visual memory. He could not have visualized the page where these paragraphs appeared on the line, although, *had he read the books,* he would have remembered their content.

I have reported these facts with the utmost accuracy, keeping in mind one of Aldous's favorite passages from a letter of his grandfather, T.H. Huxley, to Charles Kingsley:

Science seems to me to teach, in the highest and strongest manner, the great truth which is embodied in the Christian concept of the entire surrender to the will of God. Sit down before fact like a little child, and be prepared to give up every preconceived notion, follow humbly wherever and to whatever abysses Nature leads or you shall learn nothing. I have only begun to learn content and peace of mind since I have resolved at all risks to do this.

Aldous, age eight

OTHER BOOKS OF INTEREST FROM
CELESTIAL ARTS

THE ESSENCE OF ALAN WATTS. The basic philosophy of Alan Watts in nine illustrated volumes. Now available:
GOD. 64 pages, paper, $3.95
MEDITATION. 64 pages, paper, $3.95
NOTHINGNESS. 64 pages, paper, $3.95
TIME. 64 pages, paper, $3.95
DEATH. 64 pages, paper, $3.95
THE NATURE OF MAN. 64 pages, paper, $3.95

WILL I THINK OF YOU. Leonard Nimoy's warm and compelling sequel to You & I. 96 pages, paper, $3.95

THE HUMANNESS OF YOU, Vol. I & Vol. II. Walt Rinder's philosophy rendered in his own words and photographs. Each: 64 pages, paper, $2.95.

MY DEAREST FRIEND. The compassion and sensitivity that marked Walt Rinder's previous works are displayed again in this beautiful new volume. 64 pages, paper, $2.95.

ONLY ONE TODAY. Walt Rinder's widely acclaimed style is again apparent in this beautifully illustrated poem. 64 pages, paper, $2.95

THE HEALING MIND by Dr. Irving Oyle. A noted physician describes what is known about the mysterious ability of the mind to heal the body. 128 pages, cloth, $7.95; paper, $4.95.

I WANT TO BE USED not abused by Ed Branch. How to adapt to the demands of others and gain more pleasure from relationships. 80 pages, paper, $2.95.

INWARD JOURNEY Art and Psychotherapy For You by Margaret Keyes. A therapist demonstrates how anyone can use art as a healing device. 128 pages, paper, $4.95.

PLEASE TRUST ME by James Vaughan. A simple, illustrated book of poetry about the quality too often lacking in our experiences—Trust. 64 pages, paper, $2.95.

LOVE IS AN ATTITUDE. The world-famous book of poetry and photographs by Walter Rinder. 128 pages, cloth, $7.95; paper, $3.95.

THIS TIME CALLED LIFE. Poetry and photography by Walter Rinder. 160 pages, cloth, $7.95; paper, $3.95.

SPECTRUM OF LOVE. Walter Rinder's remarkable love poem with magnificently enhancing drawings by David Mitchell. 64 pages, cloth, $7.95; paper, $2.95.

GROWING TOGETHER. George and Donni Betts' poetry with photographs by Robert Scales. 128 pages, paper, $3.95.

VISIONS OF YOU. Poems by George Betts, with photographs by Robert Scales. 128 pages, paper, $3.95.

MY GIFT TO YOU. New poems by George Betts, with photographs by Robert Scales. 128 pages, paper, $3.95.

YOU & I. Leonard Nimoy, the distinguished actor, blends his poetry and photography into a beautiful love story. 128 pages, cloth, $7.95; paper, $3.95.

I AM. Concepts of awareness in poetic form by Michael Grinder. Illustrated in color by Chantal. 64 pages, paper, $2.95.

GAMES STUDENTS PLAY (And what to do about them.) A study of Transactional Analysis in schools, by Kenneth Ernst. 128 pages, cloth, $7.95; paper, $3.95.

A GUIDE FOR SINGLE PARENTS (Transactional Analysis for People in Crisis.) T.A. for single parents by Kathryn Hallett. 128 pages, cloth, $7.95; paper, $3.95.

THE PASSIONATE MIND (A Manual for Living Creatively with One's Self.) Guidance and understanding from Joel Kramer. 128 pages, paper, $3.95.

WRITE FOR FREE CATALOG TO:
Dept. D.M. CELESTIAL ARTS 231 Adrian Road Millbrae, Calif. 94030